When There's a Woman in the Room

Women MPs Shaping Public Policy

by Boni Sones OBE

*This book is dedicated to my three children,
Tanya, Jenna and Guy Barnard and their respective families.
Family life is dear to me.*

When There's a Woman in the Room
Women MPs Shaping Public Policy
by Boni Sones OBE

© Copyright Boni Sones OBE 2014

ISBN 978-0-9565871-9-0

First published March 2014 by www.bonisonesproductions.com. The complete copyright for these stories and all other rights for all purposes (including use in all media now known or which may hereafter become known) everywhere rests with the author Boni Sones OBE. No broadcast or publishing containing all or any part of this material can be made without the author's permission.

Front cover photographs by Kieran Doherty © Boni Sones OBE
Inside cover photographs © House of Commons
Inside back cover photograph © Jenna Barnard
Back cover photograph by Kieran Doherty © Boni Sones OBE

Printed by Print-Out, Histon, Cambridge CB24 9JE
Proofreading by Sarah Burton

Foreword

At the time of going to press our: www.parliamentaryradio.com Advisory Board would like to thank all those MPs, both women and men, and Peers, their researchers, academics and associates who have supported us over nine years, first with the publication of the book *Women in Parliament: The New Suffragettes* in September 2005 and subsequently with the setting up of www.wpradio.co.uk in March 2007, then also in October 2011 its sister site www.parliamentaryradio.com.

Together we have created two important historic archives of women MPs work over ten years, from 2004 to 2014.

The audio Archive of all our 350 interviews in the UK Parliament, Africa, Asia and Europe can be found at the London School of Economics.

"Your archive really is valued and I'm so enjoying working on it – the opportunity to be innovative and progressive with it is such a pleasure to me, – cataloguing born-digital archives in the UK (and in the world) is a discipline still very much in its infancy so I feel a lot of pride in what we have and will achieve together". Elinor Robinson, Digital Archivist, LSE Library.

The Harman Shephard audio Archive of the 82 interviews from the book can be found at the British Library.

Our current Advisory Board members are: MPs and Peers: Gisela Stuart, Labour MP Birmingham Edgebaston and Editor of The House Magazine, Rt Hon Caroline Spelman the Conservative MP for Meriden, Penny Mordaunt, the Conservative MP for Portsmouth North, Barbara Keeley, the Labour MP for Worsley and Eccles South.

Journalists: Jackie Ashley, the Guardian who is our Chair, and Deborah McGurran, Political Editor, BBC East and Linda Fairbrother formerly of Anglia TV.

Past MPs and Peers: Eleanor Laing MP, Baroness Susan Kramer, Esther McVey MP, Jo Swinson MP and Anne Begg MP.

Not-for-profits: Anastasia De Waal, Director of Family Policy, Civitas, Nick Aldrige, CEO Missionfish, Barbara Gorna, Film Producer and Emily Scarf campaigner. Supporters: Elizabeth Kanter.

Our founding MP members were Caroline Spelman MP, Jo Swinson MP, Sally Keeble MP, and Sandra Gidley MP. As a result of their desire for women MPs across parties to work together on issues of concern, www.wpradio.co.uk got off to a strong and stable beginning. They were assisted by the former Liberal Democrat MP David Howarth who gave us much encouragement in the early years and the former Labour researcher Dan Beagle who was a tremendous support.

Comments from our Advisory Board Members:
"Your broadcasting has been an absolute inspiration to so many of us and you should feel very proud of your achievements", Jackie.

"Glad the archive opens in March, but sad to hear you are hanging up your shoes", Gisela.

"It's quite an achievement, well done", Eleanor.

"It's been an honour to even be involved", Anastasia.

"Things will happen because of your Parliamentary Radio for Women. People will never know how much it has done to influence the debate. You may not be able to quantify that influence but others will be influenced by it," Lesley Abdela MBE, Shevolution and Britain's gender post conflict specialist.

"Boni – your book is such a fascinating read, and one which I will be referring to on a regular basis," Caroline Adams, Labour Women's PLP.

Introduction

March 2014

Margaret Sitta MP from Tanzania told www.parliamentaryradio.com recently that: "Where there is women there is talk about women's issues, which sometimes seems to be forgotten."

Fungayi Jessie Majome MP from Zimbabwe agrees: "We need to socially engineer our societies because if not we will wait forever, and we need not."

Over the past seven years www.wpradio.co.uk and www.parliamentaryradio.com have broadcast 350 interviews with women politicians of all parties, and remarkably 35 of these have been with women in parliaments in Africa, Asia and Europe.

The rights of women are on the march, and as so-called second and third World countries catch up with the hard fought for rights enjoyed by women in the First World, tensions are rising.

Even in our own UK parliament women have not felt free to express the overt or covert discrimination they feel they have been subject to even in recent times. Those who now feel brave enough to speak out about twitter trolls are breaking the unspoken taboos of the past, and moving the agenda for women forward in a most profound way.

Labour's Deputy Leader, Harriet Harman often tells the story of how when she came to power women were often refused a job on the basis there was "another woman" in that department and they would "argue" if they sat together – "you weren't allowed two women in the same room," she says.

Even as recently as January 2014 I have still been privileged to capture some of these accounts, as leading women politicians recount their earlier career paths. Labour's Louise Ellman, Chair of the Transport Select recalled how in the 1970s as a local County Councillor in Lanchashire she was greeted with the call of "go home young woman" but she says "I haven't heard that sound for a long time!" Women were not supposed to speak at meetings either.

In my previous work there were stories of how the Conservative politician and former minister, Gillian Shephard was told that her knee length skirt was too short, and should be lowered to calf length and that all women MPs were called "Betty", because their male colleagues couldn't be bothered to remember their individual names. Labour's Barbara Follett, similarly told of how the 1997 intake of 101 Labour women were greeted with "the melon gesture" when they stood up to speak in the Chamber, with Conservative men jiggling imaginary breasts in front of them as the women spoke. The younger women were most affected by this cruel targeting.

"Misogyny" was once a word used by extremists in the feminist cause, but now it more widely conveys the way many women feel they are being treated. For every broadcast interview that speaks up in favour of women's advancement the anti-lobby are waiting in the wings to hijack the debates and say why they as men now feel they are being discriminated against too.

In 2004 I commissioned a group of five women journalists to help me to write a book on *Women in Westminster: The New Suffragettes*, with the feminist academic Joni Lovenduski and the then Labour Whip and MP Margaret Moran. Together we conducted 83 audio interviews with women MPs across party, and it took me six years to get 82 of those women to agree to deposit those interviews in a special archive which I named the Harman/Shephard Archive at the British Library.

It wasn't until May 2010 just a month before the last General Election that on the second, third, fourth or even fifth time of asking that all but one agreed.

When the book was published one influential male journalist, Roy Greenslade, then media commentator for the Guardian was "big" enough to apologise and admit that when he ridiculed Ken Clarke for wearing his hush puppies he was not doing so with the same tone as when he spoke of Patricia Hewitt's dungarees.

The women Cabinet and Shadow Cabinet members Harriet Harman, Vera Baird, Tessa Jowell, Margaret Beckett, Theresa May, Caroline Spelman, Sandra Gidley, spoke as one when they condemned their treatment at the hands of male and female journalists towards them.

Move on to David Cameron's reshuffle in the autumn of 2013 when older women Cabinet members were "sacked" to make way for younger MPs to get on the ministerial ladder and again the broken promises of incoming parties and politicians regarding women's representation at all levels in Parliament had come to the fore. The Cameron Cabinet was woefully short of women, and Cheryl Gillan the former Welsh Secretary spoke her mind. "It's an amazing privilege to be a cabinet minister and I wouldn't want to make light of it. There have been lots of other women cabinet ministers but they have all been Labour," Gillan told the Huffington Post on the 29th of September 2013.

Following the publication of the book, I was invited by women MPs across all parties, to carry on campaigning and do something else. But what? It was the dawning of the internet age, and as journalism went online I saw the potential for the independent producer and broadcaster to go it alone, break from the established broadcasters, and invent their own stations.

Again I assembled a cross media and cross party team around me, a strong Advisory board, and from March 2007 to March 2014 we broadcast interviews with women MPs highlighting the positive contribution they were making every day to politics through the web on the domain names www.wpradio.co.uk and now www.parliamentaryradio.com.

We even managed to get a foothold in the lobby with the help of male journalist colleagues, and supporters, and quite honestly have never looked back. The interviews have been strong, honest, forthright accounts of women's work in the House, and never fail to give me energy to still believe in the cause of feminism and the causes they are fighting for. So much cross-party collaborative work in Westminster goes unreported, it was worthwhile to be by their sides telling their stories.

The stories in this book are private testimonies, first-hand accounts of their work, and come from those women MPs who are trying to kick issues into the political arena to try to achieve change, rather than those who have arrived and are bound by the conventions of ministerial office that would not allow them to speak honestly or frankly to an interviewer. This has been a deliberate ploy on my part but clearly we have interviewed those at Cabinet level too when there is a clear path to speak to them outside of the normal press office prolonged interview request procedures, that often impede proper and clear communications.

We never aimed to build up a large audience but through niche audiences, associations and links we have achieved our goals of influencing the influencers. With limited resources we concentrated our small team's efforts on capturing the significant interviews of the week outside of the top stories.

The celebrations surrounding the death of the suffragette Emily Wilding Davison 100 years ago in 2013 was one such occasion, it brought all the women in Westminster together from left and right, Ministers and backbench MPs and of course we were there to record their talks, speeches and celebrations.

I have consciously presented these interviews in the most accessible straight forward way possible, omitting references, calling MPs by Christian and surname only so omitting their Rt Hons, and ordering the chapters by the issues they have campaigned on both in their constituencies and in Parliament. Much good work goes on in their own backyards and it is these issues that they so often champion at PMQs that do not get reported.

The book orders these interviews from the present day to the past, so MPs titles relate to the year in which the interviews were done, not what their portfolios maybe now. It is not an academic work, it does not submit their testimonies to scrutiny and it does not champion one party's interests over another. It is their story as they told me most Tuesdays and Wednesdays. It is the reportage of listening, understanding and the "ah but" question as the other side or their opponents would put it to them. The aim was to be objective and let our interviewees speak. So much of political communication is nuanced, prefaced, bureaucratic, confrontational and impenetrable that I wanted to publish something that told the story as clearly as is possible and to allow the reader to turn the page as quickly as possible and move on. A handful of reports are listed in more than one chapter to give context to the issues being reported on.

Introduction

In the early years when online audio content was still innovative in 2007 and 2008 we did not support our reports with quotes of any kind, just getting the recordings "in the bag" was achievement enough. As the technology developed throughout 2009, 2010 and 2011 we issued press releases on our work, moving on to putting an online Hot Quote beside each report when we re-launched our website in 2011. To keep this book authentic Hot Quotes are also given beside some of the early reports too where there was a press release to support them. Listening to all the podcast interviews and reading our press releases in full will provide a lot more insight into the issues of the times, and a wealth of further quotes can be extracted from them including from those early years when we were treading particularly carefully to be "accepted". Our regular email reports to our Advisory Board were posted on our website under About Us as were our accounts. Good sound administration was a key component of our success.

This book is dedicated to all women who would want a parliamentary career, equality is worth the fight and all who have collaborated with me, men and women, as part of that struggle here and in international parliaments. Clearly there was much we did not manage to capture, but a significant amount that we all did! In particular I would like to thank the Commonwealth Parliamentary Association and ALL our long standing Advisory Board members, Caroline Adams of the Labour Women's PLP – Parliamentary Labour Party and Adrian Wright our current web manager whose creative flair inspires me.

Thanks go to those who in the first two years accepted one of my paid for commissions for a special report from freelancers including, Daisy Ayliffe, Lucy Fairbrother, Anne Garvey, Georgie Hemmingway, and Sophie Kainradl. The late Brian Shallcross of Gcap Media also reported for us. More recently I have been assisted by Amy Lee, Nigel Nelson, and Sheun Adelasoye. Special thanks to Sheun who brought much commitment to our broadcasting and Nigel who assisted us.

These seven years of broadcasting would not have been possible without the continued support of my broadcast journalist colleagues from the Eastern Region, Linda Fairbrother and Deborah McGurran. I and our

"Boni Sones and Associates" Archive is indebted to them. Gisela Stuart deserves a special thank you for championing our concerns and Jackie Ashley has stuck with us throughout.

Boni Sones OBE
Executive Producer www.wpradio.co.uk and
www.parliamentaryradio.com

Contents

1	Childcare and Parenting	13
2	Women's Representation in public life	25
3	Equal pay and low pay	62
4	Women in the Boardrooms	69
5	Violence against women, DV, Stalking, Prostitution, Forced Marriage, FGM	74
6	Women in Government and the Shadow Cabinets	90
7	The men supporting women	102
8	Campaigning women of the past	110
9	International issues and parliaments	119
10	Campaigning in the Constituency	139
11	Speaking in the Chamber and Westminster Hall	155
12	Campaigning in Parliamentary Groups	186
13	More talking points: When public discussion leads to political debate	201
APPENDICES	Web links, blogs, and press articles	216
INDEX	By name	241
INDEX	By subject	248

ONE

Childcare and Parenting

Childcare and parenting is now a political issue with all parties, but it was the Labour women of the 1997 Parliament that put the care of the under-fives on the political map. They quietly nagged and won the support of the male leaders of their party for various policy initiatives, Sure Start centres being one of their proudest achievements. The Conservatives pushed forward plans for parental leave for fathers too. Early on, the Liberal Democrats spoke up for flexible working patterns. Now it is commonplace for all parties and the Prime Minister and their Shadow leaders of the day to talk about what they and their ministers are doing to support parents, mothers, fathers, and grandparents too. The rising cost of childcare is a topical issue for all. The effectiveness of those policy initiatives are usually hotly disputed and the cost to business and Employers weighs heavy with decision makers. In Westminster a good idea is a powerful thing, and can win support from all parties who pick it up and run with it that is why All-Party Parliamentary Groups and Committees remain powerful alliances. The cost of childcare is emerging as a major electoral issue in the lead up to the next General Election in 2015. One survey by Findababysitter.com suggests that childcare costs have risen by 19 per cent in a year but the Pre-school Learning Alliance rejects those figures. The three political parties Conservative, Liberal Democrats and Labour are all looking for solutions to help working families with the cost of childcare, and those families who would like to work but can't afford the cost of working and bringing up a family. But public policy on these issues appears muddled. The Lib Dem leader, and Deputy Prime Minister, Nick Clegg, opposed the Conservative's policy of increasing the children to child minder's ratio, which may have helped reduce costs. He has instead, announced new help for poorer working families with childcare costs for two-year-olds from September 2014, which will double the number of people who receive help to 260,000 or 40 per cent of all two-year-olds. In June 2012 David Cameron, the PM, set up a Childcare Commission to see how childcare costs could be reduced and is said to favour extending school hours. The government has also just increased free education for all three and four-year-olds from 12.5 to 15 hours a week. It is also introducing tax free childcare under which parents earning less than £150,000 would be able to receive up to £1,200 towards each child's childcare costs. But it has ended universal child benefit and tax-credits for childcare and over 500 Sure Start Centres have closed.

The year: 2014
"When there's a woman in the room": The rising cost of childcare

Labour has this week gone on the offensive, with its much used theme of the rising cost of living, saying it would extend introduce "wrap-around" childcare for primary aged children, and provide help for 3 to 5 -year-olds extending free care from 15 to 25 hours per week, equivalent to £1,500 per year.

We spoke to Labour's new Shadow Minister for Childcare and Children, Lucy Powell, the MP for Manchester Central, who told us how these plans would work. Lucy has just taken maternity leave from Parliament, when it was wrongly thought she had not been voting enough.

Lucy Powell MP Hot Quote: "I would support the government looking holistically and carefully, rather than the pots of cash here, the pots of cash there, the incremental change, that's just creating a very confused environment for parents and doing nothing to address this issue. I will support the government in taking some big bold moves and measures on childcare 100 per cent and putting the early years at the centre of their social policy – they have neglected this issue!"

The year: 2013
Women and social policy – how will the parties capture our vote!

A return to family values, the issue of gay marriage and marriage, all parties it seems are out to capture the women's vote but just what are the policies that the Conservatives, the Liberal Democrats and Labour are likely to follow in the lead up to the next General Election in 2015 to actually get our votes?

Cuts in welfare, the introduction of the bedroom tax, domestic violence centres closing, and now changes to the way legal aid is administered not to mention a new financial statement from the Chancellor George Osborne for 2013/14 with yet more cuts to come, all are said to place women in jeopardy.

Here our Executive Producer Boni Sones, asks Kate Green, the Labour MP for Stretford and Urmston and Labour's Shadow Minister for Women and Equalities and Anastasia de Waal the Deputy Director of the Think Tank Civitas, specialising in family and Education, to set out what they believe the key issues will be for women and families.

First Kate on equalities and the need to gender proof government policies, then Anastasia on marriage and the family.

Kate Hot Quote: "I don't believe there is any evidence that this spending announcement was gender proofed or assessed for its impact on different equalities groups. We do know that earlier budgets and spending announcements have hit women, much, much harder than men. They have now been hit three times harder than men in terms of cuts to benefits, cuts to tax credits, and the way in which taxes have impacted on the different sexes. We suspect this latest announcement from George Osborne has probably hit women as well."

Anastasia Hot Quote: "We still feel very strongly that marriage is something that is very important to us. Marriage is the ultimate way of understanding social change, because it captures so much. It captures our understanding of partnerships, it captures our understanding of gender dynamics, and our understanding of how we raise children, and what matters in terms of personal relationships.

It really does show us a lot about household economics, and something which is thought of as the ultimate romantic indicator is in fact very pragmatically related to household economics."

Jane Ellison MP – The Queen's Speech is good for women!

The 2013 Queen's Speech has brought forward measures that are specifically designed to help women and families, including tackling the cost of child-care, capping social care costs for the elderly and giving women improved pension entitlements. Jane Ellison, the Conservative MP for Battersea, Balham and Wandsworth, is a member of the Work and Pensions Select Committee, which has been working to simplify the state pension.

Jane Hot Quote: "There was a lot in this Queen's Speech for women, and particularly older women. A measure like the single-tier pension has enormous implications for older women and for women's security in retirement in the future. It is a life changing piece of legislation. We are also grappling with the social care costs for the elderly, people will be able to plan for their old age with some certainty now. I urge the Minister Liz Truss MP to plough ahead with increasing the ratios of children to carers in nurseries – an area like mine suffers from child care costs, it is just crippling."

A Mother's Day Campaign to the door of No 10
Who will pick up the women's vote at the next General Election?

Kate Green The MP for Stretford and Urmston, and Labour's spokesperson on Women will be at the door of No 10 this Sunday – Mother's Day – to launch a new campaign on the "Mummy Tax".

Research for the Labour Party suggests that the Conservative Liberal Democrat Government's plans to cut maternity pay will, in real terms, mean that 1.2 million people, will be adversely affected. 210,000 new Mums who rely solely on benefits, will be hardest hit.

Maternity pay and maternity allowances will now be capped at 1 per cent annually, instead of being increased with inflation rises. It is estimated that new mums and their families, will lose £180 a year by 2015 as a result. At the same time, the government is reducing tax for millionaires.

Our Executive Producer, Boni Sones, spoke to Kate in Central Lobby and asked her about that "Mummy tax" and if Labour was targeting the women's vote ahead of the next General Election?

Kate Hot Quote: "Women have been hit three times as hard as men financially. This government has a real blind-spot towards the interests of women and we are making that point right now we are not waiting for a General Election to say it. We will be recognising the importance of supporting new families, the early years and enabling Mums to thrive in the workplace."

Meg Hillier MP warns of "long form filling" for parents claiming child benefit

At Prime Minister's Questions this week, Meg Hillier the Labour MP for Hackney South and Shoreditch quizzed the Prime Minister, David Cameron, about the removal of child benefit and the need for parents to fill in "long forms" in order to receive it in the future.

The government hopes to save £1.5bn a year to help reduce the deficit by taking away some of the child benefit from families with one parent with a taxable income of more than £50,000 and if one parent earns more than £60,000 it will be withdrawn entirely.

You can read the rest of this report in Chapter 11.

The year: 2012
How about requesting Flexible Working in 2013? Mary Macleod MP says you should!

The Government is trying to encourage more of us to request flexible working. But is it something only women do, or should more men be using it to further their careers and help out in the home too? If you request "Flexi time" will your employer doubt your commitment to your job and then your promotion prospects will take a back seat? Our Executive Producer, Boni Sones, caught up with the Conservative MP Mary Macleod, who is in the hot seat on this issue as PPS to the Culture Media and Sports Secretary of State Maria Miller, who is also the Equalities Minister.

Mary Hot Quote: "I don't think the flexible working revolution has happened yet, but I think it could and I think it will. What I want is for that revolution to happen because the more that men ask for flexible working as well then it will become more normal. What I don't want is for women to be penalised because they want to choose to do flexible working so the more that men do it the better, they might want to do it for different reasons but they can use it to diversify, in the way their career is developing, and that can only be good."

Hot topic – Why are childcare costs out of the reach of most families in Britain today?

In part two of her documentary series our guest reporter Sheun Adelasoye assesses the full impact that modern public policy decisions have had on the spiralling cost of childcare in Britain today.

Sheun interviews: Luciana Berger the Labour MP for Liverpool Wavertree, Claire Perry the Conservative MP for Devizes, and Ryan Shorthouse of the Social Market Foundation who is the co-author of *A Better Beginning*.

Critics say that the Conservative Liberal Democrat coalition government has withdrawn the lifeline that most families need to support childcare costs but others allege it is the fault of the last Labour government for introducing too much regulation into the system, so that the childcare costs are now unaffordable!

Luciana Berger Hot Quote: "Childcare is very expensive in this country and we need to see more being done by government to make it more affordable. We've got some of the highest childcare costs in Europe."

Claire Perry Hot Quote: "The staff to children ratios we have in Britain are the highest in Europe, or the lowest in Europe i.e you have to have more staff than in any other country for the same number of children, and why?"

Ryan Shorthouse Hot Quote: "We've come up with an innovative solution (The National Childcare Contribution Scheme), which is costless to the Government, it doesn't count as public expenditure and it mirrors what happens with the student loan system, whereby parents are given support from government, financial support, but they pay that back through their salary each month for a long period of time."

The cost of childcare and a Crèche in the Commons - Speaker John Bercow and Jenny Willott MP

In a two-part radio documentary our guest reporter Sheun Adelasoye assesses the impact that having a Crèche in the House of Commons has made to MPs and asks what solutions can be found to the high costs of childcare in modern Britain?

Insiders are known to think that David Cameron and George Osborne would be advised to think long term about moving towards tax-deductible childcare but this week's Budget has offered little redress to parents whose household budgets are being "squeezed" by changes in the benefits system. These include the now staggered withdrawal of the £20 a week child benefit for higher-rate taxpayers, which starts next January, child tax credit changes, the scrapping of the Child Trust Fund and the proposed Housing Benefit cap.

In part one of her series Sheun records an important piece of Parliamentary history by asking The Speaker John Bercow, how he reacted to much vicious personal criticism for making the House of Commons a modern workplace by setting up a Crèche on the site of the Bellamy's bar, for the use of MPs and their staff. But first she spoke to Jenny Willott the Liberal Democrat MP for Cardiff Central, who has an 18 month old son, who uses the Commons Crèche.

Jenny Willott's Hot Quote: "I don't know what I would have done if the nursery hadn't been here. I was breastfeeding, so I wanted him to be on site through the day, so if necessary I could pop over there and so on. It has made life so much easier than if I'd had a child minder off site and had to go back and forth."

John Bercow's Hot Quote: "I'm saddened, not in any way put off, not worried, just saddened by the really low grade, sub-standard down market, vitriol of some of the real rag type media outlets who are not interested in the welfare of the children, or the interests of the parents or the notions of the forward looking House of Commons, who just want to write trash for cheap stories. But if those sorts of outlets think that the House of Commons Commission or the Speaker are going to be deterred from doing what we think is the right thing by parents and children, well they're very much mistaken, then they can go on whistling in the wind, but that's all it is."

The year: 2011
Face to Face Encounters: Nigel Nelson talks to Tim Loughton MP, Under Secretary of State for Children and Families
No time to draw breath, Tim Loughton, the MP for East Worthing and Shoreham, has found himself in the hot seat since becoming the Under Secretary of State for Children and Families in the coalition government. A Foster Carers Charter, Adoption Guidance, a £11.2 million grant to the NSPCC for ChildLine and other help lines, child protection guidance, helping to launch the new National Citizen's Service, a visit to Rethink, not to mention a web chat with the Youth Parliament and speaking his mind about cut-backs to Sure Start on Twitter too. Phew!

Tim Loughton isn't frightened of speaking up for his beliefs and championing the causes close to his heart. Here Tim speaks with real passion and conviction about his plans for the future to Nigel Nelson, Political Editor of the People in the second of his series "Face to Face" encounters.

Tim pledges to get to the "heart of the more difficult communities" to help them access Sure Start Centres which he would like to see expand and open for longer in the evening and at weekends too. He is "ambitious" for them to "do more and better for more people!" You can't improve on that. Thanks Tim! Education and youth training and better care for "looked after" children are also at the top of his "to do list"!

Tim Hot Quote: Sexual exploitation: "I am not seeking to offend anybody, but at last the headlines are beginning to catch up with the problem. I think there is a really big problem with child sexual exploitation it has been going on out of the media glare for many years, but some of the high profile cases from the Midlands and the North of England earlier this year shows it affects many different communities not just cities, but in towns and rural area across the country too. This is child abuse - and we must absolutely clamp down on it, as vigorously as possible and I don't care if it is people from ethnic communities or white men it is all child abuse. We are putting together an action plan on this with colleagues in the Home Office, and we are working with Barnado's and CEOP and the police to make sure everybody knows what to do to clamp down on it. It affects an awful lot of teenagers, and one of the good things that has helped to bring this to light is the soap opera scripts in East Enders. That made a lot of people sit up and pay attention. Some of the charities involved in this think that tens of thousands of children are the victims of this up and down the country. We need to take it more seriously than it has been."

"This House would not get Married!" – A Valentine's day www.wpradio.co.uk Cambridge Union Society "partnership"
To celebrate Valentine's Day www.wpradio.co.uk went to the Cambridge Union Debate "This House would not get Married". Here William Longrigg, Partner at Charles Russell and President of the International Academy of Matrimonial Lawyers and Winston Preece, a Cambridge student, speak in favour of the motion while our Advisory Board Member Anastasia de Waal, Deputy Director and Head of Family Policy at Civitas and Anne Atkins, Author, Journalist, Agony Aunt and supporter of Christian values speak against. The Debate was Chaired by Francesca Hill, of Trinity Hall. www.cus.org will tell you who won!

The year: 2010
In 2011 we ask is the Commons family friendly? Katy Clark MP who is juggling a new baby and a demanding job says there's room for improvement!

Katy Clark, Labour MP for North Ayrshire and Arran since 2005 who has an 18 month-old-daughter, took maternity leave, and quite often uses colleagues to hold her daughter while she pops into the Chamber to vote. Katy tells Women's Parliamentary Radio about her "two-lives" with a constituency that is 400 miles and a five hour journey from Westminster and a job that is a "vocation".

You can read the rest of this report in Chapter 2.

The year: 2009
Emily Thornberry MP – Helping families through the recession

Emily Thornberry, has been the Labour MP for Islington South and Finsbury since May 2005. She has three children and was brought up in a single parent household living on a council estate. She has campaigned at a national level with trade unions and parents' groups for more family-friendly employment policies and access to childcare, particularly for women. Boni Sones, asked her to justify how the Labour government intended to help out hard pressed families during the current recession.

Emily Hot Quote: "Having been brought up by a mother who lived on benefit for many years I know the importance of the government increasing child benefit. There is no excuse for child poverty and if the government is going to do something to help families during the recession, then continuing to increase child benefit is important to ensure kids have enough to live on."

Maria Miller MP – Women and the recession

Women are said to be fairing worse in the current economic downturn than men. The Conservative's Shadow Minister for The Family, Maria Miller the MP for Basingstoke, and a mother of three children herself, tells Boni Sones what her Party would do to help families through their current economic difficulties.

Maria Hot Quote: "We must help families to get their work home life balance right. We need to make sure women are not penalised during this recession and left out in the cold. We need to look far more broadly as to how to make work more family friendly, not just for women but for families. We need to look at these problems as family problems, and take women out of the equation so they are not seen as the problem."

Eleanor Laing MP

Eleanor Laing MP, Shadow Minister for Justice, talked of the need to support women internationally by keeping up our aid budgets to the third world and the high cost of childcare for women in this country.

The year: 2008
Julie Kirkbride MP – a working mother just like you

The government has just announced it is to extend the right to Flexible working to all parents with a child under 16 from April next year. The announcement was made by Labour's Secretary of State for Equalities, Harriet Harman, at Prime Minister's Questions. At the moment the right only applies to parents with a child under 6 and there had been talk of not implementing the changes because of the recession.

Well, the Conservative MP for Bromsgrove, Julie Kirkbride, has thought carefully about her role as a working mother with an eight year old son. She has prioritised her busy life to ensure she sees as much of Angus as possible, and is happy to keep her political ambitions in check so as not to miss out on his growing up. Not unsurprisingly, Julie is an advocate of new policies.

Boni Sones, asked Julie Kirkbride MP to say why she thought flexible working was good for her family and good for business.

Dr Katherine Rake – Extended maternity leave of up to a year?

Labour's Minister for Women, Harriet Harman, wants women to be given extended maternity leave of up to a year off work. The Conservative's

Shadow Minister for Women, Theresa May, says she's lost touch with the times and men as well as women need to be given the right to take extended leave when their children are born.

Under the government's plans men would only get two weeks of leave. Dr Katherine Rake, Director of the Fawcett Society, says parental leave should be available to both parents on a paid basis. Boni Sones spoke to her about this week's political hot debate.

Katharine Hot Quote: "We have been arguing for a very long time that we want to see parental leave available to either parent on a paid basis after six months. We are currently paying mothers on maternity leave less than the minimum wage for a full time week and this shows we value that care for very young children very poorly."

The year: 2007
Flexible working practices and workplace diversity!
The MP for Solihull, Liberal Democrat Lorely Burt, has secured a debate on workplace diversity to promote her 10 Minute Rule Bill which promotes flexible working practices. She told the Trade and Industry Minister, Jim Fitzpatrick, that she wants to see more sensitive employment policies for ethnic minority women, other minorities, and also for women generally. WPRadio journalist Anne Garvey asked her to explain why she thought new laws were needed?

Lorely Hot Quote: "I think we should have women owned businesses and ethnic minority owned businesses as well, so businesses better reflect the people they are set up for. Last year I discovered that in America there are twice as many women owned businesses there than there are in the UK, and I wondered how they did that, and went off to Dallas to find out."

TWO

Women's Representation in public life

This book frequently quotes the figures for women's representation in public life. In Westminster the numbers of women MPs remains dismally low almost stuck on just 147 women MPs across all parties, just one fifth of all MPs, at just 23 per cent. In all professions the tipping point for change in organisational culture is said to be one-third representation! Academics insist that positive discrimination is needed if the UK Parliament is to achieve equality of representation, and Labours controversial introduction of All-women shortlists did lead to 101 Labour women MPs being elected in the landslide of 1997. It was the biggest change to our Parliament in the last Century, and while some leading Conservatives such as Theresa May and Caroline Spelman, have expressed support for positive discrimination in favour of women, it remains a highly controversial area of public policy with even some of the Labour women themselves who were nominated on All-women shortlists saying they would have preferred not to have been. It was the Scottish women who in the 80s started convincing the men in the Labour party that positive measures were needed, and Conservative men as well as women have helped to found the Women2Win campaign to encourage more women to come forward to stand for seats.

The year: 2014
A glass ceiling or a brick wall?
Why positive measures are needed to increase the no of women MPs
As the Liberal Democrats wrestle with continuing allegations about Lord Rennard, commentators are increasingly asking why the three main political parties, the Conservatives, Labour and the Liberal Democrats have so few women MPs. The Conservatives have 48, Labour 86, Liberal Democrat 7 and the Greens 1. 16 years after Labour's All-women shortlists increased the number of women in Westminster in 1997 to 120, of which 101 were Labour, there are still only 147 women MPs across all parties.

To reach parity with men there would need to be 325 in total and yet early indications would suggest the parties selection procedures are failing to put women into winnable seats for 2015. Even David Cameron has expressed concerns.

Here we talk to three MPs who have been steadfastly campaigning to get more women in Parliament. The Conservative MP for Braintree, Brooks Newmark, has been a leading member of Women2Win, and used to wear a badge supporting 50/50 representation.

Seema Malhotra is the Labour MP for Feltham and Heston and she has pushed forward the Fabian Women's successful mentoring scheme for those wanting to get a foothold on the political ladder.

Louise Ellman, the Labour MP for Liverpool, Riverside, has worked her way up in politics from local government in the 1970s to now being the Chair of the Select Committee on Transport, an influential role particularly in the light of parliamentary reforms which saw the Chairs of these Committees being elected for the first time. She would like to encourage more women to give evidence to Committees.

Brooks Newmark Hot Quote: "I think things are improving we have to keep working hard to get the work life balance right in Parliament. As Conservatives we need to keep working hard to try to bring more women in who want to be MPs. By 2020 of our target seats we have about one third women, we want retirement safe seats to go to at least a third women, and in the more challenging seats where Labour or LD have a large majority, ...50 per cent, of those seats I would like to see select women."

Seema Malhotra Hot Quote: "We have some tremendous candidates in our 106 target seats... Our aspiration in our rule book is for 50 per cent of our MPs to be women, we are about 33 per cent, and in the Shadow Cabinet we have over 40 per cent women. We support All-women shortlists, and we won't get 50/50 representation in Parliament unless the Conservatives and Liberal Democrat parties do this too."

Louise Ellman Hot Quote: "We have a mixture of women giving evidence to us, but I would like to see more women in higher positions come forward, but sometimes you have to look behind the organisation and identify the women who have got the information. I would certainly encourage women to give us information and we will call them. We need to keep encouraging women to be involved, we had a step change in 1997 but we need to maintain that progress."

Speaking out about "inappropriate" behaviour – a moment of political change in Parliament?

Bridget Harris a former advisor to the Lib Dem leader Nick Clegg is one of a handful of women who have gone public about "inappropriate" advances towards her by Lord Rennard a Lib Dem peer.

The party launched an internal inquiry and review of its rules on the handling of such complaints. The police have ruled out action. The QC in charge of the inquiry Alistair Webster said the allegations against Lord Rennard were "broadly credible" but it was unlikely it could be established beyond reasonable doubt.

That fudge is causing major splits within the Lib Dem party sometimes on a generational not gender lines. Baroness Shirley Williams aged 83 has spoken up for Lord Rennard.

Here our Executive Producer Boni Sones spoke to Bridget Harris, about her allegations, the inquiry and Rennard's reply. Thanks Bridget for the interview outside in the wind under the statue of Emmeline Pankhurst.

Bridget Hot Quote: "We might be looking at a moment of change in political life where Parliament is catching up with the rest of the country in terms of workplace discrimination and gender and sexual aggression towards women should not be seen as a legitimate political tool."

Put more women's bodies in a room and there is a good chance policy will change!
45 per cent of women MPs don't have children – removing the barriers to women becoming MPs!
New research suggests that there are far too few women MPs with children in Westminster. Dr Rosie Campbell, Senior Lecturer in politics at the University of Birkbeck in London, says All-women shortlists, penalties to parties that do not get enough women selected and job share MPs would help solve the problem. She would also like to see the costs of standing as a Prospective Parliamentary Candidates "capped" in some way to remove the costs and level the playing field for women.

Dr Campbell and her colleague Professor Sarah Childs, presented their new research of over 200 MPs from all Parties elected in 2010, to MPs in Westminster this week. It found that 45 per cent of women MPs had no children, compared to 28 per cent of male MPs, a far bigger divide than in the general population.

Dr Rosie Campbell Hot Quote: "This survey really shows that childcare, managing the balance of family life, and the life of a politician, is particularly difficult for women. The costs of getting selected are enormous, and we don't think about that enough. I'm an advocate of job share for MPs so there would be an opportunity to combine it with other contributions to Society. Put more women's bodies in a room and there is a good chance policy will change."

The year: 2013
Parliament Week: Women in Democracy – do women still need positive discrimination?
The Rt Hon Caroline Spelman has been the Conservative MP for Meriden since 1997 and the Secretary of State for Environment, Food and Rural Affairs in David Cameron's government. This week she joined a Parliament Week Debate to discuss women in democracy.

Caroline supports positive discrimination to get more women into Westminster, admits progress is too slow, but was surprised to find that

Woman's Representation in public life

her young audience didn't think positive discrimination was a suitable public policy tool. They wanted to climb the ladder to the top on their merit. But is there a conflict between positive discrimination and merit?

In this special Parliament Week interview our Executive Producer, Boni Sones, spoke to Caroline about her career in politics, her family responsibilities, life as a senior Cabinet minister, MPs' hours and now her new role helping and mentoring other MPs.

Caroline Spelman Hot Quote: "I am with Theresa (May) on this one. I support the use of positive discrimination. What I think is interesting, is that for the young women in the audience it is quite hard for them to understand why it is necessary to have positive discrimination. They have not experienced any discrimination yet, they want to be able to get to where they want to get to on merit."

Much to complain about and much to do! Is female representation in the UK parliament shameful?

So just 4 women in David Cameron's Cabinet, despite initial promises to ensure there would be 1/3rd representation by the end of his first term as Prime Minister. Only 23 per cent of our 650 MPs are women, totalling just 147, and the UK is now ranked 65th for the representation of women in parliaments Worldwide. What is holding women's representation back?

To shed light on "Women, Politics and Power" the Institute for Government invited three women MPs, all Ministers or Shadow Ministers, to talk of their experiences in politics: Elizabeth Truss the Conservative MP for South West Norfolk, Jo Swinson LD MP for East Dunbartonshire, and Stella Creasy Labour and Co-operative MP for Walthamstow.

Later Stella stayed behind to talk to us. As Labour's Shadow Minister on Crime Prevention, she has gained a reputation as a forceful campaigner against so called "payday loans", Wonga and abusive Twitter Trolls. We also spoke to members of the audience, including Kate Jenkins, a Visiting Professor at the London School of Economics, and three other women who were in search of female role models.

Stella Hot Quote: "It is very clearly not about you. Otherwise politics becomes showbiz for ugly people. You have to have a healthy sense that you are not the important thing what matters is the causes you are working on. When you have twenty per cent of a room being women men think it is 50/50. How do we get to 30 per cent which is the tipping point for social change?"

Kate Hot Quote: "The Liberals and Conservative parties are a disgrace to British democracy, they have the lowest representation of women of almost any political party in Europe, they should be ashamed of themselves."

Are older women "invisible" and can governments do anything about it?

Is the framing of public policy ignoring the needs of older women, who are often carers for grandchildren, elderly parents or sick partners and spouses? From the ages of 50 to 80 many women find themselves propping up the family in a variety of roles, when often it may also be really difficult for them to get proper secure employment even though they may be the breadwinners and main support for their relatives.

The Labour Party has set up a Commission on Older Women to look at these issues, and are the first political party to identify this area of public policy as of concern to voters and social policy makers. 60 percent of those over 80 are women and their votes are important too.

Our Reporter Linda Fairbrother, interviewed three guest speakers at a Conference at Birkbeck College in London recently: the Guardian Journalist Jackie Ashley who has been caring for her husband Andrew Marr, Professor Joni Lovenduski of Birkbeck, and Fiona Mactaggart the Labour MP for Slough, who is Secretary of Labour's Commission for Older Women.

Fiona Mactaggart Hot quote: "I have discussed with some of my colleagues if we ought to invite the other parties onto our terrain, but they said let them run to catch up. I think they will start running very soon."

Engineers Week – Why the UK economy needs more young girls to become engineers

The Business Secretary Vince Cable, has said there is a need for the UK economy to encourage more women to become engineers and that our position at the bottom of the league table for female engineers in Europe will present "enormous problems" for our economy in years to come.

Our Executive Producer, Boni Sones, spoke to two engineers about this shortage as they demonstrated to MPs in Westminster some of the exciting advances engineers had achieved.

Philippa Oldham, Head of Transport and Manufacturing for the Institution of Mechanical Engineers, was taking things apart and putting them back together again as a young girl, and soon progressed to working with a Formula 1 team before going to Birmingham University to gain a masters in Mechanical Engineering.

Philippa Hot Quote: "I have turned up for a meeting and been asked "do you take the minutes?", and I said "yes", I can do that as well but I am also your design engineer and I can multi-task too!"

Richard Noble, Director of the Bloodhound Project, which is being taken to primary schools across the UK, showcased his supersonic car that can travel at 1,000 miles per hour and hopefully one day will set a new world land speed record. Richard and his colleague Andy Green, have held the land speed record for 29 years.

Richard Noble Hot Quote: "The girls are being sectioned off to be hair dressers, when we know there are not enough jobs for them, it is a waste of talent. Vince is on record as saying that in 50 per cent of all the State co-educational schools there is not one girl with physics A level, and he is right."

How David Cameron can get more women into politics – let them job share!

Dr Sarah Wollaston the Conservative MP for Totnes has this week spoken up in favour of job share MPs. As the Liberal Democrat Party has to contend with allegations of sexual misconduct against one of its senior figures, Lord Rennard, Dr Wollaston has written in the Guardian that there is no place for a "casting couch" approach to appointments in political parties today. She has likened Westminster to a "boys boarding school" with just 23 per cent of MPs in the House being women!

You can read more about this in Chapter 11.

The year: 2012
A Women Bishop in South Africa but not in the Church of England
On 20 November 2012 the Anglican Church of Southern Africa consecrated its first woman bishop – Ellinah Wamukoya, will be the new bishop in Swaziland.

At the same time, the general synod of the Church of England voted narrowly against the appointment of women as bishops. The voting was 44 for and 3 against with two abstentions in the House of Bishops, 148 for and 45 against in the House of Clergy, and 132 for and 74 against in the House of Laity. Six more "yes" votes in the Laity would have swung it.

The next Archbishop of Canterbury The Rt Rev Justin Welby has said it was a "very grim day". The proviso that parishes opposed to women bishops would have been able to request supervision by a stand-in male bishop perplexed many. Parliamentarians are now suggesting all kinds of ways to bring about equality in the Church of England.

In local churches prayers have been said to unite church goers but the sense of dismay is tangible. At the theological training college, Westcott House in Cambridge the Principal, The Rev Canon Martin Seeley, put this notice and prayer on their website. It is read by our Executive producer Boni Sones, and reporter Paul Seagrove both bell-ringers at nearby St Edward's.

Job Share MPs?
Our www.parliamentaryradio.com reporter Linda Fairbrother interviews the Labour MP for Hayes and Harlington John McDonnell on the campaign to introduce Job Share MPs to help those with disabilities to enter the Commons. An issue we have been championing over the past year and

whose original supporters included the Liberal Democrat equalities minister Lynne Featherstone MP. See Linda's documentary on our More Reports Page. Copyright Linda.

Precious Awards – do join in!
Foluke Akinlose MBE tells us about the Sixth year of The PRECIOUS Awards 2012. The awards celebrate the achievements of inspirational entrepreneurial women of colour who are running businesses in the UK. We got Foulke to take a tour of the House of Commons works of Art that profile women MPs. What did she make of it all? The Awards this year feature a 'Woman In Public Life' category so do nominate someone you know.

People's History Museum, Manchester to feature our 3 portraits of women MPs across party as Object of the Month
Go to www.phm.org.uk Object Number: NMLH.2012.45.1-4 Thanks Phil, thanks Louise.

Read our brochure about the Women MPs Photos "The Day the Carlton Club accepted women".

Listen to our new World broadcasts. Women in Zimbabwe, Congo, Malawi, Afghanistan have soul. Thanks CPA.

Allowing women MPs to write their own part in History - the New LSE Archive
Congratulations to the London School of Economics whose bid for the Women's Library was successful. The content of this site and that of our earlier podcast broadcast on wpradio.co.uk will now go into this Archive.

Ellie Robinson, Archivist, tells us it should be catalogued by Christmas. Thanks Ellie and congratulations to all the Archivist team, Sue too! What an honour for all of our team here too!

The British Library Harman-Shephard Audio Archive with women MPs

The audio interviews from the book *Women in Parliament the New Suffragettes* are now housed at the Harman-Shephard collection of interviews. The 82 interviews were conducted with women Members of Parliament across Party in 2004/05 and are archived and publicly accessible at the British Library, under Sound and Moving Image collection catalogue reference C1182. See a description of the collection and search the British Library Sound and Moving Image catalogue for details of individual recordings. Thanks Rob thanks Alex.

London 2012, the women's Olympics!
Debbie Jevans, Director of Sport, Locog

When Nicola Adams won a boxing gold for GB in the 2012 Olympics she told reporters: "At first it was hard to find an opponent. I know a lot of people saw women's boxing as a bit of a freak show!" Women athletes achieved 11 gold medals in all (including equestrian events) in the first Olympics to ever include women competitors in every sport, and from Countries such as Saudi Arabia and Qatar.

www.parliamentaryradio.com for women went in search of the movers and shakers who made this incredible achievement happen. We caught up with Debbie Jevans, the international tennis champion and now Director of Sport for Locog, the London Organising Committee. But Debbie isn't going to put her feet up and celebrate until the Paralympics are successfully launched – she's responsible for them too! She tells us to watch out for double Paralympic champion Ellie Simmonds.

You'll also see (below) we've interviewed Tessa Jowell, the Shadow Olympics Minister, who has worked with Debbie, Seb Coe and others to ensure 2012 became the "Women's Olympics"!

Debbie Hot Quote: "It's a long road from when we first started to get women to be equal in these games. The first games I went to was '88 in Seoul and it was a very different story then but that curve has been upwards and it is down to people like Tessa and a lot of people working behind the scenes. Sometimes you do get a bit of opposition, it was a huge step to have countries like Saudi Arabia and Qatar competing. It was a big step change for them to have women competing but I think it's taken longer for them to realise females doing sports is absolutely right and appropriate. From Seb Coe down everyone has been very supportive."

"In the future I do personally want to see more females participating. Even though more girls do participate the drop off rate at 16 is still very, very high. I would like to see more girls competing with role models like Jessica Ennis and Victoria Pendleton helping them to understand that to aspire to be an athlete is just as important as aspiring to be a film star or a singer, or appearing in X factor with the fame you get in two seconds, you don't get that as an athlete."

The year: 2011
2012: Equality in the Commons: 100 years – too long to wait?
Tricky issue: Some issues just don't fade away, in fact as people get angrier about them they seem to come back into fashion again! In 2012 there are enough angry voices now across party to put women's representation in the Commons back at the top of the Parliamentary agenda. Here our dogged reporter Linda Fairbrother tackled that thorny issue of why at the current rate of progress we will have to wait another 100 years before there is parity in the representation of female MPs in Westminster. Thanks Linda, you are kicking off 2012 in style for us.

Joan Ruddock Hot Quote: "I think that what's happened with the appointment of a 29 year old woman Chloe Smith into the Treasury Team was that men generally think either a women can't do those sort of subjects, or that she's far too young, and also most importantly, there's an awful lot of them who thought they should have the job. And this is always the thing – women are not entitled to equal opportunity, men should always come first!"

Professor Joni Lovenduski Hot Quote: "At the current rate of progress we are going to be 100 years before we have parity. And I haven't got 100 years – have you?"

Copyright to this report belongs to Linda Fairbrother.

"Tricky Issue": Job Share MPs?

Should MPs be allowed to job share? Hot foot from one parliamentary gathering Boni Sones, our Executive Producer of www.parliamentaryradio.com, and Linda Fairbrother report on how reformers are now calling for Job Share MPs.

In this 25 minute audio documentary, www.parliamentaryradio.com reporter Linda Fairbrother analyses both sides of this month's "Tricky Issue"!

Surprisingly an idea that was once ridiculed has now been mainstreamed and is being considered seriously in those famous "corridors of power". Supporters include the Equalities Minister, the Liberal Democrat MP for Hornsey and Wood Green Lynne Featherstone who would like the Speaker of the Commons John Bercow to consider it.

Lynne Hot Quote: "I have raised it with the Speaker of the House because I think we want to get him on board. He was certainly very interested in the idea. He wants to spend more time with his children so he's always very sympathetic to a whole range of family-friendly arrangements and we are working with him and other male MPs on this.

"The men in the House who have children, particularly young children, they love them just as much as the women love their children. They do actually hate not being able to see them, particularly if they are parted because of Constituency reasons, for part of the week. It's very, very tough to miss your kid's first day at school whatever your gender."

Linda also interviews former Civil Servant Maggy Piggott and her colleague Judith Killick, who job shared in the Civil Service for 23 years, and Liberal Democrat Dinti Batstone from the Campaign for Gender Balance. Copyright Linda:

Carolyn Quinn Chair of the Parliamentary Press Gallery – the first woman!

"The Burma Road" – Our intrepid reporter Linda Fairbrother takes a tour of the press gallery fondly known as "The Burma Road" with Carolyn Quinn.

Carolyn is well known as presenter of the The Westminster Hour on Radio 4 on Sunday evenings at 10.00pm. Our audience will also recognise her voice as the presenter of the weekday PM in Eddie Mair's absence, she's presented on Today too!

Carolyn began on The Irish Post, then she was selected for a BBC local radio trainee scheme, then she worked for Radio Solent, before moving on to the local radio desk for the BBC at Westminster. She became a political correspondent in 1994.

Women weren't allowed into the Press Gallery. In the 1890s they declared: "The consequences would have been too difficult to conceive."

Carolyn Hot Quote: "Women weren't allowed into the Press Gallery. In the 1890s they declared: "The consequences would have been too difficult to conceive." Then two women sat in the press gallery to cover Nancy Astor taking her seat as the first woman MP in 1919! It took another 26 years before woman took up permanent reporting posts in the Gallery."

Women2Win: Looking Towards 2015 – The Rt Hon Theresa May MP

It was a five year birthday party and a packed celebration of the Conservative Women2Win Campaign that saw a record 49 of their women MPs elected to Parliament in the 2010 General Election. But not content with their numbers the campaign is marching on to get even more Conservative women MP elected in the next General Election probably in 2015. So could the event panellists envisage a gender balanced parliament in the next ten years? Our intrepid reporter Linda Fairbrother talked to them as the celebrations came to a lively and vibrant conclusion.

Linda began with the Guest Speaker, The Rt Hon Theresa May MP Home Secretary and Minister for Women and Equalities, then she chatted to Helen Grant MP, Priti Patel MP, Sarah Childs, Professor of Politics, University of Bristol and Jackie Ashley, Columnist, The Guardian.

www.wpradio.co.uk would like to thank: Brooks Newmark MP & Baroness Morris of Bolton Co-Chairmen of Women2Win & Alexandra Robson & Baroness Jenkin of Kennington Director of Women2Win & Co-Founder of Women2Win. Find out more...

Theresa May Hot Quote: "In terms of Constituency and boundary changes, Women2Win will carry on the work we are doing. We are looking forward to encouraging more women into Parliament in 2015 there will be boundary changes and we are now in government, not in opposition so we are not in the process of having a very large number of seats to win to get into government.

"The Party did do quite a lot, we didn't go all the way to create All-women shortlists, but the creation of the "A" list the "Priority" list, the Open primaries, the all postal Open Primaries too. We have done a lot in the past of course we will have to look at the new scenario and what needs to be done in future as well."

Priti Patel Hot Quote: "Women2Win has transformed and revolutionised the desire and conviction in the Conservative Party to get more women elected and getting more women involved in public office. We have had tremendous support from Women2Win, it has been tremendous in telling us what it is all about."

Helen Grant Hot Quote: "Women2Win was a fantastic recruitment and development organisation for women. It attracted women into politics and helped to grow them into politicians and the help could be anything from holding your hand with media interviews to attending influential events. Marvellous!"

What are they banging on about?
Wilberforce abolished slavery by "banging on" about it over many years. A year into a new Conservative and Liberal Democrat coalition government

and Parliament, three women MPs and the Labour leader Ed Miliband talk of the issues of concern to them.

Seema Malhotra Director of the Fabian Women's Network launches a campaign: "Women changing politics" to assist more Labour women to become MPs at the next General Election. 22 women have been selected to be that "crack in the glass ceiling" – we hear from two of them Chloe and Suzy. Thanks to Seema we hear from the Labour Leader Ed Miliband too.

Ed Miliband Hot Quote: "I would like to see as many women MPs as possible in Parliament at the next General Election. What I want to get to eventually is half of our MPs to be women, it's obviously going to take time to get there."

Seema Malhotra Hot Quote: "We are launching a political education scheme. We think what holds women back in politics is a lack of understanding of how politics works. It is about networks, about having confidence through knowledge and about women having aspirations about themselves.

"This political education programme is going to make a big difference about the talent coming through in our public life. Ed called the 22 women on the programme this year, as "22 cracks in the glass ceiling" which was a brilliant way to describe it. The fact we have launched the campaign in the Shadow Cabinet Room shows where the political activity is taking place. These women already have the confidence to be leaders in their own communities as well as having aspirations for themselves and others. In terms of the Labour party, further reform is only going to happen when people bring forward their own experiences and say what needs to change."

Campaigning for Liberal Democrat women MPs – where are they?

Baroness Sal Brinton, a Liberal Democrat Peer, is going to ensure her Party gets more women into Parliament at the next General Election. There are suggestions that the existing seven Liberal Democrat women MPs will all lose their seats.

Banging on they most certainly are and that's what brings success ultimately.

Baroness Sal Brinton Hot Quote: "The really good news is that we are already oversubscribed on "Inspiration weekends". I am encouraged that we have lots of strong women out there wanting to be an MP. We are also speaking to our local parties and regional organisations and the message from them is that they are ready too.

"We have agreed to do some form of twinning, not our target seats, we are much smaller than the other parties so that would be a problem. We are not calling it twinning but "groupings" to ensure we get men and women and ethnic minority candidates into seats."

How to juggle work-life balance: Does a "vocation" stop you taking a much needed break?

"A healthy selfishness" might just help us all juggle that "Work- life balance" question says Caroline Lloyd-Evans, coach, counsellor and relationship therapist. Here Caroline tells Boni Sones, our Executive Producer how women have to work harder, compete harder and climb over their own complexes to navigate that obstacle course to achieve balance. "Tweaking a little" can make a big difference. Do listen, this advice is clear!

In 2011 we ask is the Commons family friendly? Katy Clark MP is juggling a new baby and a demanding job

Katy Clark, Labour MP for North Ayrshire and Arran since 2005 has an 18 month-old-daughter, took maternity leave, and quite often uses colleagues to hold her daughter while she pops into the Chamber to vote. Here she talks about her "two-lives" with a constituency that is 400 miles and a five hour journey from Westminster and a job that is a "vocation" – often seven days a week!

Going into the New Year of 2011 Katy doesn't think the further reforms of the Commons hours suggested by Green MP Caroline Lucas would help her, but she says the "costs" of child-care are "considerable" and difficult to manage for many women wanting to become an MP! Our Executive Producer Boni Sones spoke to her.

Katy Hot Quote: "I've tried to minimise the travelling for my daughter, so she spends half her time in London and half in Scotland, I sometimes go up and down every week but she doesn't! I had a child relatively late in life and I wanted to spend as much time with her as possible so therefore you do run yourself ragged to minimise the time you are away from her. You do spend your time rushing from one thing to another.

"I was a person who always worked seven days a week in a large geographical constituency. Maybe I am using my time more wisely, and I am more efficient now, but I just can't put the hours in I used to."

The year: 2010
Shirley Williams, Baroness Williams of Crosby
Rt. Hon. Professor Shirley Williams is Co-Founder of the Liberal Democrats and is a Member of the UK House of Lords, where she was Leader of the party from 2001 to 2004. She is Professor Emeritus of Elective Politics at the John F. Kennedy School of Government at Harvard University and advises the Prime Minister on issues of nuclear proliferation. She has written many books and is regarded as an "elder stateswoman" of British politics.

Baroness Williams recently gave a talk to the "Institute of Government" on reforming politics after the expenses saga. Here Linda Fairbrother, our wpradio.co.uk reporter, asked her why she thought politics was "broke" and how we could go about "fixing it", including more women MPs in Westminster. Do listen!

Cambridge student sit in and tuition fees!
www.wpradio.co.uk caught up with two student protestors in the sit-in at Cambridge Old School's Combination Room, and asked 25-year-old Phd student "Polly" (a pseudonym) and 22-year-old history student Rachel to review the past year in politics and to look forward to 2011. They both

said they felt "betrayed" by politics and the "Big Society" and their new Liberal Democrat MP Julian Huppert, however the Conservative students in Cambridge are supporting him and the doubling in fees to £6,000 a year or more. Boni Sones spoke to them both.

Polly Hot Quote: "Fees is a bigger betrayal than expenses. The fact is I felt the expensive scandal was systematic and evidence of corruption in Westminster but this vote shows that our government is putting in jeopardy the futures of those they are supposed to be representing and it is unacceptable."

Rachel Hot Quote: "Expenses was a distraction from some of the real problems we are facing. It was symptomatic of wider lack of accountability by politicians and the fact the papers focused on this issue for so long was a major betrayal. They are not looking at the education cuts, tuition fee rises, and wider cuts, and it shows the way the media is framing the cuts at the moment. I don't trust the media to portray the cuts either."

The Big Society in conversation – Lynne Berry CEO of WRVS
Lynne Berry, the CEO of the WRVS, has told wpradio that the voluntary sector can fill gaps in services but it is not a free option. The "Big Society" builds on the tradition of people getting involved in their communities but, she says, it is not a replacement for public services.

The WRVS has over 45,000 volunteers offering practical help to older people, and has celebrated its 70th anniversary. Lynne told our reporter Linda Fairbrother that if the services of the third-sector are to expand to create the "Big Society" then more funding will be needed to professionally develop and back up volunteers with training and support. The corporate sector is already responding to the rallying cry!

The Boni Sones Harman Shephard BL Archive opens
WP Radio will be opening a new historic audio archive jointly with the British Library on August 20th 2010. The Harman/Shephard archive will

contain the full audio of 81 of the 83 cross party interviews conducted by five women journalists for the book *Women In Parliament: The New Suffragettes* published in October 2005.

If you would like access to this embargoed archive email us... Access is by permission only. The Archive will be open on August 20th 2010 for those female MPs who have allowed immediate access. Only two of the 83 women MPs interviewed for the book have declined to give permission.

The journalists who conducted the interviews are: Linda Fairbrother, Angela Lawrence, Deborah McGurran, Dr Eva Simmons, Boni Sones OBE. Each has over 25 years of broadcast journalist experience.

Jackie Ashley, used extracts from these audio interviews to broadcast a BBC Radio 4 documentary called "A Monstrous Regiment" in 2005 produced by Deborah McGurran, Boni Sones and Dr Eva Simmons.

Subsequent to that broadcast Boni has worked with the British Library to get the women MPs to give permission for the full audio interviews to go into a proper archive charting modern women MP's representation in Westminster. After four years, 81 of them have now agreed.

Boni Hot Quote: "The interviews not only charted the experiences of the so called "Blair's Babes" but we asked women MPs what they thought of changes in the hours of the Commons, All-women shortlists, the Suffragettes, how the media treated them and commented on their clothes and hair styles and what they thought of being called "Blair's Babes".

"We also discovered that some Conservative party male MPs in the mid-1980s still called all women "Betty", and some made gestures across the Chamber that demoralised the Labour women of 1997. But there were heartening stories too, both Harriet Harman MP and Baroness Gillian Shephard, warmly greeted other women MPs even if they weren't from the same party. This archive is therefore named after both of them.

"One of the most moving moments of the interviews and setting up the archive at the BL was when we got a hand written note from Mo Mowlam, in childlike writing, just before she died saying she would like her one hour fifteen minute audio interview with Linda Fairbrother and Boni Sones, to be placed in the archive. This is the last serious political interview in broadcast that Mo conducted. Mo was one of the first to reply and support us as was Margaret Beckett MP.

"I would like to thank all the journalists who conducted the interviews with me, the MPs who gave us permission to set up the project, Caroline Spelman MP, Sandra Gidley MP, and Hilary Armstrong MP, then the Chief Whip, and the British Library staff who have subsequently been documenting our work. It's been a huge collaborative effort but one that will have set the record straight for many contemporary women MPs who were being portrayed poorly by the media at that time."

"Women, Power and Politics", at the Tricycle Theatre.
Women's Parliamentary Radio interviews are on display and can be heard in a new exhibition at the Tricycle Theatre in London at the "Women Power and Politics" programme of events.

Ten interviews by Linda Fairbrother, Anne Garvey, and Boni Sones OBE, can be heard through headphones along one wall of the exhibition. Boni performed readings from her book: *Women in Parliament: The New Suffragettes* at the opening of the exhibition. The book can be purchased from www.wpradio.co.uk books.

The exhibition is a celebration of women who have made a positive political impact in the UK over the last century, whether within or outside governmental frameworks.

Incorporating rarely-seen archival material of the women's suffrage movement; political activist Olive Morris's campaigns for the rights of the black community; and the long battle of the Greenham Common Women's Peace Camp against nuclear proliferation.

The exhibition also features a little-known 1974 film by the London Women's Film Group which examines the status of women's labour under capitalism. Wpradio.co.uk has also just interviewed the Assistant Director, Amy Hodge and the Director Indhu Rubasingham, about the nine plays that are being performed in two parts.

Indhu Rubashingham Hot Quote – whose family are Tamils from Sri Lanka, which has a strong tradition of women in politics, having elected the first female Prime Minister in the world in 1960, laughed when asked if she was a "feminist". She replied: "I personally haven't got an agenda, I am not a politician and I am not a policy maker. I wanted to ask "do we need more women to represent women or do we not?", and to get people to think about it. "The reason I am hesitating (on saying I am a feminist) is not whether I am a feminist or not, I don't think that it's important for the project.... I'm interested in the unheard voice and that may or may not be women."

Amy Hodge Hot Quote – thought differently, she said: "I am a feminist. The purpose of the project is to get people thinking and engaging in the debate and the plays."

A Day in the Life of a CEO and Town Clerk on Election day

They're off. It's the day of the General Election and Antoinette Jackson is the Chief Executive of Cambridge City Council, one of a few women who run councils in Britain. She's spent months planning the fine detail of getting voters registered, staffing the 42 polling booths and getting volunteers to count the votes after the polls close at 10 pm. The results will be declared about 2.30 to 3am in the morning. Accuracy, says Ms Jackson, is essential. And there's local elections too. She spoke to our Executive Producer of wpradio.co.uk, Boni Sones.

And eight-year-old Imogen Rodgers, has managed to read ALL the election literature that has come through her door. Boni caught up with Imogen at the Good Shepherd Church Hall.

The candidates in Cambridge are: Martin Booth, Trade Unionist and Socialist Coalition; Peter Burkinshaw, UK Independence Party; Nick Hillman, Conservative; Julian Huppert, Liberal Democrat; Tony Juniper, Green Party; Holborn Old, Independent; Daniel Zeichner, Labour.

Theresa May MP – Co-founder Women2Win

Theresa May MP, Shadow Secretary of State for Work and Pensions and Shadow Minister for Women is contemplating an increase in the number of Conservative women MPs, should her party win the next General Election.

The numbers could rise from 18 now, just 9 per cent of the Parliamentary Party, to a possible 55 to 60, should the Tory Party get an overall majority.

This week another A List candidate, Joanne Cash in Westminster North, found themselves in the hot seat as she offered to resign amid a row with a senior local party member.

The Women2Win campaign was founded in November 2005 and the A-list was announced a month later, having first been suggested by Theresa May and Andrew Lansley in 2001. The roots of the Women2Win campaign pre-date Cameron but with the party leader's conversion to All-women shortlists, following the publication of the Speaker's Conference Report, the party is moving forward its progressive agenda. Research has shown that a women candidate can add 1 per cent to a party's vote.

Boni Sones, Executive Producer of Women's Parliamentary Radio, spoke to Theresa May MP about the history of the Women2Win campaign, her aspirations for future women MPs, and the issues they would be likely to champion.

Theresa May Hot quote: "I was a co-founder of the Women2Win Campaign with a number of others and the reason I did that was that we believed passionately in getting more women into Parliament and particularly more Conservative women MPs. We now have 18 women MPs and I think Parliament will make better decisions if it has a greater diversity of people and that includes the Conservative Party as well.

"It is always difficult to be precise, but if we were to get an overall majority of one, we would probably have 55 to 60 in the House as opposed to 18 and that is a step-change for us in the number of women in the House.

"I am pleased with the outcome (of Women2Win) I think we have done a great deal in the Party but I don't think we can rest on our laurels. I think we have to continue the process of saying that we want to encourage more women to come forward, and then give them the support to get selected and then get elected in the seats they are standing for."

The Hustings
Claire Ward MP Minister in Ministry of Justice team

Claire Ward, has been the Labour MP for Watford since 1997, one of the new 101 "revolution" of women who came in with that new Labour government, many on all women-shortlists although Claire was not one of these. Just 24, she was the youngest ever Labour female MP and is now a Minister in the Ministry of Justice team. She's managed to juggle the job of an MP, with a new family, and ministerial responsibilities.

Claire welcomes the Speaker's Conference report which wants all parties to do more to get women and ethnic minorities into Parliament. She tells Prospective Parliamentary Candidates it is a hard slog to get selected for a seat and that the job is "a way of life" but when you achieve success it is a "rewarding job". She applauds the planned new crèche announced by Speaker Bercow but now says there needs to be further reform of the hours of the Commons.

She is proud of her government's many achievements for women, which she says, still go largely unreported in a media which treats women MPs differently from male colleagues. Claire talks to Executive Producer, Boni Sones:

Claire Hot Quote: "It's a tremendous privilege to do the job as a Member of parliament, but there is no doubting that being a Member of Parliament isn't just a job, it is a way of life. It isn't a nine to five job, it does take up a huge amount of time and personal time and that of your family. It is also incredibly rewarding being able to see what difference you can make, being part of legislative changes like the minimum wage but also on personal cases for your constituents. When you get the success – that is what makes it a really rewarding job."

The Hustings: Maria Miller MP Shadow Minister for the Family

Maria Miller, has been the Conservative MP for Basingstoke since 2005. As Shadow Minister for Women she has been championing a better work life balance for men and women and their families and says she would support a further reform of hours in the Commons. She thinks the planned new crèche facilities announced by Speaker Bercow will benefit staff as much as MPs themselves.

Maria, who has a family and fought one seat in 2001 before being successful in Basingstoke, says the support of her husband and family was vital in helping her as a PPC to gain her seat, as well as helping her to bear the cost of it all. She says the Conservative Party could increase its number of women MPs from 17 to over 50 in the next Parliament if the Conservatives get a clear majority and that its Leader, David Cameron MP has always wanted to see more women MPs in Westminster and in the government.

Maria thinks that some of the new women MPs could find themselves with ministerial responsibilities fairly quickly, she gained her shadow cabinet role after just six months in Westminster. She names Penny Mordaunt, Margot James and Harriet Baldwin as candidates to watch. Executive Producer Boni Sones spoke to her.

Maria Hot Quote: "With an overall majority of one we'd have just over 50 MPs who would be female and that would be the first time we would have that many in Parliament and that would be a very exciting challenge for us.

"It has been an enormous priority of David Cameron, there is always more to be done, I think it would be unfortunate if we see the overall number of women drop in the next election but we have some very capable women candidates who are going to be joining the parliamentary party I hope and adding to parliamentary life."

The Hustings: Jo Swinson MP East Dunbartonshire

Women's Parliamentary Radio is beginning the New Year with a new series on "The Hustings!" We are interviewing all parties on how they are encouraging women to become Prospective Parliamentary Candidates in the forthcoming election.

We begin with Jo Swinson MP, for the Liberal Democrats who was the youngest MP in Westminster and who personally has done much to encourage women candidates. She gained her East Dunbartonshire seat in May 2005 and it was third time lucky for her.

Jo says the problem for the Liberal Democrats is not in the selection procedures, but in getting enough women to come forward. In Cambridge there are three men and three women, all local, going forward to the hustings on January 15th to replace the sitting MP David Howarth.

Jo Hot Quote: "David Cameron's policy of promoting more women as PPCs is "all fur coat and no knickers as we say in Edinburgh". I think you will find this is the case for Cameron's support of All-women shortlists, he did it for a great headline…..but actually when you look behind it I am not sure there will be that many AWS in the Tories, they have not been selecting that many women in seats where MPs are standing down. Although they should end up with some more women MPs after the next election, they are not actually changing as much as David Cameron would have you believe.

"1 in 7 of our MPS are women, but there are things to be optimistic about …at the next General Election about 40 per cent of our target seats have women candidates. Where LD MPs are standing down 4 of the 7 have selected women so although we are starting from a low base we have some good signs of success that look as if we will increase our percentage of women at the next election."

The year: 2009
Susan Kramer - Liberal Democrat MP for Richmond Park
Women and Politics

Keeping a calm head in politics has never been more needed, as more and more of MPs so called "extravagant" expenses are paraded in the "Daily Telegraph" fairly or unfairly. What's more the "WAGs" group, Women Against Gordon Brown, appear to have been orchestrating moves to make the Labour Party confront the need for a leadership challenge. Susan Kramer, the Liberal Democrat MP for Richmond Park since 2005, has been tough enough to get out there and talk about the need to reform parliament, restore trust in politics and politicians, and to say she thinks the "Telegraph" is just doing its job.

Susan made her career in finance as a Vice-President of Citibank, a leading international bank and set up her own company before moving into politics. So will women be put off going into politics and what advice would Susan give to aspiring women politicians? Boni Sones asked her.

Susan Hot Quote: "I don't want to hide that this is a tough world, it is, and you have to have the kind of hide with you that lets you cope in this World. I would hate people to think it is gentle, it isn't, but I think collectively when women are in here there is more of an atmosphere to make change happen than there has been for a generation."

The Parliamentary Education Service Question Time for Women
The Parliamentary Education Service recently held a "Question Time" event where schoolgirls were invited to meet members of Parliament and members of the Lords. They listened to speeches and talked about why Parliament would be a better place with more women politicians, and those from ethnic minorities. Boni Sones spoke to the Labour MP Anne Begg, Vice-Chair of the new Speaker's Conference, which is debating the issue, Baroness Hayman, the Speaker in the House of Lords and to the young women students themselves.

Anne Begg Hot Quote: "Hopefully we will get consensus through the Speaker's Conference, I am an optimist, and certainly we are going to try to get more women into Parliament."

Baroness Hayman Hot Quote: "I think it is important that a Parliament represents its community. It is very important that politics in the widest sense is open to everybody and that there aren't barriers to participation."

Anne Begg MP Deputy Chair the Speaker's Conference
Anne Begg, the Labour MP, for Aberdeen South, is Deputy Chair, of the specially convened "Speaker's Conference", which will look at improving the representation of women, minority ethnic people and disabled people in Parliament. Anne Begg is the first permanent wheelchair user MP in

parliament, and she said the idea for the conference had been "energised" by the election of the USA's first black President, Barack Obama. At present only 20 per cent of MPs in Parliament are women and there are still only two black women MPs, Diane Abbott, and Dawn Butler. The Conference of 17 MPs from all the Parties will report next year.

Ending WP Radio's series of interviews focusing on women parliamentarians achievements 90 years since women first got the vote, Anne Begg MP, gave this engaging exclusive interview to Georgie Hemmingway. Anne told Georgie, she could remember the time when disabled people used to have to travel in the baggage compartments of trains.

Women's Parliamentary Radio would like to thank Pete Cook of Screenspace, our sound engineer and Paul Foulsham of MagStar, our web manager for the high quality of this year's broadcasts. Thanks too to Jackie Ashley, our Chair, and all the rest of our Board and production team.

Mary Honeyball MEP "Women In Power" in European Parliament
A new book listing all the elected female representatives in the European Parliament has discovered that the typical profile of a woman MEP is white, single, aged 52 and she has never had children.

You can read the rest of this report in Chapter 9.

Sir Crispin Tickell – Women and the Recession and International Women's Day 09
To celebrate International Women's Day this week, Women's Parliamentary Radio has secured this special interview with Sir Crispin Tickell, Director of the Policy Foresight Programme at Oxford University on how to meet the "sustainable development" challenges of the 21st Century. Sir Crispin, says he is optimistic about our ability to adapt and embrace sustainable green global values despite the terrible problems that face the World. Sir Crispin believes it is WOMEN who hold the key to a sustainable global future. Boni Sones asked him why?

Thanks to CIBAM at Cambridge University for allowing us to transmit this broadcast.

Dr Noreena Hertz – Women and the Recession

It's women, it seems, who hold the future of the world in their hands as economists and politicians agree that global capitalism is in need of drastic repair.

In this new "Recession Thought Leadership Series" Women's Parliamentary Radio is asking women in business and academia to contribute their thoughts on how to fix capitalism and prepare for a greener, healthier, more sustainable planet in the future. Here, Dr Noreena Hertz, an Associate Director of CIBAM at Judge Business School in Cambridge tells Boni Sones why she thinks we are about to move from an era of "gucci" capitalism to a new one of "co-operative capitalism" and how women and families will benefit. Thanks to CIBAM for letting us transmit this podcast.

The year: 2008
"The day the Carlton Club accepted women – 90 years after women first got the vote."

A viewing of photographic images of 104 of the 125 women MPs in Westminster will be launched at a private event at the National Portrait Gallery in the autumn to mark 90 years since women were first given the vote.

The original "Blair's Babes" Reuters photographer Kieran Doherty was invited back to Westminster to take the historic group composite photographs by Women's Parliamentary Radio working in association with the Labour, Conservative, and Liberal Democrat Parties and the Independent Labour Party. They will be shown as a framed wall size set, with each party side by side.

As Caroline Spelman MP, Chairman of the Conservative Party, arrived for the first photo call on May 21st she announced that "The Carlton Club" had just voted to accept women. The display is entitled "The Day the Carlton Club accepted women – 90 years after women first got the vote."

The preliminary images can be viewed and downloaded here. The full press release can be read here. Listen to our Suffragettes International Women's Day audio report here!

Barbara Follett MP, Deputy Minister for Women, will be launching the private viewing at the National Portrait Gallery in the autumn. She said: "Britain is a more equal society today than it was on that May morning eleven years ago when 101 Labour women MPs gathered around their newly elected Prime Minister for a photograph to celebrate the fact that, overnight, we had almost trebled the number of Labour women MPs and doubled female representation in the House of Commons. That increase has been particularly beneficial to women."

Theresa May MP, The Shadow Leader of the House of Commons and Shadow Minister for Women, said: "This is a wonderful achievement which marks the 90th anniversary of women first getting the vote, but which I hope will have lasting benefit in showing women that politics is for them."

Jo Swinson MP, said: "Bringing all the women MPs together for photographic portraits is a lovely way to commemorate the anniversary. However the small number of women MPs is a reminder to us all that we must redouble our efforts to get more women elected and make equality a reality."

Clare Short MP, Independent Labour said: "I am pleased that women of all parties took part in this photographic portrait, party by party, so that there is a visual image to show just how far women have progressed and how much work there is still to do to get more women MPs in parliament.

Vandna Gohil and Southall Black Sisters

Voice4Change England has brought together leading policy makers from across Britain at a symposium in London. "Equality and Cohesion in Diverse Britain: the Making of Public Policy" set out to consider how public policy is made and whether effective policies were being pursued by public bodies. The recent court case over single group funding involving Southall Black Sisters, and the commissioning of domestic violence services, as well as the changing meanings of multiculturalism were discussed. The meeting was chaired by Vandna Gohil, the Director of Voice4Change England. Boni Sones reports.

Ann Cryer MP and Chris Bryant MP speak up for Women Bishops
Ann Cryer, the Labour MP for Keighley has tabled an Early Day Motion – 1825 – asking The House, to call on the Church of England to remove all legal obstacles which prevent women from becoming bishops; and asks the Church to end this unacceptable form of discrimination against women clergy.

Chris Bryant, the Labour MP for Rhondda, is a supporter. Both were at a conference to talk about the issue organised by the WATCH group, Women and the Church, which has urged the Church to end discrimination. Boni Sones spoke to them both.

Ann Cryer Hot Quote: "I think more women Bishops in the Church will give strength to the women clergy and that's what we have in the Commons now, 80 years since all women got the vote this week. I think the numbers do change things, they give you strength and confidence.

"A woman bishop would take a great deal of experience and thought with her, like women MPs, they are different and do raise different issues, like I have done with the issue of forced marriages."

Ann Cryer said she couldn't believe that 8,000 women in the Church had signed a petition to prevent women from becoming bishops. "It is quite shocking that that number of women, if they are from the Church, can't see the sense in having women bishops."

Chris Bryant Hot Quote: "I think this is a matter of natural justice and I can't believe either in the mind of Christ or the heart of God that we should not honour the ministries of women".

Mr Bryant was ordained in 1986 and he thinks the Church "should fully respect women".

"It's the 80th anniversary on Wednesday when women had the same voting rights as men and I believe the House of Commons has become a better place since women got involved and I think women have put issues on the agenda that men would never have thought of."

Only "One in Five" of our MPs is a woman

The NASUWT UK-wide teachers' union, held a conference in London to delve into the thorny issue of why, 90 years after women achieved the vote for the first time, only "One in Five" of our MPs is a woman. Chris Keates, the General Secretary of the NASUWT, said we needed to do more to encourage women into politics. The event was Chaired by Jackie Ashley of Women's Parliamentary Radio.

Our reporter Daisy Ayliffe spoke to Jackie and Chris and asked if lessons could be learnt from the Welsh Assembly? Her report starts with the voice of Christabel Pankhurst, the daughter of the leading suffragette Mrs Emmeline Pankhurst.

Tackling the problems of race and representation Operation Black Vote

The Conservative Party is actively encouraging the Black Minority and Ethnic community to get involved in politics at a grass root level.

At a conference in London more than 50 delegates listened to how they could get their "VOICE" heard in the Conservative Party. They heard speeches from Simon Woolley of Operation Black Vote, Sonia Brown, of the National Black Women's Network and Theresa May MP the Shadow Leader of the House and the Shadow Minister for Women.

The Conference was organised by the Women's Officer, Liz St Clair. Boni Sones spoke to them as the Conference adjourned for lunch.

Baroness Shirley Williams and the Annual Women's Library speech

The Liberal Democrat Peer, Shirley Williams, has had a distinguished career in British politics. She was a member of the Wilson and Callaghan Governments in the 1960s and 1970s. In 1981 she co-founded the Social Democratic Party, becoming the first MP elected for the SDP in 1981. She is now writing her autobiography to be published next year. As the daughter of the renowned feminist Vera Brittan, it will no doubt contain many gems on British political history. Shirley has just delivered the annual Women's Library speech celebrating 90 years since women got the vote. Here she tells Boni Sones, what she thinks of women's political progress throughout the World.

ERS Debate "The Reform of the Voting Systems"

The Government's long awaited report on "The Reform of Voting Systems" has been greeted with mixed reactions from those who have long been advocating a change in the way we elect our MPs to Westminster. Reformers say that the current voting system of FPTP - First Past the Post – discriminates against women and ethnic minorities in favour of the sitting candidate – overwhelming white males. In this special WP Radio documentary debate, sponsored by the Electoral Reform Society, we asked MPs from all parties why they are or are not in favour of electoral reform.

The debate is Chaired by Jackie Ashley of the Guardian and BBC. Round the table the MPs are Chris Huhne, Shadow Home Affairs Spokesman for the Liberal Democrats, Caroline Spelman Chairman of the Conservative Party, the Labour MP Stephen Pound and academic Professor Nina Fishman who sits on the ERS Board.

Diana Wallis MEP – Liberal Democrat Vice President of the European Parliament

The British Liberal Democrat MEP for Yorkshire and the Humber, Diana Wallis is Vice President of the European Parliament. Diana is the first British female of any party to be elected to this position. Her roots in politics began in 1994 as a councillor on Humberside County Council. She became an MEP in 1999. In Europe Diana, a solicitor, is a spokesperson on the Legal Affairs Committee, she is also a full member of the Petitions Committee, in which she has championed citizen friendly legislation. On a flying visit to Westminster, she snatched a few moments to talk to Boni Sones.

WP Radio Mentioned in International Women's Day Debate in the Chamber

WP Radio was mentioned in the International Women's Day debate in the House of Commons Chamber. We are in Hansard.

Jo Swinson: It is also important to note that better representation of women changes the issues that are discussed. I highly recommend an excellent book called "Women in Parliament" by Boni Sones and the hon. Member for Luton, South (Margaret Moran), which chronicles interviews with many women MPs. I read it a few months after my election and found it contained a few tips...

Margaret Moran: I thank the hon. Lady for that unanticipated plug and for her support for the follow-on project that Boni Sones and I have been involved in – women's parliamentary radio – through which we can provide unmediated information about women in Parliament and about what we are doing, rather than the stereotypes about women in this place that are often promulgated in the media.

Jo Swinson: The hon. Lady is absolutely right; the project is an excellent one that deserves support and its website is www.wpradio.co.uk. I would certainly encourage hon. Members to become involved with that excellent project.

Channel 4 Political Awards 2008

The WP Radio team was nominated for the Hansard Society Democracy Award at the Channel 4 Political Awards this year presented by Jon Snow. Our congratulations to Operation Black Vote which won and our thanks to the Hansard Society and Channel 4.

Congratulations to our team: Pete Cook, sound engineer, Paul Foulsham of MagStar for the website design. Our journalists: Linda Fairbrother, Anne Garvey, Deborah McGurran. Our Chair: Jackie Ashley. Production assistants: Dan Beagle, Sophie Kainradl and Lucy Fairbrother. See clip of WP Radio featured in the 2008 Hansard Society Democracy Award on Channel 4.

Andy Williamson eDemocracy Programme Director, Hansard Society
"WPR calls itself "the Woman's Hour of Westminster", in reference to the long-running BBC Radio 4 series. But it isn't a traditional radio station, it's a website that provides online streaming and downloads of audio anywhere, anytime. This is a really powerful form of eDemocracy that is often ignored and overlooked in the conversation. It's a good example of a clearly targeted niche product that has harnessed the internet to overcome the significant barriers to entry that exist for traditional broadcast media. In doing so, it provides a rich source of information to an audience that could not possibly be reached by a traditional radio station.

"WPR is just one of many examples of why eDemocracy remains a contestable discourse and why that is a good thing. By keeping the definition fluid we allow people to innovate, coming up with ideas beyond labels and silos. And that's a good thing for democracy."

Thanks Andy for that glowing tribute. Read our WP Radio Newsletter written by our intern Lucy Fairbrother, telling you of a year in our life.

Women in the World Today the Conservative agenda for women!

Theresa May MP has launched a new report on the Conservative Party's priorities for women in the UK. "Women in the World Today" puts down the foundation on which the Party's women's policy will be built. Four Conservative Prospective Parliamentary Candidates: Flick Drummond, Lorraine Fullbrook, Helen Grant and Penny Mordaunt told Boni Sones of the issues that confront women in their constituencies.

Charlotte Leslie

Charlotte Leslie, is the Conservative Party's Prospective Parliamentary Candidate for Bristol North West. You can read the rest of this report in Chapter 10. Learn more about PPCs.

Sal Brinton – Liberal Democrats

Sal Brinton is a leading Liberal Democrat at local and national level. She is the Party's Prospective Parliamentary Candidate for Watford and has been involved in politics for 30 years. She has been a County Councillor and a PPC. Sal is now standing for a winnable seat and is helping the Liberal Democrats to train women who want to become parliamentary candidates. So what tips do women need to help them get selected for a seat and why should they stand for one they are not likely to win? Boni Sones talked to Sal.

The year: 2007
Women supporting Women

In WP Radio's new series: "Women supporting Women" our reporter Anne Garvey talks to two women MPs who are helping to change women's lives inside and outside Westminster.

Jo Swinson MP

Jo Swinson is the Liberal Democrat MP for East Dunbartonshire. She is the youngest MP in Westminster and her party's equality spokes person. She has championed issues such as the pay gap and also become a respected campaigner displaying her environmental concerns on issues such as unnecessary packaging.

Eleanor Laing MP

Eleanor Laing is the Conservative MP for Epping Forest. In July 2007 Eleanor was appointed Shadow Minister for Justice. She's previously worked as Shadow Minister for Children, and Women and Equality. She has a son Matthew who was born one week after the 2001 General Election. Eleanor believes women can stand up for themselves at the dispatch box, and has a few good tips for Prospective Parliamentary Candidates.

Women supporting Women

In WP Radio's new series: "Women supporting Women" our intern reporter Sophie Kainradl goes in search of women in other campaigning roles who are helping to change women's lives.

Joy Greasley on the Women's Institute

The Women's Institute was founded in 1915 with two aims: to revitalise the rural community and encourage more women to help with food production during World War I. Today the WI describes itself as 'a modern voice for today's woman' and is even suggesting that brothels should be licensed in order to protect prostitutes. But can an organisation with such a strong sense of tradition ever really represent such a great diversity of women? WP Radio reporter Sophie Kainradl talks to Joy Greasley, head of the WI's Training Committee, to ask how the WI is living up to its new image and if it really has as much power as its slogan suggests?

Frances O'Grady on the TUC

Frances O'Grady became the Deputy General Secretary of the Trade Union Congress in 2003. She is the first woman to hold such a senior position in the organisation. Frances is a staunch campaigner for women's rights in the work place, from equal pay to better maternity cover. She told WPR Radio reporter Sophie Kainradl what the government must do to improve the lives of female workers, why women make great politicians and how society desperately needs to change to cater for working mothers.

Are women fairly represented at Westminster?

Women MPs still only make up 20 per cent of MPs across party and it could be several hundreds of years before we have a fifty fifty gender balanced Parliament. Boni Sones, asked feminist academic, Joni Lovenduski, Professor of Politics at Birkbeck College at the University of London, why women's representation at Westminster was making such slow progress?

Women Championing Women

So what have women in Parliament been doing to champion issues of concern to women in the Country? Well if you asked them they'd say quite a lot. Sally Keeble for Labour, Caroline Spelman for the

Conservatives, and Sandra Gidley of the Liberal Democrats have been talking to Linda Fairbrother about how Women MPs are helping us.

Theresa May Interview and Women2Win
On the 23rd November the Conservative's 'Women2Win' campaign celebrates its first birthday. So how effective has the campaign been? It has had its fair share of negative headlines but some positive ones too as more women creep onto the Cameron 'A list' of candidates. Women now make up almost 40 per cent of the candidates chosen to fight the most winnable seats. Yet even the organisers admit "there is still so much to do." Boni Sones talked to Theresa May as she travelled back from one event on the train.

Monstrous Regiment
The 1997 election was extraordinary in many ways but not least because of the numbers of women in Parliament doubled from 60 to 120. Never before had the House encountered anything like it. And nor, it seems, had most of the women who joined it. Boni Sones, Deborah McGurran and Eva Simmons produced this documentary. It is presented by Jackie Ashley.

THREE

Equal pay and low pay

Equal pay was a battle that most women thought had been fought and won when the veteran Labour politician and Minister, Barbara Castle agreed to meet with the Ford Dagenham women who went on strike in support of their demands for equal pay rates to the men. Their strike began on 7th June 1968 when women sewing machinists at Ford Motor Company Ltd at the Dagenham plant in London walked out. The women made car seat covers and when the stock ran out the strike eventually resulted in a halt to all car production. Their jobs were graded in Category B, a less skilled production job, then Category C, with more skilled production jobs. As a result they were paid 15 per cent less than the full B rate. It was very common then for women to be paid less than men. Thanks to Barbara Castle, the Secretary of State for Employment and Productivity in Harold Wilson's government, the strike lasted just three weeks and the women, later portrayed in the Film "Made in Dagenham", received a pay increase, meaning they were then only paid 8 per cent below that of the men. Later the then Labour Government passed the Equal Pay Act of 1970, which said men and women had to be paid the same, but clever manipulation of job descriptions can still and does still disguise a lot. Later, Labour's introduction of a National Minimum wage in 1999 was a victory for women, many of whom were employed on low wages. It was as significant as the Dagenham strike. Now David Cameron, the Prime Minister has just announced that the Conservative Coalition government will raise the minimum, wage which will undoubtedly be beneficial to women and families in times of benefit cut backs. Sadly surveys of the public and private sector still show women are paid significantly less than men. More transparency in pay systems and as Sheryl Sandberg COO of Facebook advises "leaning in" could help to redress this balance.

Equal pay and low pay

The year: 2010
Fawcett's Challenge to the budget:

Rachel Reeves, the new Labour MP for Leeds West, is supporting attempts to force the government to analyse the impact of George Osborne's budget on low income households, particularly the regressive effects of the VAT increases. As a former economist with the Bank of England she is backing the Fawcett Society's judicial review of the budget and its impact on women. Boni Sones asked her why?

Rachel Reeves MP Hot Quote: "The evidence that we do have that was commissioned by Yvette Cooper, The Shadow Works and Pensions Minister, from the House of Commons Library, shows that the cuts in the Budget have a disproportionate effect on women, 72 per cent will impact on women compared to 28 per cent on men, so 6 billion of the 8 billion cuts will fall on women. I don't think it is right or fair, and I want to know if the government knew that when it put forward the budget, and if not why didn't it look at the impact on women and children as well?"

"…..In my constituency women are already struggling to get by. As we bring down the deficit we need to do it in a fair way and the Fawcett Society are trying to ensure that the government take into account the impact on women and people with disabilities and ethnic minorities as well, in line with the new Equalities Bill, and none of these things has the government attempted to do."

The year: 2009
Baroness Prosser – Equal Pay

The Treasury Select Committee is spending the autumn asking prominent men and women in banking, finance, politics, academia and the fields of equality, what their views are on whether a so called "Lehman Sisters" approach could have helped avert the financial crisis in the City.

The Committee is looking at how many women are in senior positions in major financial institutions, how widespread is the glass ceiling, pay inequalities, flexible working, and sexism in the City. One of those to give evidence was Baroness Margaret Prosser, Deputy Chair of the EHRC.

Our reporter Linda Fairbrother caught up with her and asked what she told the Committee?

Baroness Prosser Hot Quote: "The collapse of the banking system was so dramatic, maybe with a good mixture of women it still would have happened, but there is evidence to show that if you have a mixed workforce men and women together then behaviours are modified,.. ....women are much more thoughtful much more grounded and so that mixture makes people check their behaviour."

Baroness Prosser also spoke on the gender pay gap in the City, which stretches to a massive 80 per cent in some cases, saying the long hours are an issue for women.

"At the high earning end of financial services the employment is hugely male dominated, the age range of people operating at that high earning end goes from around 25 to 39, when women will be stopping to have children, and that is the time they want people to work all hours, so that is not suitable for women, and that alone shifts the emphasis and creates a pay anomaly."

Lynne Featherstone MP promotes equality for job applicants with the "no name" application form

Lynne Featherstone the MP for Hornsey and Wood Green and the Liberal Democrat's Equality spokesperson, has tabled an amendment to the government's Equality Bill calling on names to be taken off job application forms.

The Solicitor General, Vera Baird MP QC, who is leading on the Bill in the House, has indicated that the amendment is likely to be accepted in due course despite opposition from some quarters. She said they were looking into the research that had been conducted on this particular issue.

Lynne Featherstone MP told Women's Parliamentary Radio that the original proposal came about because two of her interns with the family names of Hussain and Patel had spoken to her of their inability to get through the job recruitment process.

Lynne told our Executive Producer Boni Sones, that she was optimistic that her "Featherstone" amendment would succeed:

Lynne Hot Quote: "My hope is that it will become mandatory throughout firms over a certain level of employees. I think it will make a huge step change to that bias which exists in the selection process. Work in American has shown, that the issue is not about racism or ageism or sexism it is more to do with brain patterns, that the person reading the CV has, so they will accept what is familiar and reject what is not familiar. That is what we are trying to do, to get through that first hurdle, then it is down to you at the interview."

WP Radio takes a sideways look at the Government's new Equality Bill through the eyes of two women leaders – one in the TUC and the other in Management Studies.
Kay Carberry, Assistant General Secretary TUC
Too much or too little? The Government's New Equality Bill has been published this week almost 40 years after the Equal Pay Act came into force.

It brings together all of Britain's Equality Legislation into one Act. As well as covering race, disability and gender the new Bill turns its attention to maternity, age, sexual orientation, religion, belief and gender reassignment.

Public sector bodies such as government departments, local authorities and health authorities, will have to comply with the provisions of the Act. The many businesses that supply them with services won't be awarded contracts until they do too.

The Minister for Equality Harriet Harman says the Bill will "make Britain more equal" however, Shadow Minister for Women Theresa May remains broadly supportive although sceptical about the actual measures in the Bill.

With the pay gap still standing at 17 per cent, Boni Sones, asked the TUC's Assistant General Secretary, Kay Carberry, if she was happy that the Bill went far enough?

Kay Hot Quote: "The TUC warmly welcomes this Bill and we would like to congratulate the womens' ministers on what they have achieved, there is lots of very good stuff in this Bill. On the Equal Pay aspects of the Bill we are a little bit disappointed…..we would like to have had fully fledged gender pay audits, but the Bill goes a little short of that."

It has been agreed that the TUC and CBI will be working with the Equality and Human Rights Commission on getting the strongest possible recommendations for equal pay measures in order to get sufficient voluntary take up, if not the government will legislate.

Ms Carberry continues: "We are very pleased to have been invited to participate in the exercise in drawing up what the measurements are going to be and what the reporting requirements are going to be. We are going into this very seriously, whole heartedly and we want to make sure it is a very successful exercise."

Dame Professor Dawson, the KPMG Professor of Management at Judge Business School at Cambridge University

Professor Dawson tells www.wpradio.co.uk her thoughts on how women can progress in business, what distinct qualities women managers have, and if these can help get them to the top. She also grapples with those other sticky problems of the so called "glass ceiling" and gender pay differences.

Professor Dawson has managed to juggle bringing up a family, with a high flying career in business and management herself. She was Director of Judge Business School from 1995 to 2006 and has specialised in studying organisational structure and change. She is also now Master of Sidney Sussex College in Cambridge. Those close to you at home, she says, can help determine the success of your career.

Professor Dawson Hot Quote: "I think individual managers have a style, women are certainly not one sort of style. In general you could say that probably more women than men are more empathetic, have more consideration for understanding other points of view and looking at a bigger picture, but there are some men who can do this as well and some women who can't do it at all. I don't think women are like this and men are like that, but on the balance of probability you might say some women managers have a greater humanity in the way they manage."

On the Government's new Equality Bill Professor Dawson said: "This is something I have changed my views on over the years. I used to think, would making a law really make that much difference? But over time it does change people's mind sets, it does change what they regard as legitimate..."

She continues: "Increasingly, board rooms, directors of human resources, operations managers will get into their mind that it is not legitimate to seriously discriminate against women in terms of pay, which all the evidence suggests there is...not necessarily deliberately but that is the result.

"I do think legislation makes a difference. I think it begins to change what is legitimate and it begins to change the mind set so that things that were thought normal and natural become illegitimate over time."

Her tip for the top: "I got used to having very little sleep when I brought up my children, ...I do think stamina and I do think optimism... a sense you can do something, you can do a job and making sure, if you can, you have relationships with people who also support you.

"If you go home to someone who does not share your commitment to your development it must be deeply frustrating and debilitating both for your relationship and your career. ...choosing who you are with outside work is as important to your work situation as what happens in the work situation."

Thanks to Cambridge Judge Business School for allowing us to broadcast this podcast.

International Women's Day Women and the Recession:
Women across party celebrated International Women's Day 09 with a heartfelt debate in the Chamber on Women and the Recession. You can read the rest of this report in Chapter 11.

The year: 2008
Judy Mallaber MP – Labour and the gender pay gap!
Judy Mallaber the Labour MP for Amber Valley in Derbyshire has been at the forefront of work in the Commons to eliminate the gender pay gap. There's still a 17 per cent difference among women's full-time salaries and that of men, and this rises to 40 per cent for those working part-time. In London it stands at 25 per cent. Judy sits on the Women and Work Commission and has recently led a Select Committee inquiry and report into what more can be done to make faster progress. The Report "Jobs for Girls", concluded that the Government should be doing more to keep the issue high on its list of priorities across departments. Boni Sones spoke to Judy about her work, ideals, and ambitions as an MP.

FOUR
Women in the Boardrooms

It has recently become a hot topic, but as the interviews we have conducted illustrate women's representation in the Boardrooms has been an idea that has been long in the making, and cuts across all the parties, Conservative, Labour and Liberal Democrats. The Conservative women of the 2010 intake have given this issue extra push with Liberal Democrat support at the highest level. Some began their careers in the City, and their links and associations not to mention sponsorships of important events has allowed the issue of women in the boardroom to gain extra prominence. In Europe it is an issue too. In October 2013 the Business Secretary Vince Cable welcomed a report by Lord Davies on "Women on Boards". The figures showed that the number of women directors in FTSE 100 companies has risen to 19 per cent. This was an increase from the 12.5 per cent of two years previously. The coalition government hopes to meet its target of 25 per cent representation on FTSE 100 boards by 2015. But even so, only 6.1 per cent of executive directors are female. A previous report by the Equalities and Human Rights Commission showed that, if no action was taken, it would take 70 years to achieve gender-balanced boardrooms in the UK's top 100 companies. Vince Cable earlier in the year wrote to all companies with no female board representatives. There are presently three women running FTSE 100 companies, Angela Ahrendts at Burberry, Alison Cooper at Imperial Tobacco and Carolyn McCall at EasyJet.

The year: 2013
What's stopping women executives running FTSE 100 Companies?
A new report from the Conservative Women's Forum wants to encourage more women onto Boards and to get to be CEOs and Directors. There are just 3 female FTSE 100 CEOs. Remarkably the percentage of senior female executives running the UK's top companies day-to-day is actually lower than in 2007! That really is food for thought.

Well, this Report makes a series of practical recommendations to ensure we build "The Executive Pipeline of Talent for Future Women on Boards"! Measuring data, clear objectives, improving careers advice and women themselves seeking sponsors and mentors to assist in their careers are just some of the reports practical recommendations – not to mention encouraging and supporting young mothers back to work and helping with the cost of child care. It was launched by its co-authors, Mary Macleod MP and Dr Therese Coffey MP. Our Executive Producer, Boni Sones, spoke to Therese.

The year: 2012
Do our Boardrooms need more women?
Against – EU legislation but for more women in our Boardrooms – Therese Coffey MP
Therese Coffey the Conservative MP for Suffolk Coastal is one of a growing number of Conservative women MPs and Peers spearheading the campaign to use "voluntary" measures to get more women into our Boardrooms. Therese herself sat on a major UK Board, as Finance Director, and thinks women can with the right encouragement get their voices heard at the most senior level. The new Equalities Minister, Maria Miller MP, the Secretary of State for Culture Media and Sport, has also spoken in favour of improving women's representation on Boards. Therese talks to Boni Sones, our Executive Producer.

Therese's One Minute Solution: "This issue still needs to be addressed but it is how you go about doing it. There are some people who believe that laws change behaviour but I don't think they necessarily do. It may do in the initial shock reaction and tick box approach. But if you want to change behaviour, if you want to change culture that has to come from the inside and from the ground up.

That's why we need to be asking the questions, pressing for good examples, showing that it makes a difference and being tenacious with it. By just resorting to law making you have actually lost the argument."

Do our Boardrooms need more women?
For – EU legislation to get more women into our Boardrooms – Vicky Pryce, Economist

Vicky Pryce, Author of *Greekonomics – The Euro Crisis and Why Politicians Don't Get It*, tells us why she is in favour of proposed new EU legislation to get more women into our Boardrooms. The proposal has been put forward by the EU Justice Commissioner Viviane Reding but the UK is leading a delegation to oppose the suggestion. The plan would force public companies across the EU to reserve at least 40 per cent of their board seats for women. Vicky, who is former Joint head of the United Kingdom's government economic service, says we shouldn't have to wait 40 years before there is a 40/60 balance on the male dominated Boards of our Footsie 100 Companies. The top 100 footsie companies now have just three women CEOs, following the departure of Marjorie Scardino from Pearson's. However, Business Secretary Vince Cable thinks voluntary measures are working, now that the number of women on UK footsie 100 Boards has gone up from 12.5 per cent to 16.7 per cent in a year.

Vicky's One Minute Solution: "I agree with the EU Reding proposal entirely. I don't think culture can change overnight and just having targets of sorts voluntarily won't work. But that is not the real issue. Women on Boards will not make a huge difference, if you have just one or two, so what! The really important issue is having women executives who are on Boards and promoting women in senior positions in both the public and private sector is absolutely essential."

The year: 2010
Janet Hanson - CEO and founder of 85 Broads

The title might seem slightly disrespectful but Janet Hanson's global network of women called "85 Broads" was named after the office address of Goldman Sachs where she worked in New York, not the other type of "Broads"! As global CEO and founder of "85 Broads" Janet Hanson has built up a global network community of 20,000 trailblazing women who want to create greater success for themselves, each other and the communities in which they live to affect change for women globally.

"85 Broads" recently launched its Cambridge Chapter at Judge Business School at Cambridge University where Boni Sones, Executive Producer of wpradio.co.uk met up with the ebullient, entertaining and wise Janet Hanson.

Janet Hot Quote: "I think at Goldman Sachs, it was luck that made me form 85 Broads. I felt so lucky to have an extraordinary career there that when I left, I thought to myself how do I make sure that other women who are coming up the ladder know how much fun it is?

"The purpose of 85 Broads was to feed all of that excitement and inspiration to them and to cheer from the sideline, that was the real impetus behind it. There are lots of women out there who want you to succeed and help you build your career. I wanted them to know they were supported by us even after we had left."

The year: 2009
Women in Business

Lorely Burt, the Liberal Democrat MP for Solihull, has just come back from an international conference in America to study how public procurement policies are helping to advance women in business and the equalities agenda. Lorely is her party's spokeswomen on Business, Enterprise and Regulatory Reform, and is the first female Chair of the Parliamentary party. She wants to see a big increase in women in business over here. Boni Sones spoke to her about the trip. www.weconnect.org.uk will tell you more.

The year: 2008
Peter Day and Harriet Harriett Harman MP, Minister for Women and Leader of the House of Commons

Presenter Peter Day, goes to Norway to find out why others aren't following its lead to make it legally binding for all the boards of companies to have 40 per cent women. He compares Norway with Spain and Britain, and talks to Harriet Harman, Minister for Women and Leader of the House of Commons and others.

Producers: Sandra Kanthal and Rosamund Jones Editor: Stephen Chilcott. Thanks to the BBC for allowing us to broadcast this.

FIVE

Violence against women, DV, Stalking, Prostitution, Forced Marriage and Female Genital Mutilation

When the Labour women MPs came to power in 1997 they had previously conducted their own research on "What Do Women Want", in order to address the policy areas which were of most concern to women. Their Leader, Tony Blair, had written a speech for She Magazine, on 29th March 1995, with the same title: "What Do Women Want?" They were surprised to find that high on that list were measures to combat domestic violence. As they occupied the corridors of power they incredulously wrote into their speeches, that until 1891 it had been legal for a husband to be able to inflict "moderate corporal punishment" on his wife, in order to keep her "within the bounds of duty". They set up an All-Party Parliamentary Group on domestic violence which included their male colleagues, thereby pushing DV up the agenda and onto the desks of the Ministers in the Home Office and Justice Departments. Labour made tackling violence against women and girls a priority. They set up specialist DV courts, specialist police units and prosecutors, and formed partnerships with councils and housing departments and charities to support victims of DV. This all helped reduce the incidents of DV, and the number of cases referred to the CPS (Crown Prosecution Service), rose by 23 per cent. In 2008 Theresa May MP launched the Conservative Party's priorities for women in the UK, in a document called "Women in the World Today" which formed the Party's women's policy initiatives. Since 2010 when the new Conservative Liberal Democrat Coalition government took power, there has been a 13 per cent decrease in the number of cases being referred to the Crown Prosecution Service. The figures are stubbornly stuck even after 16 years of policy initiatives from all parties. 1 in 4 women will be a victim of domestic abuse at some point in their lives and on average, 2 women are killed a week by their former or current partner. The issue now cuts across countries and continents and a 2002 study has estimated that at least one in five women in the world had been physically or sexually abused by a man sometime in their lifetime. International conferences on the issue suggest that "gender-based violence" accounts for as much death and ill-health in women aged 15–44 years as cancer, and is a greater cause of ill-health than malaria and traffic accidents combined. Forced Marriage, Stalking, FGM, Female Genital Mutilation and Sexual exploitation of women, including sex trafficking and modern day slavery are now part of the violence against women agenda too. All parties in the UK are now co-operating to tackle these issues, women and men and they have formed All-Party Parliamentary Groups to work on the issues together.

The year: 2014
One Billion Rising for Justice on February 14th
Today Trafalgar Square, London will be overflowing with One Billion women Rising for Justice to prevent violence against women globally. Campaigner Eve Ensler, writer of the Vagina monologues, has organised a second year of protest, which embraces over 160 countries World Wide. Here we asked Labour's Shadow Home Secretary Yvette Cooper, and Baroness Helena Kennedy, why they as leading women politicians in the UK "were rising" today. We then spoke to three female activists, Anti FGM campaigner, Leila Hussein, who welcome the government's announcement that doctors will be asked to report FGM, Sophie Barton Hawkins, a prison advisor, and Rahela Sidiqi from Afghanistan, campaigning against detention centres for female asylum seekers.

Yvette Cooper, Shadow Home Secretary Hot Quote: "I am joining One billion Rising because there are too many hidden crimes, too many forgotten victims of violence against women and we should have zero tolerance of it across the World…we should have compulsory sex and relationships education for all our young people growing up so that they learn zero tolerance of violence in relationships and learn to respect themselves and each other, we shouldn't let this go on for another generation."

Baroness Helena Kennedy QC Hot Quote: "I go to other Countries and I see again that women's issues are not on the agenda and violence against women is not recognised as a serious crime. It is undervalued as a crime...and they can't get the police to take it seriously. Violence against women is in every community in the World and it can only be countered by men and women coming together to address it... I am rising because I have been talking about this for 40 years and it has to be addressed internationally by politicians, governments and communities."

Leila Hussein anti FGM campaigner: "I am rising because my grandmother has undergone FGM, my mother has too, I have and I need to rise for my future grand-daughters and I want them to live in a World where they are free from all forms of violence. I didn't want my daughter to go through what I went through."

Madeleine Moon MP calls on the government to set up an independent ombudsman for the armed forces

An inquest in Salisbury, Wiltshire, has heard how a young military policewoman Anne-Marie Ellement took her own life after the allegation she made of rape against two soldiers was not properly investigated. Now the Welsh MP for Bridgend, Labour's Madeleine Moon, who is a member of the House of Commons Select Committee on Defence, has called for a new post of Ombudsman to be set up to investigate such complaints properly.

The Ministry of Defence (MoD) said it had zero tolerance of bullying, but the most recent survey of military staff found that one in 10 said they had been victims of discrimination, harassment or bullying. Our Executive Producer, Boni Sones, asked Ms Moon MP why women who complain about harassment come up against a brick wall?

Madeleine Hot Quote: "The armed forces complaints officer does not have enough powers. They have to pass over the complaint to the chain of command for investigation, that is why the Ombudsman powers are going to be the critical point of the change. The investigation must come from the Ombudsman and their staff not the chain of command, that is the big change."

The year: 2013
Domestic Violence

Helen Goodman the Labour MP for Bishop Auckland, spoke at a Labour fringe event meeting on the need to provide access to a refuge for women leaving homes where they have been subject to domestic violence. Two women a week are killed as a result of domestic violence.

The Home Secretary, Theresa May is investigating the way police forces respond to incidents of domestic violence with the Inspector of Constabulary, but charities want her investigations to become a public inquiry into police and other state agencies response to DV.

Helen Goodman MP says refuge provision across the Country is still very patchy and that there needs to be a consistent approach taken by providers whatever part of the Country you live in.

Helen Hot Quote: "I think provision is about 50/50. To get into a refuge you would have to have documents from the police, documents from your doctor to be able to prove abuse has taken place, and of course not everyone has that. There are a whole range of problems. I am quite alarmed about the amount of violent pornography on the internet and we think this is influencing people's behaviour."

Modern Slavery – Fiona Mactaggart wants tough new measures to help trafficked people

Fiona Mactaggart, the Labour MP for Slough and the new chair of the All-Party Parliamentary Group on Trafficking has been a long standing campaigner against human trafficking and the sexual exploitation of young children. She introduced her own Private Member's Bill on the use of trafficked labour in the Supply Chain to supermarkets.

Now she is waiting to see the full details of the Government's proposed new Modern Slavery Bill, details of which are not yet known. In Scotland this week a Labour MSP Jenny Marra, has introduced her own Human

Trafficking Bill calling for it to be made illegal to punish people forced to commit a crime as a result of trafficking. Here Fiona tells our Executive Producer, Boni Sones, what measures she would like to see in the new UK Bill.

Fiona Hot Quote: "I think that a critical thing, which I hope the government will do, is to make sure that within the legislation there is a mechanism to make sure that the data about who is trafficked, how and where to, is much better than it currently is. Until we know who is affected we won't get solutions to this evil problems."

Helen Goodman MP campaigning for an age verification system on the viewing of internet porn following the murder of April Jones And a message for Emily

Helen Goodman the MP for Bishop Auckland, and Labour's Shadow Minister of State for Media Reform, is calling on Google and other internet providers to introduce new measures to crack down on internet porn, following the murder of five-year-old April Jones, and the conviction of Mark Bridger for life for her abduction and murder. Violent images of child pornography were found on Bridger's computer. Helen wants internet providers to be more proactive, in order to cut the demand for viewing extreme pornography and child abuse. Our Executive Producer Boni Sones, spoke to Helen.

Helen's Hot Quote: "The stance at the moment for internet providers is reactive. We need them to be proactive, by introducing safe search as the default, so the filters are already there rather than having to download them. I would like a proper age verification system so that people who want to view extreme pornography and child abuse lose anonymity and pause before they press the "yes" button. I am very disappointed the government has shelved their Green and White Paper on Communications, I was hoping they would have a Bill in the Queen's Speech."

Helen's message to Suffragette Emily Wilding Davison, who died 100 years ago today: "I don't think we are campaigning as vigorously, she was an inspiring person and I hope young women in particular draw strength from this story and realise that they can achieve things, they can make a difference!"

Jane Ellison MP – FGM new moves to impose safeguards in Schools
Jane Ellison the Conservative MP for Battersea, Balham and Wandsworth is Chair of the All-Party Parliamentary Group on FGM – Female Genital Mutilation – and has been working actively with others to get "zero tolerance" to the practice in the UK.

There has not been one single prosecution yet in Britain, despite the fact that The Royal College of Midwives say that one in three of their members surveyed came across women who had undergone this procedure. Conservative and Liberal Democrat Ministers, including Theresa May MP, Justine Greening MP and Lynne Featherstone MP have all put forward departmental measures to tackle this issue. Recently the Department for International Development said £35 million of the government's aid budget would go to tackling FGM in the developing World. The Home Office has also facilitated a conference on the issue. Now school inspectors will be asking teaching staff to report the issue.

Jane Hot Quote: "Ofsted will now ask a specific safe guarding question where there are girls in schools from potentially at risk communities or practicing Countries of origin. This will be important because schools will have to look again if they don't have a safeguarding policy, but there is no two ways about this, just one police prosecution would send a very important signal – in 25 years in Britain of this being a crime no-one has been prosecuted."

The year: 2012
Head to Head: Why have so many organisations been "blind" to sex abuse?
Sheun talks to Simon Danczuk MP
Our reporter Sheun Adelasoye continues her special investigation into the Rochdale sex-trafficking cases with this extended interview with the

Labour MP for Rochdale Simon Danczuk. Mr Danczuk is continuing to campaign on this and other sex abuse cases, such as the investigation into the sex abuse allegations against the late Jimmy Savile. He wants the criminal justice system to take into account that girls and women who commit crimes have often been abused themselves. He has recently held a Westminster Hall debate on the issue and is giving evidence to the Home Affairs Select Committee looking into these issues.

Simon's One Minute Solution: "What these cases have done is to raise awareness that this type of behaviour is completely unacceptable, so there is a much greater awareness in all communities about what is acceptable and what isn't. The organisations and institutions have been blind to the abuse and not just in Rochdale Social Services but elsewhere too. The police, the BBC, they were blind to the abuse allegedly being committed by Jimmy Savile. So there has been institutional blindness to abuse across a whole range of different organisations. The good to come out of these types of cases is that it brings it to the fore that this isn't acceptable and that it should be reported."

Theresa May's Forced Marriage Bill
Amber Rudd MP for Hastings and Rye

The Home Secretary Theresa May is introducing a new Law to protect women and men against Forced Marriage. Supporters say that bringing together all existing legislation and orders into one new all-embracing Law is an important way to reinforce the message that Forced Marriage is wrong. However, some groups think that the government may be introducing new legislation when existing laws such as rape are enough and that a family law approach is sufficient. They argue that criminalising Forced Marriage might prevent families reporting it, and that the government is showing a lack of sensitivity to divergent cultural norms.

An estimated 8,000 young women a year are forced into marriages. Executive Producer, Boni Sones, put those questions to one of the Conservative "sisterhood" Amber Rudd, the MP for Hastings and Rye who supports the new legislation.

Amber Rudd Hot Quote: "This is a much needed important piece of new legislation to protect women and men's rights and I am delighted that the Home Secretary, Theresa May has brought this forward and I think it is an important part of safeguarding women. There are existing laws on rape and kidnapping for example, but it is not such a clear message and it is a completely different way to explain to people that forced marriage is illegal. It is a very important message to send out to the communities and it should have been done before."

A special report on sex trafficking and culture by Sheun Adelasoye

A hidden issue or a one-off case? Following a high profile trial policy makers are getting to grips with how the issues of race, culture and religion are impacting on the procurement of vulnerable white girls by Asian men into the sex trafficking industry.

In this special two-part audio documentary our www.parliamentaryradio.com reporter Sheun Adelasoye talks to the Rochdale MP Simon Danczuk (Labour): Usama Hasan (Sheikh and Senior Researcher at the Quilliam Foundation): Dr Kay Chalmers (pseudonym) a white Anglo-Saxon female who converted to Islam: Alison Worsley, Deputy Director – Policy & Research, Barnardo's.

Six members of a gang who preyed on under-age white girls in Rochdale, Greater Manchester became the first people in Britain to be convicted of sex trafficking and were jailed.

The six and three other men used a one-time victim to recruit other girls so they could be driven to "chill" houses around the north of England for sordid sex. Of the 11 defendants on trial at Liverpool Crown Court, 10 were Pakistani and the other an Afghan asylum seeker.

Simon Danczuk Hot Quote: "I've consistently said that race is a factor in these particular crimes, I'm absolutely convinced of that. I know that there are other parliamentarians that have said that race isn't a factor, but I disagree with them."

Usama Hasan Hot Quote (Senior Researcher at the Quilliam Foundation): "It's really more to do with a breakdown in our Society in some sense. There are many young vulnerable women out there on the streets, and unfortunately some men are sexual predators, which is really very sad and they exploit these women."

Alison Worsley, Barnardo's Hot Quote: "I think it's a hidden issue, which is why we are obviously trying to raise awareness of it. We do an annual survey of our services to find out what the picture is, and last year we worked with just short of 1,200 people. That was an 8.4 increase on the previous year – we are seeing greater detection of the problem."

Dr Kay Charmers Hot Quote: (pseudonym): "Thank goodness the case has come to light. I am Anglo-Saxon indigenous British I am seen as an oddity because I converted to Islam. That's a very positive thing because being Muslim doesn't have a face or a uniform for want of a better word, religion is I think a private spiritual matter for those people."

Hot topic – The battle for "access" to Legal Aid for victims of Domestic Violence
Amber Rudd MP and Kate Green MP – go "head to head" on this Tricky Issue!

Victims of Domestic Violence can take years to summon up the confidence to report offences to the police. They may not, initially, tell anybody else, even friends and family yet alone those in positions of authority, about their abuse. But reforms to how Legal Aid is "accessed" in the future for Domestic Violence victims is leading to concerns that women will not be able to "qualify" for Legal Aid in order to take their cases to Court. New time restrictions are being imposed and new processes are being put in place for those in authority to legitimate that abuse did actually take place.

The Women's Institute, Mumsnet, Netmums and Rights of Women, have written to the Justice Secretary Ken Clarke, saying that the new reforms to Legal Aid will be detrimental to Domestic Violence victims. They have copied their letter to the Prime Minister, David Cameron.

The Labour Women MPs want more reforms and concessions to the proposals but Ken Clarke says the amendments he has already made are sufficient, including broadening the definition of domestic violence for legal aid purposes to include emotional and psychological harm, not just physical abuse.

Women admitted to a refuge, those receiving social services support, and any victim whose partner or ex-partner has a caution for violence against them will now also be entitled to claim legal aid. Originally only those in a refuge would have been able to claim.

The various amendments have been "ping ponging" between the House of Lords and the House of Commons. So who is for or against the various amendments?

We talk to Amber Rudd MP, the Conservative MP for Amber Valley and Kate Green, the Labour MP for Stretford and Urmston and Shadow Equalities Minister. Both have supported a number of the amendments. They spoke to our Executive Producer Boni Sones in Central Lobby.

Amber Rudd Hot Quote: "I feel it is an example of democracy in action because it gave us time to make the case to the Secretary of State. It gave the interest groups like the WI and Mumsnet time to make the case about widening the definition of Domestic Violence and a lot of Conservative MPs, Conservative women MPs in particular, took the opportunity to speak to the Secretary of State Ken Clarke.

"There have been very important concessions made which do safeguard women's rights, and this will be the end of the "ping pong". I hope the message comes across of the facts: that if you have been a victim of Domestic Violence you will get Legal Aid – the only thing is you have to have evidence from someone else, and that is a very reasonable position to take."

Kate Green (Co-author "Everywoman Safe Everywhere" Report) Hot Quote: "It is a very confused situation with accessing Legal Aid. The government are putting women and sometimes men at risk of further abuse. We need further concessions. There is quite a lot of slow reporting, in the first few months, there can be up to a couple of dozen incidents before a victim is able to report abuse. If there are doubts about the remedy you can access, women will be all the more deterred from seeking advice and support. This is happening against a backdrop of many other changes to Legal Aid which will restrict access to advice, for example welfare benefits and housing and family law arrangements too. It is not just the DV cuts that are serious but all the other things someone fleeing DV can find themselves dealing with."

Clare's Law and Hazel Blears MP – "Two people every week die from domestic violence"

Hazel Blears the Labour MP for Salford and Eccles has been campaigning for a new law to give women more information about violent partners who have a previous record of domestic violence.

Her constituent Clare Wood, was murdered by her former partner George Appleton after she ended the relationships. He stalked her, threatened her and then eventually strangled her in February 2009 and later hanged himself. In the past he had repeatedly harassed women.

The Home Secretary, Theresa May, has just announced that "Clare's Law" is to be piloted in four areas including Salford and Greater Manchester. Hazel has been working closely with Clare's father Michael Brown for two years to secure this change. Sheun Adelasoye, reports.

The pilot "Clare's Law" scheme is based on two options: the 'right to ask' and the 'right to know' and will test the methods used by the police to disclose information to victims or potential victims of domestic violence. Our guest reporter Sheun Adelasoye spoke to Hazel about it. Thanks Sheun. Congratulations Hazel!

Hazel's Hot Quote: "Two women a week – 100 women every year - are killed by their violent partners and for many of them there will be a history of domestic violence, before it gets to the point of killing someone there has been a serious of incidents taking place. The police estimate that across the country there are probably 25,000 people who are deemed to be serial perpetrators with a history of domestic violence so it is a big, big problem."

International Women's Day 2012 "The Campaigners"!
Slavery and FGM – Three Campaigners and two Hot Topics that refuse to go away!

Jane Ellison MP and Amber Rudd MP – Raising awareness of FGM – still practiced in the UK today!

Two Conservative women MPs, Jane Ellison the MP for Battersea and Amber Rudd the MP for Hastings & Rye have helped establish a new All-Party Parliamentary Group on Female Genital Mutilation (FGM), which Jane Chairs.

The new Group is made up of over 50 MPs and Peers from all the main political parties. It has been formed to raise awareness of FGM in the UK and overseas and to work with the Government and NGOs towards eradicating the harmful practice.

2001 figures suggest that around 20,000 girls in the UK are living at risk of having FGM committed against them and 66,000 girls and women are already living with the consequences. It is believed that the problem might now be a lot bigger, especially in London.

Jane Hot Quote: "It is heart-breaking. The headmistress who spoke to me about the problem of FGM said I saw the little girl go off a happy little eight year old and come back a shadow of her former self, a depressed inward looking child."

Amber Hot Quote: "This is something we will be raising on International Women's Day with the International Development Minister, Andrew Mitchell. I will certainly let my constituents know about it."

The year: 2010
"Prostitution Regimes in Europe" the Liberal Democrat Dr Belinda Brooks-Gordon, fights back!

Concern over the last Labour government's so called "wash-up" legislation is growing. Critics believe some of the laws passed in the last year to further equality and help women, are detrimental to those they seek to help. Already the Conservative-Liberal Democrat government has dropped moves to remove anonymity for rape complainants, after protests from the Labour ranks, but now some Liberal Democrats want to see Labour's prostitution laws reformed, they had made it an offence to buy sex from individuals who were "procured for gain". At Birkbeck College, the University of London, academics from all over Europe met to discuss "Prostitution Policy Regimes in Europe". Boni Sones, our Executive Producer, spoke to Dr Belinda Brooks-Gordon, a leading Liberal Democrat and Reader in Pscyhology and Social Policy at Birkbeck, Daniela Danna Reader in Sociology at the University of Milan, and Marjan Wijers a Human Rights lawyer from the Netherlands.

Chapter 6 has more on women in the government and DV.

The year: 2009
Clause 13 of the Policing and Crime Bill

On the first day back after the long summer recess, Labour MP and former Home Office Minister, Fiona Mactaggart, held a briefing meeting in the Commons to campaign for Clause 13, of the Policing and Crime Bill. There are fears the Clause maybe diluted or rejected in the Lords, where the Bill is now being debated, and Fiona told the meeting that 54 organisations supported it. See Chapter 11 too.

She was joined by Catherine Briddick, Senior Legal Officer at Rights of Women, who said it was the first time she had wholly supported the Home Office but she believed it was "completely right" to make it a "strict liability" offence to pay for sex from a person who is "procured for gain". Some other countries have legalised prostitution but supporters of Clause 13 say this has been shown not to work. Boni Sones spoke to Fiona and Catherine.

Alan Campbell MP, Home Office Minister and Lynne Jones MP
Prostitution

The government is changing the laws that govern prostitution in a bid to protect women who are trafficked or "procured for gain" by making it illegal to pay for sex from them if they are being controlled in this way. The amendment in the Policing and Crime Bill, now passing through Parliament, is contentious.

Alan Campbell MP, a Minister in the Home Office responsible for crime reduction says the government is right to be taking a firm line on protecting those women who are most vulnerable. The government's new laws would also attempt to rehabilitate sex workers by making an Order for them to attend meetings aimed at tackling addictive behaviour.

But the Labour MP, Lynne Jones, has put down an Early Day Motion, saying her own government's measures are "deeply flawed".

Our reporter Georgie Hemmingway, spoke first to Alan Campbell MP about how the new government measures would work in practice, and then to Lynne Jones MP.

The year: 2008
Caroline Spelman MP – Conservative women tackling women and violence!
Caroline Spelman is the Chairman of the Conservative Party and has been the MP for Meriden since 1997. As a working mother she says her children are her top priority. She is working with the Conservative Women's Organisation to challenge Society's attitude to violence against women. In her West Midlands constituency she has helped set up a charity called MABL (Make a Better Life) to help women affected by violence access services. Now she is taking on the issue of stalking, to ensure the police, policy makers, and government realise what a serious crime it is and how it can, in some cases, lead to murder. She is interviewed by Boni Sones.

In an exclusive interview with wpradio.co.uk Mrs Spelman, the MP for Meriden said Hot Quote: "I think stalking is an under-estimated issue by the general public and by a lot of women. Statistically few people know that 1 in 5 women will be stalked at some time in their life – and as a constituency MP it really comes home to you when you first have to deal with a case when you realise the law isn't adequate and the protection and support is not adequate for the victims who are mostly women."

Talking of the two cases documented in the Conservative policy document: "Women in the World Today" which refers to the death of

Rana Faruqui, and Claire Bernal, she said it was clear stalking did lead to murder.

"There have been a number of tragic cases. This is a crime which is essentially escalatory – it gets worse. The harassment increases in severity the whole time and although the stalker maybe prosecuted and may go to prison for some period of time, they do come out again and the victim does know they are vulnerable."

Mrs Spelman said she wanted to see two changes: An increase in the penalty so repeat offenders are not released from prison so soon without more safeguards. Secondly, she wants to change the way police treat the offence to ensure stalking is taken more seriously as a potential homicide.

She said that if the Conservatives became the party of government subjects like stalking would not be neglected. "We will have a significant increase in the number of women on our benches."

She said she had "no doubt" that David Cameron, the Party Leader, would give 30 per cent of his Cabinet posts to women as he has promised.

"We are expecting to have over 60 women on our benches when we form a government after the next election ......and that will mean there will be more women on the front bench."

She said there was a high proportion of female MPs in Labour's 100 most marginal seats but that there was likely to be "no reduction" in the percentage of women in Westminster if the Conservatives win the next election."

The year: 2007
Caroline Spelman MP
The Chairman of the Conservative Party, Caroline Spelman, MP for Meriden, has been working with others in her party to address the issue of forced marriages. She says women feel solidarity with others across party to stop women being exploited in this way. The Conservatives and Labour have supported Lord Lester's (LD) Forced Marriage Bill. This aims to outlaw forced marriages as well as supporting people who are victims of the practice. WPRadio journalist Linda Fairbrother asked Caroline how big a problem forced marriages were in Britain?

Margaret Moran MP

Margaret Moran, the Labour MP for Luton South, chairs the All-Party Domestic Violence Group. After talking online to women survivors of domestic violence through a project called "Womenspeak" MPs have now turned their attention to children who experience violence in their own home. They joined with children's charities and Women's Aid to listen directly to children's voices through an online project called "KIDSPEAK" which Margaret helped shape. The aim is to provide a safe, anonymous and secure online environment where children and young people affected by domestic violence can share their experience with the police, judges and parliamentarians. She explains in her own words why the project is so important.

Baroness Uddin

Baroness Uddin is a Labour peer who has dedicated her life to public social reform and equal rights. She was appointed to the Lords in 1998 for her work on women and disability rights where she has continued to champion diversity issues and issues affecting the Bangladeshi community. She's worked on the problems surrounding forced marriages and more recently the collapse of the First Solutions company, which was involved in money transfers from Bangladesh. Boni Sones spoke to her at length about her 30 year career in politics first in the community and now as a campaigner in the Lords. She started with her childhood in Bangladesh.

SIX

Women in Government and the Shadow Cabinets

So how many women should there be in a Cabinet or Shadow Cabinet? The answer would appear to vary according to whether you are aiming to achieve power or have it. The Prime Minister David Cameron, once said he wanted a third of his Cabinet members to be women, but has just four. Theresa May is the Home Secretary, Justine Greening, the International Development Secretary, Theresa Villiers the Northern Ireland Secretary, and Maria Miller the Culture Secretary. Cameron himself says he is disappointed, and when he sacked two of the older women members of his first Cabinet, Caroline Spelman, and Cheryl Gillan, there were accusations of ageism levelled against him. Of the four Liberal Democrat members of the coalition Cabinet, none are women. Jo Swinson the most senior Liberal Democrat woman, is a Parliamentary Under Secretary of State at BIS, the Department for Business, Innovation and Skills. She has just taken maternity leave. In the Labour Shadow Cabinet, Ed Miliband, has eleven women, with Harriet Harman, as Deputy Leader. They recently introduced a quota system to ensure that one-third of its Shadow Cabinet are women. Harman likes to goad the other parties by telling them they are "raining men"! At a PMQs on February 5th 2014 Ed Miliband told David Cameron that the Conservative Party had a "women problem". This followed the resignation of four Conservative women MPs from the 2010 intake, and the deselection of Anne McIntosh the MP for Thirsk and Malton. Miliband told Cameron: "There are as many men who went to Eton or Westminster as there are women in his cabinet. Does he think it's his fault the Conservative Party has a problem with women?" David Cameron said that he was proud that under his leadership the number of women MPs had gone up from 17 to 48 but admitted they needed to do "much more". Cameron said he wanted to see "more women at every level of our public life" and that the Conservative Party had elected the only woman Prime Minister, Margaret Thatcher! When Labour was in government, female members of the Cabinet used to informally write on their ministerial papers asking their senior civil servants if the policy they were introducing had been gender proofed and what exactly were the implications for women and families. The Conservative women in the current Cabinet may have similar informal systems, but they are probably not as bold as their predecessors in speaking up for positive discrimination in public policy making. Luckily for us we did get early on the support of one leading female member of the Lobby for our broadcasting, the Times sketch writer Ann Treneman. Ann gave us "specials" on her yearly timely diaries and the sketches she had written on women in the Chamber. She also interviewed leading women politicians on their reforms to Commons procedures for us and as an eye witness sitting regularly in the Press Gallery Ann was well placed to do these interviews. See Chapter 13 for more of Ann's interviews.

The year: 2013
The Movers and shakers in 2015!
Esther McVey MP shows young girls that if "Esther" Can then so can they!
Here we want to say that Ministers can make a difference to public policy and showcase our documentary interview with Esther McVey, when she had just become an MP, and rolled up her sleeves to promote a career booklet for young women in Merseyside called: "If Chloe Can". Esther is now the new Employment Minister.

Esther showed much initiative in launching the booklet in Westminster in Autumn 2010 alongside a formidable line-up of successful women who could act as role models to others and also with the Work and Pensions Minister, who she then went on to work for, Iain Duncan Smith. Before speaking to Esther, we spoke to the "real Chloe" from her local Belvedere Academy. And then we recorded a round table debate with those business women attending Esther's event. The documentary begins with Debbie Moore of Pineapple Studios.

More women in the Cabinet and Shadow Cabinet line-ups!
While there are still only four women in David Cameron's Cabinet: Theresa May, Maria Miller, Justin Greening and Theresa Villiers our

congratulations go to Esther McVey, the Conservative MP for Wirral West, who becomes the new Employment Minister, and Nicky Morgan who has been promoted to Economic Secretary to the Treasury.

Helen Grant, Shailesh Vara, Jane Ellison and Anna Soubry also get promotions, to parliamentary undersecretary at sport and equalities, justice, health and defence respectively. Karen Bradley becomes a Whip and Amber Rudd and Clair Perry become Assistant Whips.

For the Liberal Democrats Lady Susan Kramer becomes the Minister of State for Transport, a surprise for her she told us! Baroness Kramer sits on our Advisory Board and we have appreciated her support. You can hear our earlier interview with her on Welfare Reform.

In Ed Miliband's Labour Shadow Cabinet reshuffle, there are eleven women, with Rachel Reeves promoted to Shadow Work and Pensions, and Gloria De Piero to Shadow Minister for Women and Equalities. Harriet Harman, Deputy Leader of the Party, and Yvette Cooper, Shadow Home Secretary remain the most senior Labour women, alongside the other familiar names of Angela Eagle, Caroline Flint, Rosie Winterton, Margaret Curran, and Baroness Royall. Maria Eagle and Mary Creagh have swapped places in Transport and Environment. Emma Reynolds, Emily Thornberry, Liz Kendall, will also be allowed to attend Shadow Cabinet meetings as junior shadow ministers.

The year: 2012
On the Spot – Lisa Nandy MP tells us why 16-year-olds should vote!
Lisa Nandy, the Labour MP for Wigan supports a lowering of the voting age to 16. Lisa, who is aged 32, is one of the youngest MPs in Parliament and she has recently authored a Compass think tank report on the issue. As her Party's Shadow Children's Minister Lisa has the support of her Leader, Ed Miliband and her Party who have been pushing for a change in policy since the last General Election. Now for the first time 16 year olds will be allowed to vote in Scotland's 2014 Referendum on Independence. So with "push" for policy change coming from different directions will the voting age soon be lowered? Our Executive Producer Boni Sones spoke to her.

Lisa's One Minute Solution: "My Party went into the last General Election with a commitment to lower the voting age to 16 so we are not introducing it by the back-door. There is a really compelling case for 16-year-olds and 17-year-olds to have the vote in every election, it is entirely right to say they shouldn't have it in one election and then not in another. Decisions are being taken right now that will affect 16-year-olds for the rest of their lives and future generations. If you don't get involved you can't change it."

Dame Tessa Jowell MP – Women and the Olympics
Sheun and Tessa go "head to head"!

Our reporter Sheun Adelasoye caught up with Dame Tessa Jowell, the former Labour Secretary of State for Culture Media and Sport, who with the former Prime Minister Tony Blair succeeded in getting the 2012 Olympics to London. Tessa, the Labour MP for Dulwich and West Norwood, and an Olympics Minister, has always campaigned for the greater representation of women in Olympic Sports including boxing and cycling. So how does she view the chances of women athletes in Olympic sporting events?

Tessa Hot Quote: "We campaigned to increase the number of cycling events women could compete in and also for the first time women's boxing, so women will box in our Olympics and take place in a wider number of cycling races too.

"It is very rare in public life that you have the opportunity to see something through from the beginning to the end and that gives me enormous satisfaction. It has been a great privilege."

Extending Birth Control to women in the developing World

Baroness Lindsay Northover The Liberal Democrat Peer who is the Government Spokesperson on International Development and Government Whip on Health, Justice and Women and Equalities tells us what she thinks of DFID's and Bill and Melinda Gates' campaign to extend birth control to many more women in the developing world. Lindsay reveals what her

Government is doing to facilitate women's rights in new democracies by supporting women and girls.

Lindsay Hot Quote: "The Family Planning conference which has just been held, co-sponsored by DFID and the Gates Foundation, is extremely important because family planning can be the key for so many women worldwide. At the moment we know that about 4 out of 10 women have access to family planning, and about 7 out of 10 wish to do so, so they can choose when to have children, and how to space them. That is extremely important to the position of women."

Jo Swinson a campaigner in government

Jo Swinson, the Liberal Democrat MP for East Dunbartonshire on why we need a UK representative on the UN CEDAW Committee, (the Committee on the Elimination of all forms of Discrimination Against Women). Jo also has a Private Member's Bill to make it easier for consumers to understand price labels on supermarket goods and those 2 for 1 'special offers'! Jo answers her critics on her and Equality Minister, Lynne Featherstone's 'Body Image Campaign', which is already having an impact to stop the air brushing of images in magazines. Oh, she's also Nick Clegg's, the Deputy Prime Minister's, PPS! With just 7 LD women MPs, does she wish she'd supported All-women shortlists?

Jo Hot Quote: "I take up issues that affect people in their everyday lives. Although people do like to trivialise body image, I strongly believe it is an issue up and down the Country in terms of health, and education and opportunities.

"AW Shortlists is no guarantee. Our Leadership Programme is giving women opportunities not provided to other candidates and that should help I think for us at the next election. But we should never be complacent there is always more to do."

They year: 2010
Two at the top – Lynne Featherstone MP the new Equalities Minister
Lynne Featherstone MP for Hornsey and Wood Green is the new Equalities Minister. Alongside Theresa May MP the Home Secretary and Minister for Women & Equalities she will be spearheading the coalition government's equalities plans. Lynne "loves" coalition government, thinks "thrashing out" compromises is a good way to work and says she's looking forward to implementing the Labour government's Equalities Act, which she says is a "three party" success story. She's pledged to narrow the gender pay gap and wants all teenagers to see the film "Made in Dagenham"! Lynne and Theresa are busy progressing their own equalities agenda too including flexible working, a Transgender Action Plan, kite marking air-brushing in magazines, more women in the Boardrooms, and moving the civil partnership agenda forward. Boni Sones OBE our Executive Producer, wanted to know more.

NB: This interview was conducted before the government announced it will drop Labour's proposed new socio-economic Equality law duty requiring councils to tackle social deprivation.

Lynne Hot Quote: "Firstly I am living proof miracles do happen, I had never thought of being a government minister in the way that this had happened. The Liberal Democrats were not necessarily starred to go straight to government. But opportunity has knocked."

"I love coalition – two heads are always better than one and interestingly, the Equality Act which I am commencing, it was a Labour Bill, but both the opposition parties supported it. I did put down so many amendments on women's issues, particularly on pay, which Labour didn't accept. The Bill is going ahead, nine-tenths is already commenced and the outstanding issues are coming on stream, they were not all timetabled to start at the same moment. The clauses on positive action, goods and services, old people, dual discrimination are being worked out with business too. You could say it was a three party success."

"I thought "Made in Dagenham" was a brilliant film! I think children of 12 young girls and boys should see it, it shouldn't have an adult rating because it is such a significant part of our social history and made that huge differential step that led to the Equal Pay Act. Now forty years later I am trying to deliver what those women started, and it's a fight still. We are moving the agenda forward, such as the removal of gagging clauses, and how the gender pay reporting parts of the Bill are going to work the voluntary side. We are progressing women on Boards, it's still a pitiful seven per cent, and we're looking at how we can break down those barriers for women at all levels including the psychological ones."

Caroline Flint MP – On The Frontline

Caroline Flint MP for Don Valley, is Shadow Secretary of State for Communities and Local Government in Ed Miliband's Shadow Cabinet. New rules meant MPs had to choose at least six female MPs but ended up giving them eight of the 19 elected places. Caroline in now on the frontline attacking coalition plans to reform housing benefit, even though she thinks some reform is needed and is leading the charge for a programme of building new affordable homes. She also told Boni Sones OBE, Executive Producer of www.wpradio.co.uk she was no longer a token woman in a Labour cabinet line-up but was now a "first among equals".

Caroline Hot Quote: "I think we have always been in favour of reform, I was a former employment and welfare reform minister, and we have looked at ways of adjusting housing benefit and allowances and allowing people going into work to keep more of their benefits, but housing benefit can be a very complicated issue. One of my concerns now as Shadow Secretary of State for Communities and Local Government is that there is not enough affordable housing for people to move into and that is why local authorities turn to the private rented sector to house families. We are not hearing enough from this government about supply.

"The housing cap, that gets most press coverage, does affect some people, but the biggest changes that will affect 700,000 people across the country are the changes to the sort of properties that you can seek to live in and get help with your rent with. This is being tightened and reduced and that affects pensioners and working families too."

What they did for us! The Labour women's fight for equality

The dissolution of Parliament brings to a halt thirteen years of a Labour government. It began in 1997 with Tony Blair and those historic 101 Labour women, many selected by the device of All-women shortlists. It meant in total Westminster had the highest number of women MPs ever, 120 and also Betty Boothroyd the Speaker. This special two part documentary series looks at the Labour women's achievements.

Vera Baird QC MP

Vera Baird QC MP for Redcar talks to our reporter Linda Fairbrother about the Labour women's Equality Bill, which she has just steered through Parliament.

It was a hard fought for piece of legislation that has eventually won the backing of all parties.

It sets out to create a fairer society for all combating discrimination on the grounds of age, disability, race, religion or belief, sex, sexual orientation, gender reassignment, marriage and civil partnership, pregnancy and maternity.

Vera Hot Quote: "It has been a great privilege to have my hand on the tiller of this Bill, it has been extremely good. The purpose of it is to try to require those who discriminate not to have the situation as it is now, whereby people bring an action in a Tribunal, what we require now in the public sector and some of the private sector is that they must engineer out inequality. There is a major change of emphasis here, and I am pleased to be part of a process which I hope will change society's concept of how equality should be dealt with."

"We had unequal equalities in that you could still discriminate in the sale of goods and services to somebody on the basis of their age though we had outlawed that for race and gender years ago. We needed to streamline and pull together the legislation that we have got already, we had passed a lot of legislation on race, disability and gender and more recently about age and sexual orientation too but they are all creatures of different ages, and we have now put them into a shape so that they fit together and that is more accessible. We have also made it a Plain English Bill so there is a straight forward explanation of the clauses and there is an Easy Read version intended for those with low literacy levels and with pictures too."

"This Bill is powerful stuff, make no mistake our Equality legislation has made a massive difference over the years, the pay gap has gone down, the employment gap between disabled an able bodied people has gone down, it is now about 25 per cent and the race employment gap has gone down into the low teens. Our legislation has worked but it has reduced too slowly and we have significantly beefed it up now. If you put a duty on a public authority to reduce equality you are going to have them watched by all around them, and if they fail they will have to pay a penalty."

Ann Cryer MP – Campaigning on Forced Marriage
Ann Cryer MP for Keighley, who is stepping down from Westminster aged 70, has gained a reputation for plain speaking and doggedness. Her husband, Bob, was an MP and when he died she decided to stand too, she was then followed into Westminster by her son John, becoming the first mother and son MP team in Westminster.

Here Ann tells Executive Producer Boni Sones about her suffragette grandmother, the roots of her political passions, and her much acclaimed work on Forced Marriages and now first cousin marriages.

Ann Hot Quote: "Women do live different lives, we have more caring responsibilities, with children, parents, grandchildren, and I think women have an ability to juggle things, and I think because we can do that, it is vitally important we have that 52 per cent of the population represented in parliament to boost women's issues that affect their lives. The Speakers' Conference report is making a difference even now."

"The Labour Women in the party have championed maternity leave, the Sure Start scheme of childcare, flexible working, these have all been terribly important for women, and now we are getting a crèche here in 1 Parliament Street for MPs and staff who work here."

"I feel proud of the changes I have got in legislation about grooming of girls, about forced marriages, those things I shouted for and saw into legislation. I think it only worked because there were women in the Cabinet and on the backbenchers. I think women should understand what the 13 years of this government has meant to women because women here have been shouting on their behalf."

"My real inspiration came from my paternal grandmother who was a member of the Women's and Social and Political Union in the Rosendale Valley, there was a real thrust for suffragettes in the NW from working class women. My grandma Dianh Place, lived at Waterfoot, and was an active member there, and able to do this because she only had one child. My father was political too a member of the ILP and a pacifist, my mum was a Christian, so I participate in various Christian things too and my whole being is representative of what came before me in my family."

The year: 2009
Tessa Jowell MP Minister for the Olympics
Men & Olympic events = 164 Women & Olympic events = 124

Tessa Jowell, MP, as the Secretary of State for Culture Media and Sport helped London win its bid to host the 2012 Olympics. Now as Olympics Minister, she is pressing the case for sports women to be able to compete in as many Olympic sports as the men. Currently men can compete in 164 events and women 124. Olympic gold medallist cyclist Victoria Pendleton and others are supporting her campaign, which would allow women to compete in heavyweight wrestling and men in synchronised swimming.

Yvonne Ball of the British Wrestling Association said it was highly unlikely women would want to compete in heavyweight wrestling. Never-the-less Ms Jowell thinks this misses the point and that sportswomen of the future should have equality as a goal and their glass ceilings removed. She told Boni Sones, that she has written to the UK sports chiefs and is optimistic that there will be some change before 2012.

The year: 2008
Maria Eagle MP
Parliamentary Under-Secretary of State and Minister for Women and Equality

The Queen's Speech contained new measures to promote equality through a new all-embracing Equality Bill. The measures will replace nine current laws, drawing them together to address discrimination on the grounds of gender, race, sexual orientation or disability.

The new Bill deals with tough issues such as equal pay, age discrimination in the provision of goods and services, discrimination on the grounds of sexual orientation, and who gets what job in the promotion stakes. But should it have included the private sector too, and is there a need for compulsory pay audits?

In this exclusive interview, Parliamentary Under-Secretary of State and Minister for Women and Equality, Maria Eagle MP told Boni Sones, why critics of the Bill had got it wrong and why, 90 years after women got the vote, the suffragettes would have been proud of the Bill.

Vera Baird QC MP – Solicitor General on women in the justice system

Vera Baird, the Labour MP for Redcar, in her new role as Solicitor General is at the forefront of helping women get a fairer deal from the criminal justice system. She is working on new procedures to help women who take rape charges to trial and wants to challenge society's myths about the nature of serious sexual violence and its impact on victims. She's also been to Sweden recently where those who visit prostitutes can be prosecuted. Boni Sones talked to her about her work and what motivated her to take on these tough challenges.

Joan Ruddock MP – Parliamentary Under-Secretary of State

Joan Ruddock MP is the Minister in charge of Climate Change, Waste and Recycling and Biodiversity in the Department for Environment, Food and Rural Affairs. She finds her job demanding but also deeply rewarding. Here she talks to Boni Sones about the issues she is working on to cut down the CO2 emissions we create, including new guidelines for manufacturers of white goods.

Make 2008 the Year in which you cut your carbon footprint:

To help people take action against climate change in 2008, the Government has developed the Act on CO2 online carbon calculator which enables people to work out the size of their carbon footprint and provides them with a personal action plan to reduce it.

Individuals are responsible for more than 40 per cent of CO2 emissions in the UK – mainly from energy use in the home and travel - but there are many simple, low cost ways to cut down the amount of CO2 emissions we create. Check how you rate on the carbon calculator.

The year: 2007
Hazel Blears MP

Gordon Brown's new Cabinet has five women in it. The new Home Secretary is Jacqui Smith, the first woman to hold this important office. Harriet Harman, fresh from her deputy leadership victory, is Leader of the Commons. The Leader of the Lords is Baroness Ashton of Upholland. Ruth Kelly moves to Secretary of State for Transport, and Hazel Blears, the former Party Chairwoman, is to take over Communities and Local Government. WP Radio journalist Anne Garvey caught up with her as she was saying goodbye to her former colleagues and before she knew of her new role.

SEVEN
The men supporting women

It was very clear early on in the Tony Blair government, that the women MPs could nag and cajole their colleagues to change public policy in favour of women. When the 101 Labour women of the 1997 landslide victory got to Westminster they demanded change. It came about slowly by what some have termed "nagging"! As they walked the bewildering miles of corridors in Westminster and queued to vote as the division bells rang, they collared the ministers who passed them and listed their demands. A crèche, breastfeeding in the Commons, the publication of the Speakers' List, allowing them to know when they would be called to speak and most importantly a change in the hours and the late night sittings too. These changes were highly charged and controversial with their male and some female colleagues too and the women themselves did not always agree. Were late night sittings into the early hours of the morning an essential part of parliamentary life or could Westminster be family friendly? A demand by one Labour woman MP, Margaret Hodge, for job share MPs printed in a leading Sunday newspaper sent her powerful Labour colleagues into a rage. How dare she say such a thing! Now that demand for MPs to be allowed to job share, post the MPs' expenses scandal, is voiced fairly regularly. Oh how times have changed, and only on Mondays does Westminster sit late into the night. But even in January 2005 scuffles were breaking out in the corridors of power between competing MPs when the reforms to MPs' hours gained by the Labour women, were later revised a bit. Surprisingly it was the late Robin Cook, who as the then Leader of the Commons was handed the calendar for the Canadian Parliament, and that convinced him that perhaps the demands of the women could be met. Various Committees and sittings were held on how to reform Westminster, including the Modernisation Committee and the so called earlier Jopling reforms. Publication of the Parliamentary Calendar led to MPs knowing when they could take holidays and be with their families and children, and when they would be at work. FGM, Stalking, Sex Trafficking, DV,

Forced Marriage, reforms have all relied on men and women working together to change policy for the better but it is the women who admit that "nagging" is extremely helpful. Fiona Mactaggart, says that this vice is in fact an asset. Harriet Harman, and Tessa Jowell, pushed back childcare for the under- fives with Labour's Sure Start Centres, by enlisting the support of Tony Blair and the Prime Minister's Chancellor, Gordon Brown. They were told they could do it and a few years later others caught up with what was one of the boldest and most successful policy initiatives of the Labour government over three terms in power. David Cameron and Nick Clegg as Prime Minister and Deputy Prime Minister now regularly wade into debates on policy issues affecting women such as childcare and the need for more women in Parliament.

The year: 2012
The Campaigners – fighting in the front line of politics for social justice!
The need for a new law on stalking – sooner not later.
Should the UK follow some parts of the United States and Scotland in introducing a law specifically to create an offence of stalking? The Independent All-Party Parliamentary Inquiry into Stalking Law Reform, Chaired by the barrister Elfyn Llwyd, and Plaid Cymru MP has just concluded that a new law is needed specifically to deal with stalking.

At the moment stalking can only be dealt with in a Magistrates Court, as a lower tier harassment offence under the Protection from Harassment Act 1997 which was passed to deal with the problem of fixated behaviour.

Mr Llwyd's Committee also wants perpetrators of the offence to be put through clinical psychology courses. In all the report makes 30 different recommendations.

Elfyn Hot Quote: "There were people who had reported stalking offences to all the authorities and the stalking continued and they were murdered. We heard of two or three such examples and their parents came and gave evidence to us. How they managed to do it I don't know but without their help we wouldn't have got anywhere. In some cases there wasn't a dry eye in the room.

"There has never been a stalking law as it has never been identified in law as the offence of stalking. We need a dedicated stalking law nothing else will work. There are 120,000 reports of stalking each year, very few are prosecuted, and of those that are prosecuted fewer than 3 per cent end up in prison sentences."

"The Campaigners"! What determined MPs are doing to campaign for social justice.

Andrew Stephenson the Conservative MP for Pendal: "Justice for Jane Clough" and "Justice for the Yousaf Family". In both campaigns Andrew is working with families whose relatives have been murdered and through using parliamentary processes he is making a real impact on public policy and social justice. Andrew's Ten Minute Rule Bill, to change Bail laws, was drawn up with the help of Jane's parents, whose daughter was murdered while her attacker was on Bail facing charges that he raped her. It is now being incorporated into a Parliamentary Bill. It would give the prosecution a right to appeal against a Judges' decision to grant bail.

Andrew has also used his Maiden Speech, an Adjournment Debate and visits to the Foreign Office to fight for culprits in Pakistan to be brought to justice for the murder of three members of the Yousaf family when they were paying a visit to Pakistan: Mohammed, his wife Parviaz and their daughter Tania.

Andrew Hot Quote: "Jane's parents wanted to ensure that lessons were learnt from what happened even though it wouldn't bring Jane back. We had meetings with Ministers and others and that led to my Ten Minute Bail Amendment Bill. We kept up the pressure from there and I was delighted that we got All-Party support, from Labour, the Liberal Democrats and the Conservatives. That led to the government agreeing in principle to support the Bill and bring forward our amendments as part of the Legal Aid Sentencing and Punishment of Offenders Bill."

"The Yousaf family case was a real learning case for me. I was staggered when I invited the family to come down and listen to the Adjournment Debate and 300 people came down to listen to that debate at 11 at night, it showed the strength of feeling amongst the community."

The year: 2009
Stop press: Congratulations to John Bercow MP for becoming the new Speaker of the House of Commons and thanks for this interview...
John Bercow MP Contender for the role of Speaker in the House of Commons.

The Conservative MP for Buckingham John Bercow, is standing for the position of Speaker in the House of Commons. He is well liked and respected in Labour circles, even though he is a Conservative, and he is said to have the backing of more than 100 Labour MPs. Members of his own Party aren't so sure though, as some believe he leans too much to the left. For the past 17 years the Speaker's Chair has been sat in by Labour members. Some think a left leaning Conservative who is relatively young and forward looking would help to modernise the House in the wake of the MPs' expenses row. Mr Bercow is 46 years old, one of the youngest contenders for the job.

John, a member of the wpradio.co.uk Advisory Board, told our reporter Georgie Hemmingway, how he would help further equality in the House, and clamp down on sexist exchanges in the Chamber.

Other contenders for the role include: Margaret Beckett, (Lab); John Bercow (Con); Sir George Young (Con); Ann Widdecombe (Con); Sir Alan Beith (LD); Sir Alan Haselhurst (Con); Sir Patrick Cormack (Con); Parmjit Dhanda (Lab); Richard Shepherd (Con); Sir Michael Lord (Con).

Dr Evan Harris MP – women and their right to the throne
The Liberal Democrat Equality Campaigner, Dr Evan Harris MP, attempted to introduce a Private Member's Bill to modernise our monarchy by allowing a woman to be first in succession to the throne rather than being superseded by a younger male sibling, the so called rule of "primogeniture". Dr Harris's "Royal Marriage and Succession to the Crown Bill" also wanted to allow those in the line of succession to the

throne to marry a Catholic. Boni Sones, asked Dr Harris, why his Bill was needed now?

Evan Hot Quote: "The idea that deep at the heart of our constitution there is something so sexist as that and anti-Catholic means that it doesn't serve our reputation very well as a Country and I think it is an opportunity for the government to live up to its commitment to get rid of unjustified discrimination wherever it exists even at the heart of the establishment."

John Bercow MP

The Conservative backbench MP for Buckingham John Bercow is a supporter of human rights and women's rights internationally. A former backbencher of the year, Mr Bercow sits on the International Affairs Select Committee and chairs a committee looking into Genocide. He is a supporter of All-women shortlists for his party, something others oppose, to get more women into Westminster and talks movingly of his visits to a Darfur refuge camp where he believes women and the love of their children, have been instrumental in rebuilding their war torn communities. Boni Sones asked him why he has championed women's rights here and internationally with such commitment and passion.

John Hot Quote: "The National Minimum Wage, "could usefully be increased". He continued: "I have argued that there seemed to me to be quite a powerful case in the present economic climate for increasing it somewhat more sharply. This may seem counter intuitive in a recession but I think there would be a good case for a sizeable increase which would boost the spending power of the lowest paid workers and that might actually generate a bit of demand in the economy.

"I think there is room for blue sky thinking in the Low Pay Commission, and over a period of time I think it would be perfectly affordable."

Mr Bercow MP also supports Labour's Deputy Leader, Harriet Harman MP's quest for a new Equality Bill. "I don't regard it as something that can be signed up to by only Labour or Liberal Democrat politicians, I have long been a supporter of Equality legislation and I think the government should get on with it. My attitude as a Conservative is to be pragmatic, the issue is what works, does it help, is it fair and will the Country benefit?

"My view is that a sensible, reasonable, carefully thought through piece of Equality legislation can be of great advantage to the Country and my attitude is that if the Labour Party doesn't get on with it then the next Conservative government should, and I hope in the national interests that the government will not procrastinate and delay and I wish Harriet Harman MP well in her internal discussions."

The year: 2008
Anne Jenkin on Hyett Dickinson

The name doesn't exactly roll off the tongue, but the Liberal MP for North St Pancras, Sir Willoughby Hyett Dickinson, should be a hero to the women's movement. He introduced the first Women's Suffrage Bill in 1907, as a Private Member's Bill. Sir Willoughby Dickinson was an early pioneer of votes for women. He had two highly educated sisters, one a doctor, and he couldn't understand why he could have the vote and his two sisters couldn't.

The story is told in this ninetieth year since women got the vote, by the energetic, dynamic, formidable and witty, Anne Jenkin, wife of the Conservative MP Bernard Jenkin. Anne is a political force in her own right, as a fund raiser, campaigner and co-founder of the Conservative's Women2Win Campaign. Boni Sones spoke to Anne by the new exhibition to the suffragettes in Westminster and then by the statue of Margaret Thatcher, who is a friend, one of many in her legendary contacts book.

James Purnell MP Works and Pensions Minister

One of the surprise changes of 2008 was when the Works and Pensions Minister, James Purnell, announced hundreds of thousands of women will win the right to a full state pension. Carers, full-time mothers and other women who have not paid enough National Insurance to qualify will be allowed to make one-off payments to bridge the gap and catch up. Pensions campaigners across party were jubilant. It will benefit up to 555,000 people.

Purnell said women will be able to buy back up to 12 years of missed contributions instead of the present six. The changes will relate to any person, but in reality mainly women, who will retire between April 6th this year and April 5th 2015, and who has 20 years or more of their National Insurance record. Pensions campaigner, Alexandra Kemp, of the West Norfolk Women and Carers Pensions Network and a member of the powerful coalition for Human Rights and Women and Pensions, told Boni Sones what she thought the original suffragettes would have thought of these changes, 90 years since women won the vote.

The Human Fertilisation and Embryology Bill Evan Harris MP

The Human Fertilisation and Embryology Bill Report stage will be debated by the Commons this week. Proponents of change to our current abortion laws are going to be proposing some further liberalising amendments, including reducing the number of doctors signatures from 2 to 1 that you need to get an abortion, allowing midwives to carry out abortions and for them to be carried out in GP surgeries. Diana Abbott, MP is also going to be proposing an amendment that would allow women from Northern Ireland to have abortions on the NHS in Britain. Currently Northern Ireland's abortion laws are governed by an Act that was passed in 1861, before women even had the right to vote. Dr Evan Harris MP, is a leading advocate for change as are other MPs across party. Boni Sones spoke to him, Ann Furedi, of the British Pregnancy Advisory Service, and Kate Paterson, an NHS Consultant obstetrician at a briefing meeting.

Charles Walker MP – Conservative

Charles Walker the Conservative MP for Broxbourne, has been trying to get more support for victims of rape. He's held an Adjournment Debate in the Commons this week on the issue and is working across party to ensure more resources are given to rape crisis centres, and to improve the rape conviction rates for reported offences. He is interviewed by Brian Shallcross of GCap media. Thanks to GCap for the interview.

Women Matter:

Andrew Selous the Conservative MP for South West Befordshire has signed a motion in Parliament calling on the government to help women affected by HIV and AIDS in the developing world. The Women Matter campaign, has been launched by the leading international development charity VSO. It is asking the UK's Department for International Development to put women at the heart of its new global HIV and AIDS strategy. Brian Shallcross of GCap Media spoke to him. Thanks to GCap for the interview.

The year: 2007
Paul Goggins MP

Paul Goggins MP, the Minister of State for Northern Ireland, has been at the forefront of pioneering complementary medicine on the NHS. In his previous role as Health Minister for Northern Ireland, he announced a new £200,000 fund to pilot the integration of complementary medicine into the NHS. He said that these therapies should be made available to all people, not just people who can afford to pay privately. The pilot project is being operated by Get Well UK and will aim to treat 700 patients initially. Boni Sones, went to Ulster to speak to four patients and their health practitioners to find out how the Get Well UK programme was improving their health.

EIGHT

Campaigning women of the past

It was only recently in February 2007 that Parliament put up a statue to the Conservative Prime Minster, Margaret Thatcher in the Members Lobby in the House of Commons, and she was still fit enough to unveil it herself. It was the first time a former Prime Minister has been honoured in this way before he or she died. Elsewhere in Westminster the representation of women in Parliament is thin on the ground but now improving thanks to an active House of Commons Works of Art Committee who are commissioning portraits of modern women politicians, such as Diane Abbott, the first black woman MP and Margaret Beckett, the former Labour Minister. Mo Mowlam has made it to the National Portrait Gallery but few other modern women politicians have not even the high profile women, Harriet Harman or Theresa May. Also of interest is the white stone statue of Viscount Falkland standing in St Stephen's Hall, to the left just before you enter Central Lobby. It is a common myth that the crack in the stone sword was made when a suffragette had chained herself to it and had to be cut free, but this is not true. There is documentary evidence to show it broke shortly after its installation in the 19th century. The suffragette action caused the spur on Falkland's boot to break, and apparently it was the weight of the chain that caused the damage and not the process of being cut free! It was up that St Stephen's walkway that the suffragettes used to walk to demand to speak to their MPs so that women could "get the vote". The militant suffragette Emily Wilding Davison hid herself in the Chapel of St Mary Undercroft, in the crypt of St Stephen's Hall, on the night of the census on 2nd April 1911 so she could say she was in Westminster. We actually managed to broadcast from there! Some MPs do take people on their own suffragette tours and there is a Parliament and Votes for Women display on the principal floor, which recounts the history of women's suffrage and those early women MPs. These are recent developments and the Labour MP Judy Mallaber, a member of the House of Commons Works of Art Committee spoke up for them. Another interesting stop in such tours is the statue of Emmeline Pankhurst which still sits just outside in Victoria Tower Gardens, although admittedly she was honoured in this way very early on, just two years after her death in March 1930. Women MPs like to gather round her statue, lay wreaths, and sing songs with their male colleagues too, on celebration days such as International Women's Day in March each year. In Westminster itself one campaigner, the writer and film producer Barbara Gorna, has been particularly influential in loaning the scarf that Emily Wilding Davison, is said to have worn when she ran under the King's horse at Epsom races and later died. Barbara loaned the scarf to Danny Boyle who staged the 2012 Olympics, and it proudly led the procession of suffragettes in the stadium. Thanks to Melanie Unwin, the Deputy Curator, and her colleagues the scarf is now in a glass case at the entrance to the public gallery as part of the suffrage exhibition, but it is on loan from Barbara. Modern day campaigns to get significant women in politics recognised may not be as radical as the past but it does most certainly take years to achieve change. Barbara has written a film script of Emily's life, and Parliament did do Emily proud when it celebrated 100 years since her death in 2013 with public celebrations in Westminster Hall when both Theresa May and Harriet Harman spoke of the achievements of women in Parliament from then to now. In 2008 www.wpradio.co.uk commissioned the Blair's Babes photographer, Kieran Doherty to take four photographs of our women MPs party by party to celebrate 90 years of women and the vote, and the Commons acquired a copy of each and hung them in the Upper Committee Corridor. The walls of Jericho came tumbling down for a short time at least but so much more could be done.

The year: 2013
Campaigning for a Statue of Emily in Parliament
Harriet Harman MP and Theresa May MP – Two women at the top of their parties

Women MPs across party, the Speaker John Bercow and other friends came together in Westminster Hall to celebrate the life of Emily Wilding Davison, the suffragette who died after being knocked down by the King's

Horse at Epsom racecourse 100 years ago. They are now campaigning for a statue of Emily to be commissioned and placed in Parliament.

In this special documentary our Exeuctive Producer Boni Sones, and Adivsory Board member Deborah McGurran talk to Jane Garvey, the co-presenter of Women's Hour, Sandi Toksvig the presenter of Radio 4's News Quiz, and Labour's Emily Thornberry MP, who organised the event. You can also hear snippets of the speeches made by The Speaker, and the two most senior women in British politics today, Labour's Harriet Harman MP, and the Home Secretary Theresa May MP.

Jane Garvey Hot Quote: "Of course there should be a statue of Emily Wilding Davision! I want my daughters to know about her, I want my granddaughters to know about her, the statue needs to go up and it should go up quickly."

Sandi Hot Quote: "Every time you go past a news stand and see a tabloid newspaper where the front page is a woman showing her bottom, take a sensible newspaper and put it on top!"

100 years since Emily Wilding Davison, the Suffragette died Parliament pays tribute to her

Westminster has paid tribute to the Suffragette Emily Wilding Davison 100 years after she was knocked down by the King's Horse at Epsom races. (5th June 2013).

"Parliament and Votes for Women" The Speaker's Advisory Committee on Works of Art and Parliament Week, paid tribute to Emily with a special tour of the places in Westminster Emily and others targeted with her Suffrage militant activities.

Boni Sones, our Executive Producer, spoke to the Labour MP Alison McGovern, Elizabeth Crawford, the suffragette historian, and Irene Cockroft, of the Bourne Hall Museum in Ewell, Surrey. All had their own Emily stories, including an eye witness account of Emily's funeral procession from Kate Frye.

Campaigning women of the past

Celebrating the life of Emily Wilding Davison – 100 years since she died

Congratulations to Clare Balding and writer, Barbara Gorna for the super Channel 4 documentary on Emily Wilding Davison, who died 100 years ago in June after trying to pin a suffragette scarf to the King's Horse at Epsom races on Derby Day. Thanks to Barbara and others that scarf is now in a glass case in Westminster itself.

We have over the past six years, often told this story on www.wpradio.co.uk and www.parliamentaryradio.com. One of the very special moments of parliamentary history we recorded was in 2008 when MPs of all parties, men and women, celebrated 90 years of women and the vote.

They laid flowers at the statue of the suffragette Emily Pankhurst, which is still outside Parliament, and then walked into the Commons to commemorate the life of Emily Wilding Davison. They visited the broom cupboard where Emily actually hid herself in the Chapel of St Mary Undercroft, in the crypt of St Stephen's Hall, on the night of the census on 2nd April 1911 so she could say she was in Westminster.

Here is the twenty minute documentary that our Executive Producer Boni Sones made. Beware there are many MPs singing suffragette songs!

MPs and former MPs who appear in this documentary in order of appearance are: Caroline Spelman, Maria Miller, Baroness Uddin, Lynda Gilroy, Fiona Mactaggart, Hilary Armstrong, Judy Mallaber, Barbara Follett, Harriet Harman, Jo Swinson, David Davis, Barbara Keeley.

Why Emmeline Pankhurst needs a home in Westminster

A group of women MPs are campaigning to get this Manchester portrait of Emmeline Pankhurst by artist Charlotte Newson, into the Palace of Westminster, somewhere!

We spoke to two Labour MPs, Kate Green and Gisela Stuart, about women's representation in art and in numbers in Parliament, and also to the artist Charlotte Newson, and Yvonne Edge, the former manager of the Pankhurst Centre in Manchester.

Kate Green MP Hot Quote: "This portrait has been touring here and abroad. I would like it to make its home here in Parliament. I think we should be adding it to the Parliamentary Art collection, you don't see many women on the walls here in Parliament and this is probably the one woman we should all celebrate, I would like her to come here."

The year: 2012
The discovery of a return train ticket rewrites history for Emily Wilding Davison
Stop press: On 8th June 1913 it will be 100 years since Emily died
One scarf, one dogged journalist, and women MPs working across party, have helped to re-write how the Suffragette Emily Wilding Davison was fatally injured at Derby Day on June 4th 1913 at Epsom racecourse when she tried to pin a "Votes for Women" scarf onto the King's horse. She died four days later.

It has always been said that Emily "threw" herself under the horse, but now campaigner, writer and film producer, Barbara Gorna, has told how Emily purchased a return ticket back to London for that same day indicating that she was not expecting to die. Barbara journeyed to the Women's Library, now part of the LSE, to sift through various objects to make her "discovery" and with the help of her friends, MPs and curators, managed to find a place for Emily's scarf in Westminster itself. Here our Own Correspondent Linda Fairbrother, tells Barbara's story, from an article she has written for House Magazine.

How Barbara, Joan and Danny Boyle, took 'Emily' to the Olympics
When the Suffragettes appeared in the opening Ceremony of the 2012 Olympics, their procession was led by the scarf Emily Wilding Davison wore when she was knocked down by the King's horse at Epsom races, and later died. What an achievement. Olympics procession organiser, Danny Boyle "borrowed" the scarf from the House of Commons where it hangs in a small display near Central Lobby, called "Parliament and Votes for Women".

But the scarf belongs to script writer and producer Barbara Gorna, who with Film Producer Joan Lane of WildThyme Productions Ltd are making a film of Emily's life. Emily ran onto the track in support of the women's right to vote campaign and was knocked over by the King's horse, but as this film reveals for the first time 'Emily' did not commit suicide – her death was an accident.

In Spring 2011, Boni Sones OBE spoke to Joan and Barbara as they stood under the 'Emily' scarf and progressed to Central Lobby.

We are sure Emily would want to congratulate Dame Tessa Jowell, an Olympics Minister, who worked so hard to ensure women competed in all the Olympic sports for the first time. Tessa's podcast is further down our Home page. What an Olympics it has been for women athletes and those much prized Gold medals. We're sure Emily must be watching too!

"A symbol of Hope" ... celebrating a very special woman campaigner of the present!
Aung San Suu Kyi speaks to both Houses of Parliament in Westminster Hall. (22nd June 2012).

Burmese opposition leader Aung San Suu Kyi has made an historic address to both Houses of Parliament in Westminster Hall. Described as a "symbol of hope" can she inspire women leading resistance movements elsewhere in the World? Portsmouth North Conservative MP Penny Mordaunt, and Seema Malhotra, the Labour MP for Feltham and Heston came hot foot from the speech to Central Lobby Westminster to talk to us. Penny also told us why she is opposed to her own Government's Bill to reform the House of Lords.

The year: 2009
Chloe Smith MP for Norwich North
December 1, is the 90th anniversary of Nancy Astor taking her seat in Parliament
Chloe Smith the new MP for Norwich North is now the youngest MP in Parliament after being elected in a by-election in July this year. At 27 she is two years younger than the previous "baby of the House", Lib Dem Jo

Swinson, but Chloe insists "If you are good enough you're old enough, the age isn't the thing!"

Chloe describes herself as a Norfolk girl "through and through" and whilst a candidate for 18 months she was an energetic local campaigner. Her mentor was Baroness Gillian Shephard of Northwold, a former Norfolk MP and minister, and Chloe says she herself has mentored other potential candidates through the Conservative's Women2Win Campaign jointly led by the Rt Hon Theresa May MP.

She's already given her Maiden Speech, on further education in her constituency and although she says she isn't a fan of positive discrimination she does want to see women supported in their attempts to gain seats. Here our reporter Linda Fairbrother secured a special interview with Chloe, but first she visited Cliveden House in Berkshire, the former home of the first women MP to take up her seat in Westminster – the Conservative Lady Nancy Astor, where she spoke to Annette Scudamor, a National Trust guide.

Maggie! Maggie! Maggie!
Is Margaret Thatcher the "Mother of the Nation" or the "Monster from the Blue Lagoon"?
That's the question The Cartoon Museum in Bloomsbury, London, is asking from 6th May to 26th July with an exhibition of satirical cartoons of Britain's first woman Prime Minister 30 years since her election. It features work by Steve Bell, Gerald Scarfe, Trog and many others for newspapers and magazines across the political spectrum. The cartoons reflecting her 11 years in power, were chosen by Steve Bell of the Guardian and one of her former trusted ministers, Lord Baker of Dorking. Clearly they find it hard to agree about her legacy but the exhibition brought out the humour in both of them. Boni Sones began by speaking to Lord Baker and then Steve Bell.

In their spirited and lively "ding dong" over the legacy of Margaret Thatcher, **Lord Baker, says Hot Quote:**

"She was remarkable she was undoubtedly the most successful peace time Prime Minister we have had in the last Century. To begin with I was rather cool about Margaret, but I was one of those who came to like her more and more, and as I was getting to like her more and more there were quite a lot of the real Thatcherites moving away from her and quite a lot of the Thatcherites did her in."

While Steve Bell retorts Hot Quote: "What it can't really convey is the full pain of living under Margaret Thatcher …it was the sheer agony, if you were opposed to Margaret Thatcher it was murder three general elections on the trot with Thatcher, then one with John Major, it was hard to take and it was relentless. It wore you down, and you had to find solace in symbolic attacks."

Together Lord Baker and Steve Bell chose 100 cartoons across the media reflecting her 11 years in power and they had: "great fun, I enjoyed it very much," said Lord Baker. Steve Bell said "it's been a fascinating exercise".

But surprisingly Lord Baker says: "Margaret never looked at the cartoons ever, she never watched "Spitting Image". When you are a very strong personality you don't worry about what others say about you, she never looked at them, she was so confident."

Showing how Emily was knocked down by the Kings Horse

To celebrate International Women's Day 09 Film maker Barbara Gorna has kindly allowed WP Radio to show HER film on the life and tragic death of the suffragette Emily Wilding Davison, the only suffragette to die for the cause. The former Speaker of the House of Commons Betty Boothroyd and the former Labour MP Tony Benn, tell Barbara why Emily's life is so important to them today, more than 90 years since women first got the vote in Britain. The film shows the scarf Emily wore when she was knocked unconscious at Epsom races. That scarf is now on display in a special permanent exhibition in the House of Commons thanks to women MPs of today across party and Barbara. THANKS to Barbara and good luck with her movie on Emily.

The year: 2008
Gwyneth Dunwoody MP

WP Radio would like to pay tribute to the Labour MP Gwyneth Dunwoody, who has died aged 77. She was the longest serving female MP in Parliament and had been the MP for Crewe and Nantwich since 1974. She was known as a "fighter" and chaired the Transport Select Committee where she stood up for MPs rights. Hear her interview the BBC in June last year.

International Women's Day
Mo Mowlam MP (Labour 1987–2001)

WP Radio is celebrating International Women's Day by releasing this five minute extract of one of the last political interviews the Labour politician Mo Mowlam gave. Mo has given permission for the whole one hour interview to be available after the next General Election as part of an audio archive held at the British Library with women politicians. Mo Mowlam, Labour MP for Redcar between 1987-2001, oversaw the talks which led to the 1998 Good Friday Agreement. She had the conversation with broadcast journalist Linda Fairbrother in her garden in August 2004 a year before she died for the book: Women In Parliament: The New Suffragettes. In this extract she talks of the Blair's Babe picture and why young women should get involved in politics. 90 years since Women got the vote we thought it fitting to release it now. Happy International Women's Day Mo!

The year: 2007
Women supporting Women
Emily Wilding Davison

It is 90 years since women over 30 were first given the right to vote. In 2008, Women's Parliamentary Radio is campaigning to get a plaque to the militant suffragette Emily Wilding Davison at St George's Church in Bloomsbury where her funeral procession started and a statue of her in Westminster. Writer and Producer Barbara Gorna has the sash Emily was trying to pin to the King's horse when she was killed and she told Boni Sones why she wants it to be known Emily's death was a tragic accident not suicide.

NINE
International issues and parliaments

It was only relatively recently that each year Westminster started to hold a regular yearly International Women's Day debate which is by tradition held on March 8th every year. It was the Labour women who got Parliament to devote time to this debate in the second term of the Blair government, and all parties, men and women now join in with debates in the Commons and the Lords. The first debate that was officially called "The International Women's Day" was held on 6th March 2008, but in previous years the women MPs had held special debates in the Chamber on issues such as women and justice, or women and violence. It was a radical departure from the past and as with most progress in Westminster the reforms are often hijacked so only recently attempts were made to shorten the length of time the issues affecting women on international women's day could be under discussion. International Women's Day was first declared in 1910 with the first event held in 1911. In March 2011, a group of Peers made their maiden speeches on the 100 Anniversary of International Women's Day. They were – Baroness Heyhoe-Flint, Baroness Brinton, Baroness Jenkin of Kennington, Baroness King of Bow (Oona King), Baroness Lister of Burtersett and Baroness Morgan of Ely. The debate focused on the global and domestic challenges for women in the centenary year of International Women's Day. Westminster often plays host to women MPs from elsewhere in the World, and www.wpradio.co.uk and www.parliamentaryradio.com have been privileged to be invited to these events to interview these formidable parliamentarians. We have thanked both the Commonwealth Parliamentary Association UK (CPA UK) and the British Group of the Inter-Parliamentary Union (BGIPU) for these interviews. We were also aware of the modern technology changes that were transforming broadcasting of the time, and the fact that modern audio recording equipment allowed interviews to be conducted on phone lines country to country, rather than expensive line bookings. We therefore in 2011, very early on, got our MPs in Westminster to interview women

MPs in South Africa and Africa "down the line". On January 28th 2011 we claimed a World First in broadcasting when we got Dame Anne Begg to interview women MPs in the Kenyan Parliament. A week later on February 4th 2011 we hooked up the Liberal Democrat MP Jo Swinson to speak to a woman MP in the South African parliament who was campaigning there to end violence against women, much as our parliamentarians do here. Women MPs across party form formidable international alliances and are part of a strong global network of women in parliaments and in the United Nations campaigning for change. Together they are working towards realising the UN's Millennium Development goals setting targets for national governments to achieve from DV to breast feeding. The UN did become a fan of www.wpradio.co.uk and asked if it could use our four photos of women MPs for an event it was staging, and we agreed. The fame of women in Westminster spread, and our spirits were again raised when one Canadian listener nominated our Emily Wilding Davison 100th celebrations suffragette coverage of 2013 for an international radio award.

The year: 2014
When there is a woman in the room...

The Prime Minister David Cameron is reported to have expressed his concern about how few women have been selected to fight winnable Conservative seats at the next Election in 2015. When he came to power he promised that he would have one-third women in his Cabinet and he had hoped to increase again the number of Conservative Women MPs, which rose from 17 to 49 at the 2010 election.

"..After the 1931 general election, there were 13 Conservative women MPs. After the 1997 general election, there were 13 Conservative women MPs." Source: Conservative Women's Organisation.

Here to assist David Cameron, and the other Party leaders, Ed Miliband for Labour and Nick Clegg for the Liberal Democrats, in their bids to get more women elected to the UK Parliament we have made a special New Year 2014 documentary. "When there is a woman in the room", lets women from Parliaments all over the World tell the male leaders of our political parties in the UK why they need to "have a woman in the room" to shape social policy. Positive discrimination in favour of women is allowing women to put women's issues on the agenda assisted by the men in their parliaments too.

The Documentary begins with Margaret Sitta MP from Tanzania, then Eve Bazaiba Masudi MP from the Democratic Republic of Congo, Shinkai Karokhail MP from Afghanistan, and Fungayi Jessie Majome MP from Zimbabwe.

Margaret Sitta from Tanzania begins the documentary by telling us **Hot Quote**: "Where there is women there is talk about women's issues, which sometimes seems to be forgotten."

Fungayi Jessie Majome MP from Zimbabwe ends the documentary by telling us **Hot Quote**: "We need to socially engineer our societies because if not we will wait forever, and we need not."

Our thanks to the Commonwealth Parliamentary Association UK (CPA UK) and the British Group of the Inter-Parliamentary Union (BGIPU) for letting us record these interviews in November 2012 and December 2013. Interviews by Boni Sones, Executive Producer, and Linda Fairbrother reporter.

The year: 2013
How sharing experiences across the World is helping to improve women's lives
International Parliamentary Conference on the post 2015 UN Development Agenda.

The Millennium Development Goals that the United Nations established in 2000 for all its members, set targets in eight areas which were to be completed by 2015, but what progress has been made?

The targets included eradicating poverty to setting goals for primary education, gender equality, child mortality, maternal health including breast feeding, disease, the environment and global partnerships for development.

In support of these goals www.parliamentaryradio.com and our sister site www.wpradio.co.uk has for seven years worked to connect women in parliaments globally to let them share their stories through our web based radio channel. Better communication can change lives too.

Recently around 100 delegates from all over the World, gathered in the UK Houses of Parliament to review progress to date, and in particular to look ahead to 2015 when the next set of goals will be put before their governments for agreement.

Our reporter Linda Fairbrother spoke to three delegates: Senator Fauzaya Talhaoui from Belgium, Cynthia Forde from Barbados and Margaret Sitta from Tanzania.

Margaret Sitta Hot Quote: "For now it is not possible to empower every woman but for the future it is better to invest in girls education. Where there are women there is talk about women's issues." Copyright Linda Fairbrother.

The year: 2012
From Our Own Correspondent – A Day in the Life of Angela Larkin who runs a very special project in South Africa
Angela Larkin, founder of the Thanda After-School project for more than 325 HIV/AIDS orphans living in the Kwa Zulu Natal district of South Africa, has been nominated by our supporters Christa Botha and Liz Kanter to feature in our "From Our Own Correspondent" special report. Here our Correspondent Linda Fairbrother describes their first ever Christmas Party for the children.

You can find out more on the Thanda After-School website to donate this Christmas. "Thanda" means Love in Zulu! Thanks Linda. Copyright Linda Fairbrother.

Women in Africa, Europe and the Middle East – fighting for their human rights
Women from Parliaments all over the World came to Westminster this week, to take part in The International Parliamentary Conference on Gender and Politics. The Commonwealth Parliamentary Association UK (CPA UK) and the British Group of the Inter-Parliamentary Union (BGIPU) hosted the event.

The issues they have successfully put on the agenda in their Parliaments are much the same as women across party are tackling in our own Houses of Parliament. Education, health care, domestic violence, better representation of women in politics, inheritance rights and giving a helping hand to those women who want to succeed in business. Their rights in these areas have been hard fought for and require tremendous tenacity and resilience to keep up the momentum for change. War and food shortages are the reality in many of these countries still.

Here Linda Fairbrother, Barbara Gorna, and Boni Sones spoke to six of them and their representatives. Do listen, their voices have soul!

The year: 2011
Hidden Stories from Afghanistan

Afghan Women's Hour journalist Zarghuna Kargar has just published her new book "Dear Zari". Based on 13 real life stories of women in Afghanistan today, including her own, she tells how these heart-breaking and empowering stories are transforming women's lives, simply through their "telling".

Zarghuna was part of the first team of journalists to report for Afghan Women's Hour which in two years became the second most popular programme on the Radio. The telling of stories and the sharing of experiences through radio has transformed the lives of many women and their families. Zarghuna, who now lives in London, tells our Executive Producer, Boni Sones OBE, how every time she wrote or read lines in the book tears came to her eyes.

Zarghuna Hot Quote: "Emotionally it was very hard, just listening to those women and hearing about their experiences was very touching for me as an Afghanistan woman. Meeting women as a woman journalist in Afghanistan, is not so hard, because I would just go to neighbours in Kabul, and people living around me and working with me. I talked to women who had suffered in attacks of war, or women achievers in Afghanistan."

"All of these stories I tell have affected me in a very personal way. One woman married a gay man, and was struggling to get a life without a husband. This convenience marriage to a gay man, was a very difficult life and she wanted to get divorced, but because she was not educated she found it very difficult. Divorce is a very big taboo in Afghanistan, and I went through a divorce too. It really touched me emotionally because I made those decisions in my own life which is against my traditions and against my society."

www.wpradio.co.uk VSO UN "Godmothers" documentary presented from Central Lobby, Westminster
1,500 women are dying a day in childbirth. Forced marriages, rape, violence, poverty, equal pay: Michelle Bachelet's new UN Agency for Women has some vocal supporters in the UK who want to ensure it gets the funding it needs to make a difference. To make sure that happens, VSO has just launched the 'Godmothers' campaign www.thegodmothers.org.uk which calls on DFID to become a leading donor to UN Women by making a financial contribution of around 21 million dollars.

In this special Two Part 50 minute UN "Godmothers" documentary our Executive Producer Boni Sones OBE, caught up with Sharon Hodgson MP, campaigners themselves, and Anas Sarwar MP, as activists met their MPs in Central Lobby, Westminster.

Sharon Hodgson the Labour MP for Washington and Sunderland West Hot Quote: "It will be a talking shop if it has no money to do anything with, other Countries have started to put up the money, Spain has put up £13 million, Australia £8 million and when I asked Andrew Mitchell, the International Development Secretary, what the UK government was going to do he said they were going to have a strategy review in June and they would look at it after that. We need this money now if not the UN Agency for Women will be a talking shop."

"There are many major issues that need confronting on behalf of women and we really need the UN Women to have some teeth to say what is acceptable and what isn't and for the UK government to back that."

"We hear about landmarks but at this point in time with all of the changes in the World, the Middle East, Egypt and other revolutions, I think the UN Agency for Women can be a real revolution for women across the developing World."

Anas Sarwar the Labour MP for Glasgow Central, who sits on the International Development Select Committee, Hot Quote: "More than three-quarters of the poorest one billion people in the World today are women. Women have to be at the heart of our development strategy as a Country and that is why I support the UN Agency for Women and that is why the UK has to commit to it."

"Some of the greatest challenges we face in the developing world is to champion the role of women on issues such as access to education, violence against women, land ownership, women's representation, all of which will be championed by the new UN Agency. Spain has committed £13 million but the UK hasn't committed a single penny to this new Agency and we need to lead from the front. I will press the Secretary of State, Andrew Mitchell on this."

"My constituents are natural internationalists; ordinary hard working people give generously to global disasters, even in the most difficult times. What people want is peace, prosperity and justice for every man woman and child throughout the World, and we as the UK most show leadership on this new UN Agency for women. We need to lead from the front on development."

In Part 2 of UN "Godmothers" Boni talks to Lesley Abdela of Shevolution while she chatted with activists in Central Lobby.

Lesley Abdela Hot Quote: "The "Godmothers" has been set up to keep an eye on the British government and the UN Agency for women to make it work. This VSO initiative embraces a variety of supporters, ordinary people and organisations such as the WI. They want DFID to invest £21 million dollars, the same as it gives to UNICEF, a relatively modest amount."

"What I have seen time after time after time, women are in the front of campaigning for democracy, peace and progress but the moment it gets formalised they are pushed out. We are not where it matters at the top table; we are not opening the doors for women enough. In the Middle East talks for instance, there should be equal numbers of women."

"We are not asking for extra money into DFIDs budget, but for something like 0.2 per cent of DFIDs budget to be allocated to this. We either go full tilt and set up UN Women for success or why bother to do it at all?"

Baroness Jay and Laura Moffatt MP help VSO tackle global poverty
Baroness Jay of Paddington and Laura Moffatt the Labour MP for Crawley have both done stints working as volunteers for VSO in a bid to help tackle global poverty.

VSO is the world's leading independent international development organisation that works through volunteers to fight poverty in developing countries.

Baroness Jay was among six parliamentarians to participate in the Parliamentarian Volunteering Scheme this summer, where they helped to advise community organisations on matters relating to advocacy and campaigning.

In South Africa Baroness Jay ran a workshop on reducing the burden of HIV and AIDs care on women and girls. Last summer former nurse Laura Moffatt MP spent three weeks immersed in the health system of Sierra Leone, the poorest country in the world.

Linda Fairbrother spoke to them both with Katy Peach, Policy and Advocacy Manager at VSO.

Philippa Reiss Thorne – Gone Rural in Swaziland
Philippa Reiss Thorne is the Managing Director of Gone Rural in Swaziland. She is a 30-year-old social entrepreneur with a mission who has led a community of 700 women from 13 different communities throughout Swaziland, marketing and selling their Fair Trade products all over the world and to top fashion designers and stores.

These rural communities now find themselves under more financial pressure than ever, having to pay for transport to clinics, school fees and to support more children. 80% of their women rely on Gone Rural as their sole income; each woman supports an average of 8 dependents; 82% of their husbands and partners are unemployed. Although extremely poor by western standards, these families will often take in neighbours' children who have been orphaned by HIV/AIDS.

Here Boni Sones spoke at length to Philippa about Gone Rural, its ethos and how it had managed to treble the daily wage of the women who work with it in just three years. You can find out more at: http://www.goneruralswazi.com

Jo Swinson MP "Guest Editor" and Lindiwe Mazibuko, MP South African Parliament

Jo Swinson the Liberal Democrat MP for East Dunbartonshire, PPS to Business Secretary Vince Cable, sits in our www.wpradio.co.uk "Guest Editor" Chair this week. She recently meet Lindiwe Mazibuko, the opposition Democratic Alliance Spokesperson in the South African Parliament and the Shadow Deputy Minister of Communications. Lindiwe is one of the Parliament's youngest members, as was Jo herself.

In this special "hook-up" to celebrate 100 years of International Women's Day in March 2011, Jo asks Lindiwe about how she was elected and what the impact of apartheid and the ANCs 1996 Constitution has been? Lindiwe told Jo how the women in the Parliament were progressing the pressing issue of young women being kidnapped and raped as some sort of marriage courtship practice, and to stop women being treated as "objects" culturally. Here Jo is co-founder of "The Campaign for Body Confidence".

Lindiwe told Jo Hot Quote: "I was elected in 2009 in the last General Election for the Democratic Alliance, we have a full PR list system and I was number three on the list. I had been working for the Party the Democratic Alliance for some time, they were looking for people who were competent and diverse and who could represent a better mix of South African's and as a young politician I made the cut. The Party was looking to diversify and I was ready and waiting."

"Almost half of the MPs in the National Assembly are women and the same is true of the ANC's Cabinet, almost half of them are women. In the governing party certain positions are sometimes reserved for women and some for men but in our Party it is a far more open approach and we have a female leader. Women's issues are everyone's issues is our approach, the challenges that face women in South Africa stem from the rich culture of patriarchy. The representation doesn't always translate into as much activism as it should."

"Politician's are quick to make glib speeches but it is not always translated into policy implementation for instance on the issues such as polygamy, we have never made a serious issue about this. Women are still having to subscribe to a patriarchal society even when half the women in the Cabinet are women."

"Issues of poverty such as HIV, Aids and sexual violence are of importance too, the rate of infection is much higher amongst women than men, particularly young women. One survey found a third of men admitted to committing sexual violence against a woman, figures like this are astonishing. Women as objects that have to be treated like a child or as a possession is something that stems from the deep patriarchy which was part of apartheid and there is a little bit of a time warp here. In deep rural parts of the Country the most astonishing practices still take place like women being kidnapped and raped as part of some pre marriage courtship practices. People are frightened to champion women as equals."

"We in the DA are trying to convince South African's our rights in the Constitution are only of value if we are willing to protect each other, and someone who doesn't come from my racial or cultural group. It is such a difficult process because the scars of apartheid are deep and longstanding, and the hope is coming from young people and young leaders. It is difficult to break that racial deadlock, but we are working as hard as we can to make that happen."

"We need our partners in Parliament's all over the World to fight the fight with us to fight the culture of patriarchy and attitudes surrounding women, and others must be willing to discuss the challenges we face. To celebrate 100 years of International Women's Day it would be good if we could join hands with women in other Parliament's where women are more emancipated in order to give us a bit more momentum too."

A first for internet broadcasting – www.wpradio.co.uk invites our Guest Editor of 2011 Dame Anne Begg to interview women MPs in the Kenyan Parliament
Our first Guest Editor Dame Anne Begg interviews four women MPs from the Kenyan Parliament.

In our new Global podcast broadcast series of 2011 www.wpradio.co.uk will be inviting women MPs from the UK Parliament to interview women MPs from other Parliaments all over the World. Technology now allows these "hook-ups" with relative ease compared to broadcasting conventions of the past.

When Dame Anne Begg, MP for Aberdeen South, Chair of the Works and Pensions Select Committee, met a delegation of women from the Kenyan Parliament recently to talk about how Committees work in the UK Parliament, she invited them to be interviewed in this new series and they agreed. They were the guest of the Commonwealth Parliamentary Association UK.

There are now 22 women MPs in Kenya, 10 per cent of the 222 MPs in all. Six of these 22 are nominated, to represent special interests.

The Kenyan women MPs went on strike in 2003 when they were banned from taking their handbags into the Kenyan Parliament. They argued handbags were part of their "attire" and the ban was lifted.

Here Anne asks the delegation about the ban, and changing family structures in a global world that is now allowing women to take out bank accounts and giving them new rights to the inheritance of land. The responsibilities of men are now changing too.

That all important new Kenyan Constitution and Bill of Rights approved in 2010, gives people new rights to "self actualisation". This will lead to more women in the Parliament, and the allocation of 47 safe seats for women, one for each County, and 16 women in the newly created Senate House.

Dame Anne, the first full-time wheelchair user in Westminster, spoke to Hon. Dr Joyce Laboso MP, Hon. Shakila Abdalla MP, Hon. Linah Jebii

Kilimo MP, Hon. Rachel Shebesh MP. This podcast broadcast was produced by Boni Sones OBE.

Dr Joyce Laboso MP spoke for her colleagues when she said **Hot Quote**: "We currently have ten per cent of women in our Parliament, six of which are nominated by the political parties to represent special interests. We really are excited about what the new Constitution has offered to us, we know it is not going to be easy, we have to do a lot of civic education and capacity building for women to take up the positions at National and local level. We will start to change the World in 2011 the anniversary of 100 years of International Women's Day but there is a lot to do to make the changes happen."

Dame Anne Begg, Hot Quote: "It is an exciting time for broadcasting through the web and by allowing women MPs themselves to be "Guest Editors" www.wpradio.co.uk is giving us a public voice to explore the issues that affect and impact on women in countries and Parliaments all over the Globe.

"We can share our experiences and our voices, and by joining together in this way the World will seem a smaller more accessible place, where our stories really do matter to one-another and can change how we conduct affairs and what issues we decide to bring to the fore in our respective parliaments. That handbag protest was a small thing but very symbolic for the Kenyan women in the same way getting Ladies toilets in the voting lobbies was the big change here. Thanks to www.wpradio for allowing us this thought provoking opportunity that audiences can listen to all over the Globe, via a computer or a mobile phone application."

The year: 2010
VSO "Women & Development": In debate Noreine Kaleeba of Uganda and Marg Mayne, CEO VSO
What is the best way to embark on empowering the lives of women and girls in developing economies? Here VSO's Chief Executive, Marg Mayne talks to Noreine Kaleeba a patron and founder of The AIDS Support Organisation (TASO) in Uganda, and Deputy Chair of Uganda National

Health Research Organisation. They tell wpradio.co.uk reporter, Linda Fairbrother, that the education of girls and women's involvement in politics is key to lifting women out of poverty and enabling their participation in the economy. VSO now works with partners across a range of programmes in the developing world.

Dolma Gyari and Ngawang Lhamo, Tibetan Parliament.
The Tibetan Parliament-in-exile is located in the hill town of Dharamsala in northern India. Formed by the Dalai Lama less than a year after the uprising in Tibet against Chinese rule that led to his exile, the Parliament looks after the Tibetans across the world and provides a model for their homeland.

Dolma Gyari is the first woman to be elected as Deputy Speaker of the parliament-in-exile, and has since been re-elected three times. She has been a political activist for a number of years, and believes passionately about the power of women to make change.

Member of the Tibetan parliament Ngawang Lhamo was born in Tibet, escaping into India as a child. Originally a teacher, she became General Secretary for the Tibetan Women's Association before founding a school for children with special needs.

Lucy Fairbrother spoke to the two women MPs about why their roles are so important to them as they visited the UK parliament.

The year: 2009
Lesley Abdela MBE – Shevolution
Lesley Abdela, of Shevolution, has been working with other British based NGO groups to ensure that the UN Security Council Resolution 1235 is implemented, to help women's rights to be put top of the international agenda in conflict zones like Afghanistan, Congo, Nepal, Northern Ireland, and Sri Lanka.

Lesley has helped write a report for the Associate Parliamentary Group on "Women, Peace and Security", which draws up a global checklist for women in these conflict zones. Lesley has looked closely at what is happening in Nepal. Boni Sones spoke to her.

Betsy Kawamura – international campaigner against gender based violence

Betsy Kawamura, is an international campaigner against gender based violence. She was herself a victim of gender based violence in Okinawa during the Vietnam war, and Betsy believes the voice of past victims of gender based violence can help heal others. She has told her story in the USA, Japan, Europe, Sri Lanka and now to various UN related agencies, to help raise awareness of all those exposed to GBV, including militarized GBV, prostitution and trafficking on an international level.

Writer Barbara Gorna first asked Betsy why she was a fierce champion of gender based violence. Then Barbara spoke to Betsy about the representation of women in International Parliaments.

The interviews took place in the House of Commons by the permanent exhibition to the suffragettes and the scarf of Emily Wilding Davison who died staging a protest after being knocked down by the King's horse at Epsom races.

Mrs Sherry Ayittey
Honourable Minister for Environment, Science and Technology, Government of Ghana

There's still a lot of work to be done if the world is to reach agreement on reducing greenhouse gas emissions in Copenhagen in December when the G20 countries meet. But while politicans prepare for the "Road to Copehhagen" talks, academics from all over the World met at Cambridge University to look into the impact of climate change on water resources in Africa.

"The Global Water Initiative, Implications of Climate Change and Variability on African Water Resources" conference heard from keynote speaker Mrs Sherry Ayittey, Honourable Minister for Environment, Science and Technology Government of Ghana. A Bio-Chemist by training Mrs Ayittey, believes the issue of water resources is one of basic "human rights" and that in this inter-connected world the developed world needs to embrace the problems the developing world is facing. In speaking up for the voice of the voiceless Mrs Ayittey says that with "trust" in each other we can work towards a dialogue of understanding in Copenhagen. Thanks to Cambridge Judge Business School for allowing us to broadcast this podcast.

Lucy Changme – Zambia

Lucy Changme, is the deputy minister for gender and women in development in the Zambian government. She is passionate about improving the education of girls, and getting more women into politics. Our wpradio.co.uk reporter Georgie Hemmingway caught up with her recently at a One World Action event to celebrate International Women's Day 09. Lucy told Georgie how she was pushing ahead with a gender based violence Bill in Zambia this year.

Lesley Abdela

Lesley Abdela needs no introduction in the world of women and politics. She has worked in over 30 countries advising on gender and democratic development. She is now Vice-President of the Electoral Reform Society and is a partner in Shevolution and Chief Executive of Project Parity. In 1980 she co-founded the 300 group, to get more women into the UK parliament, has received a UK Woman of Europe award, and written and broadcast on the subject of women in politics. 90 years since women achieved the vote Boni Sones asked her how she rated the UK's progress on female representation in our parliament against other countries.

Lesley began by talking about Rwanda and Sweden which have the highest number of women in their parliaments of any country, and she's convinced that Britain needs both a proportional voting system and quotas to achieve change here. Thanks to the Electoral Reform Society for sponsoring this interview.

Sandra Gidley MP

Sandra Gidley is the Liberal Democrat MP for Romsey and the Health Spokesperson for her Party. She has used her professional training as a pharmacist to champion all kinds of health issues here and globally. In the UK she has been at the forefront of getting men to take health prevention seriously, improving alcohol awareness, and she is working across party on mental health issues. As a member of the All-Party Parliamentary Group on Aids, she has visited Africa. Boni Sones asked her what could be done to further the Millennium Development Goals on health for women.

The year: 2008
The Mothers' Union

The Christian organisation "The Mothers' Union", is a formidable campaigning organisation globally with 3.6 million members in 78 countries. It is asking governments to give financing to help achieve the UN's Millennium Development Goal 3. This uses the elimination of gender disparity in primary and secondary education as the indicator of the empowerment of women.

Boni Sones spoke to three MU members about the Mothers' Union work. Rachel Aston, Social Policy Officer, Vivian Kityo from Uganda, and Elizabeth Brown from Canterbury.

Mary Honeyball MEP "Women In Power"

A new book listing all the elected female representatives in the European Parliament has discovered that the typical profile of a woman MEP is white, single, aged 52 and she has never had children. She holds a postgraduate degree in a science related subject and has worked in various scientific posts prior to her election. Like most political institutions across the world, women remain underrepresented in the European Parliament. Only 246 out of 785 MEPs are women – just 31 per cent, but this is still higher than the UK Parliament were women MPs make up 19.8 per cent of the total. *Women in Power: A Guide to Women Members of the European Parliament* has been written by Mary Honeyball MEP. Boni Sones spoke to her. The book is to be published soon.

Britain's youngest MP Jo Swinson interviews Malalai Joya, the youngest person in the Afghanistan Parliament

Malalai Joya defied death threats to travel on London's underground to be interviewed by 28 year old Liberal Democrat MP for East Dunbartonshire, Jo Swinson for Women's Parliamentary Radio at the House of Commons recently. She has just been given the Anna Politkovskaya award by the charity RAW on War in memory of the Russian journalist murdered two years ago in Moscow. "She lives a life of courage and truth-telling in the face of grave danger as Anna did," said Mariana Katzarova of RAW in War.

Malalai, now 30 years old, is currently suspended from the Parliament for saying: "A stable or a zoo is better than the legislature". She continues to campaign against the warlords. In this special documentary podcast Jo Swinson talks to Malalai and Boni Sones reads from the words of her friend, the campaigning journalist Glyn Strong who uses her family name "Joya" in her article.

Malalai Joya tells Jo Hot Quote: "Some women in some big cities have access to jobs and education but most do not. Women are being kidnapped and raped, girls too, and they are burning the schools and building schools with cheap materials that will fall down."

She says the next election could see democracy fail if the corrupt warlords get more power. "We could have built two Afghanistan's with the 14 billion of aid this corrupt government has received since 9/11.The warlords are getting more powerful in this corrupt government and if they get more power at the next election we are worried democracy will fail. Security is more important than food and water, let's rebuild Afghanistan, the schools and the hospitals."

Jo Swinson MP said Hot Quote: "As a woman MP in the UK we might talk about how male dominated and difficult it is but listening to Malalai Joya, it just blows me away because nothing we face is on the same scale of her bravery and courage. If there are more people in Afghanistan like her then there is a bright future for the Country and I sincerely hope that will be the case."

Malalai Joya makes a moving appeal at the end of the documentary for peace. She says:" The Nation who liberates itself is free but the national who liberates others will lead them into slavery as in Afghanistan. Those who struggle may fail but those who do not struggle have already failed. Please join me in our struggle in Afghanistan."

Jo tells Malalai Joya: "Your bravery is an inspiration to us all."

Mums for Mums, Ethiopia

90 years since women in Britain first got the vote the UK Parliament still has only 20 per cent of women as MPs. In the United States, expectations for women to be in the very top jobs in politics are at the fore of the Presidential race. However, in Africa, some countries have achieved gender balanced parliaments after long internal struggles and wars. Ethiopia is working towards gender balanced parliaments at a regional and national level. It is one of the few countries in the developing World to be on course to meet the United Nations Millennium Development Goals for the education and health of girls and women.

A project in the northern Tigray Region "Mums for Mums" is helping young single mothers in Mekelle, learn work based skills to provide for their children. It is run by Tebereh Woldegabriel, the Voluntary Executive Director. Her husband, Dr Solomon Inquai, is the retired Parliamentary speaker and head of social affairs in the Tigray region. Boni Sones spoke to them both. You can make a donation by going to www.mumsformums.com.

Lucy Fairbrother – free Tibet!

Lucy Fairbrother is a 23-year-old political activist who put her ideals to the test at the beginning of the Beijing Olympics. Together with a friend, Iain Thom, she put a "One World One Dream Free Tibet" banner at the top of a lighting pole just outside the Bird's Nest stadium. After being questioned by the Chinese police she and Iain flew home to Britain. www.wpradio.co.uk reporter Daisy Ayliffe spoke to her on her return to find out what motivated her to be an activist.

International issues and parliaments

Electoral Reform Society: Women MPs

The United Kingdom Parliament is waiting for a revolution. Despite the best attempts by all three parties, Labour, Conservative and Liberal Democrats the number of women in our Parliament is still dismally low, just under 20 per cent. Women may have had the vote for nearly 90 years but we still can't get an equal split of male and female MPs in Westminster. In this special documentary commissioned by the Electoral Reform Society, WP Radio journalist Linda Fairbrother spoke to parliamentarians here and abroad. Amongst others, Linda talked to Sweden's Margot Wallstrom, Vice President of the European Commission, the Spanish MEP Barbara Duhrkop, and Professor Pippa Norris, of Harvard University in the USA.

The year: 2007
A New Year wish for "Disarmament and Globalisation" from Baroness Williams of Crosby

Shirley Williams is an unofficial advisor to the Prime Minister, Gordon Brown, on Nuclear Proliferation and Safety. She was a member of the Wilson and Callaghan Governments in the 1960s and 1970s. In 1981 she co-founded the Social Democratic Party, becoming the first MP elected for the SDP in 1981. Here she tells Boni Sones, why disarmament is the most pressing problem the World now needs to address.

Rhoda Kalema Mother of the Ugandan Parliament

Rhoda Kalema, the "Mother" of the Ugandan Parliament, tells here in her own words her story of imprisonment in Uganda before going on to become an MP herself and helping to set up a Commission to help women and their families. She talked to Boni Sones.

A Rising Tide in Uganda

Women in the UK have been at the forefront of helping women internationally to progress their careers in politics. Many have to struggle to get their voices heard and suffer at the hands of oppressive regimes. No more so than in modern Uganda. A book "A Rising Tide", tells the histories of modern women politicians there from the 1940s through to the present time. *A Ugandan women's Struggle for a Public Voice 1940–2004* is published by Forwode. Here Sue Woodsford, tells how she supported one of those women, Rhoda Kalema, when she was in prison. Sue begins by reading Rhoda's story. Other stories in the book are read in this one hour radio documentary by Patricia Lashely, of Momentum Arts, and Boni Sones.

TEN
Campaigning in the Constituency

The weekly half-hour Prime Minister's Questions, PMQs, has a reputation for being a shouting match between the PM, David Cameron and his opposite number the Labour Leader, Ed Miliband. Accusations and counter accusations, name calling, baying and shouting are knocked into line by the Speaker John Bercow, who shouts "order, order" at them from time to time. This is the most familiar visual image of British politics that the public sitting at home observes. Yet much else goes on in Westminster and even at PMQs that you may never see. After the first fifteen minutes of shouting, and finger pointing, and bad body language, an MP will get up to ask the Prime Minister a question on behalf of their constituents. It is a humbling experience to watch and observe. You may well see the constituent sitting in the public gallery, waiting for their MP to ask their Prime Minister that question on their behalf. Questions to the Prime Minister on behalf of constituents or the constituency concerned can be "called" from all sides of the House, Conservative, Labour, Liberal Democrat or the Scottish or Irish MPs or the Independents. Campaigns fought in the constituency help to shape public policy, and feed into the work that All-Party Parliamentary Groups and Select Committees do in the upper committee corridors. These additional PMQs may not be reported by the national media, but they are frequently picked up as news stories in the home towns of the MPs who were lucky enough to get their question asked.

The year: 2013
Three MPs who made a difference in 2013 for their constituents and their New Year wish list for 2014!
The last Prime Minister's Questions of 2013 saw the Prime Minister David Cameron and the Labour leader Ed Miliband, robustly fighting their corner on the economy, employment, energy prices, and food banks once more. With unemployment falling across all categories, women and youth

included, to 7.4 per cent or 2.39 million, the lowest level since the beginning of 2009 the Conservatives felt their plans for the economy had come good, with the private sector providing more jobs than before.

But Labour insisted that there was a real cost of living crisis with low paid part-time work not providing enough money for families to pay their household bills and more people needing food banks and pay day loans than before.

Here we asked three MPs to reply to the issues raised at PMQs and the questions put to the Prime Minister.

Penny Mordaunt, the Conservative MP for Portsmouth North, has been working round the clock to attract new jobs to her constituency in the face of hundreds of ship building job losses at the City's naval base and has recently written to David Cameron with a list of seven demands.

Sandra Osborne, the Labour MP for Ayr Carrick and Cumnock, says poverty is a real issue in her constituency and has been out with others collecting food for the increasing number of food banks in her area.

And finally, we spoke to Nick Raynsford, the Labour MP for Greenwich and Woolwich, who asked David Cameron a PMQ on so called "compassionate conservatism".

Penny's New Year 2014 wish: "We should be the Maritime capital of the UK, the place to go for design, for development and build. That is the vision I have and it is a vision that is shared by a huge number of companies and individuals. If you are not an optimist you shouldn't be in politics."

Sandra's New Year 2014 wish: "For the Scottish Referendum next year I hope people will vote "No". On the issue of energy bills we should adopt Labour's policy and we should do more to get young people back to work. The bedroom tax should be abolished in 2014."

Nick's New Year 2014 wish: "Cancel the bedroom tax. People are trapped there are not enough small units for them to move into... These people are the victims of government policy and there should be an early Statement in 2014 to say it will be repealed... I feel angry today because of the hypocrisy of people who sought office making a prospectus about their commitment to compassionate conservatism but are now pursuing very harsh, crude, unkind policies that are causing enormous suffering and misfortune amongst disadvantaged people. I find that deplorable *and I am very angry.*"

Rachel Maclean the new Conservative PPC for Birmingham Northfield

Battles are now being fought for those new to their political careers who are standing as PPCs – Prospective Parliamentary Candidates for the next General Election in 2015. As the parties line up to get their candidates in place we wanted to find out who the key players are likely to be.

Here we interview Rachel Maclean, the new Conservative PPC for Birmingham Northfield, at the next General Election, which as a result of the Fixed Term Parliaments Act is for the first time a date set in stone.

Rachel has been a resident of the Birmingham area for over forty years and a Birmingham employer for two decades. She has over twenty years' experience in international business management, including work in India, the Far East and the U.S. Rachel currently runs an IT book publisher – a business she founded and built with her husband – creating 40 local jobs in the process and employing 250 people worldwide. She is also a mother of four children. She is a graduate of Oxford and Aston. So why does she now want to be a politician and how does she want to change public policy? Rachel spoke to our Executive Producer Boni Sones.

Speaking Up!
Social Care, Schools, Road, Rail and Welfare Reform – Spending in 2015 under review!

The Chancellor George Osborne has this week set out his Spending Review for 2015/16. He outlined measures that will impact on health, education, further welfare reform, and his capital spending plans for roads, the railways and infrastructure that are said to be some of the most significant since Victorian times. Here before the full impact of that announcement had been fully digested and hot foot from the Chamber, we asked two

MPs to assess how they thought it would impact on their constituencies.

First we spoke to Dr Sarah Wollaston, the Conservative MP for Totnes, Brixham and the South Hams, and Dr Julian Huppert, the LD MP for Cambridge. Both pinpointed the reform to the school funding criteria as having a beneficial impact on their constituencies. We also asked Dr Wollaston, who was selected on an Open Primary, about her idea for the "E" selection of candidates in the future.

Dr Wollaston Hot Quote: "There's been a real move forward in integrating health and social care. There is another £2 billion going from health to social care, on top of the £1 billion already announced. It will stop the "silos" where we know never the two join up, so I am very positive about that. I was very interested that we are moving forward on the issue of fair funding for schools too."

Julian Huppert Hot Quote: "There was extra support for the science budget. But for me one of the great achievements was the extra support for schools funding. Cambridgeshire schools have been under-funded for three decades now, we are right at the bottom of the pile, we get £600 per pupil per year less than the pupil average. The Chancellor has said that will change and that there will be a new formula, much fairer. That's incredibly welcome. But I don't like the way the two Parties are trying to outbid each other on this welfare cap, we need to make sure we do look after some of the poorest in our Society."

Helen Goodman MP lives off £18 a week to prove the Bedroom Tax is unfair

When the Labour Bishop Auckland MP, Helen Goodman, received many complaints from her constituents about the unfairness of the Conservative Liberal Democrat government's new "Bedroom Tax" she harnessed the powers of social media, and launched a series of Youtube videos showing her living on a food budget of £18 for one week. That's the exact amount some of her constituents will be left with to feed themselves when the new Tax is introduced in April this year. It imposes a reduction in housing benefit for "under occupancy" and one, or more spare rooms.

Over 1000 people in her constituency are likely to suffer, sacrificing a healthy diet for a home, and there are less than 100 available smaller homes for them to move to. Our Executive Producer, Boni Sones, spoke to Helen, about the new tax and her food choices for the week.

Seema Malhotra MP – Helping Women in Business get started in 2013

Seema Malhotra, the Labour MP for Feltham and Heston, is to launch a pilot scheme in her constituency next month to mentor women who want to start businesses. Surprisingly, research shows that just 10 per cent of small and medium-sized businesses in London are run by women.

However, the government has just announced that it will increase the Start-Up Loans scheme by £30million to £110million over three years and that it is extending the age limit to access it from 24 to 30, following "high demand" for the scheme.

Boni Sones, Our Executive Producer, spoke to Seema, as she made her way to her office in Westminster.

Seema Malhotra Hot Quote: "This is about everybody having a way in which the pathway to setting up your own enterprise, managing risks effectively, getting the training you need getting the advice you need is set out clearly. Somebody was emailing me yesterday about how they should identify the right location and how they get a start-up loan, those practical questions are what people want answers to. It is about making the pathways much easier and making advice easier to access. It is also about men and women supporting others coming through too and accelerating their pathways to growth."

The year: 2012
Penny Mordaunt MP, defends the Health and Social Care Bill

Just imagine. You are a Conservative MP out on the doorstep having to defend your Government's much criticised NHS Reform Bill. You knock on the door and your constituent asks you to say why you want the Bill to succeed when others are talking of scrapping it altogether?

Critics have dubbed The Bill David Cameron's poll tax moment, and Nick Clegg has admitted it is more unpopular than the controversial raising of tuition fees.

The Bill will pass accountability down to the local level with GPs and local authorities being responsible for commissioning services and larger bureaucratic structures such as PCTs scrapped. We asked Penny Mordaunt, the Conservative MP for Portsmouth North, to explain clearly what the Bill does and why she supports it?

Penny Hot Quote: "The people that are deciding whether someone should have a drug or not is not that person's GP or their consultant or their specialist, it is not based on clinical need, and for me that is the killer change that we need to happen that this Bill will bring about. The people making those decisions should be your GP your oncologists, your hospital consultant."

Esther McVey MP – If Chloe Can!

Esther McVey the Conservative MP for the Wirral West – "If Chloe Can": Esther's careers booklet for young women, with case studies of positive role models of women who have succeeded in their careers in many different walks of life, is now a play. An extract from the play was staged by The National Youth Theatre in Speaker's House this week, thanks to the Speaker John Bercow.

We got Chloe, played by Sophie Wardlow, and her fellow actress friend, Carly-Jane Hutchinson, to interview well known politicians including David Davis, Harriet Baldwin, Esther herself, the Speaker John Bercow, and Michael Portillo. We also caught up with Esther's Dad, Jim McVey, who told us some secrets of Esther's success too. Thanks Sophie and thanks Carly, we'll give you a job!!

Iain Duncan Smith, Secretary of State for Works and Pensions Hot Quote: "I have known Esther for a while and I love the project "If Chloe Can". It is helping girls from difficult backgrounds to realise that everything is open to them if they make the effort to work hard and to try hard there are lots of women who have gone before and who have achieved. I think it is really important for "If Chloe Can" to be able to say actually you are only ever limited by the limited nature of your own ambition. If you try hard you may not reach the sky but you will get somewhere better than you ever thought you would. I thought the performance was excellent Chloe!"

The year: 2011
Jo's marathon for leukaemia research Target: £2,620.00 Raised so far: £2,770.40 If you would like to sponsor Jo go to: www.justgiving.com/jo-swinson
Jo Swinson the Liberal Democrat MP for East Dunbartonshire, a PPS to Vince Cable, and co-founder of the Campaign For Body Confidence is about to compete in the Virgin London Marathon 2011 on April 17th.

Jo is only the second women MP ever to run the London Marathon following in the footsteps of her colleague Patsy Carlton, a former LD MP for Cheadle, who ran it four times, but subsequently died of cancer in 2005.

At her height Jo has trained for between 35 to 40 miles a week, and fitted in five work outs during the week. She eats plenty of complex "carbs" but also confides that while she is running long distances she snacks on sports drinks and jelly babies too.

Jo who completed the Loch Ness Marathon in 2007, says running is a good way to "respect" your body and give you confidence. Our Executive Producer Boni Sones OBE caught up with Jo as she was climbing the stairs to her third floor office in Westminster:

The year: 2010
Helen Grant, the new MP talks about her parliamentary year!
Our www.wpradio.co.uk reporter Linda Fairbrother spoke to Helen Grant the new Conservative MP for Maidstone and the Weald, the former seat of "Strictly" star Ann Widdecombe. But from her first "biggest, best" day as an MP, through to her Maiden Speech, Helen says it's "issues" she's concerned with and there will be no dancing for her:

Helen Grant Hot Quote: "The Chamber takes some getting used to, even though I am a Solicitor and had been to Court, there's nothing quite like the Chamber, there's tradition, there's procedure, you have to notify the Speaker before you make your Maiden Speech, it's not a moment to mess up, there's pressure. I waited for five hours that day, but it was a lovely opportunity to listen to others, I spoke about social mobility, aspiration, family and enterprise, which have been key to getting me here.

"I don't talk about being the first female black MP, but if it breaks down those ceilings it's a good thing. I'm just Helen and all I wanted to do was become the next MP for Maidstone and the Weald and thankfully I am here. I now want to work hard and you have to prove yourself to be useful, reliable and loyal."

The new faces on the block!
Helen Grant MP Conservative and Rushanara Ali MP Labour.
Helen Grant the Conservative MP for Maidstone & The Weald and Rushanara Ali the Labour MP for Bethnal Green & Bow are two of the new faces at Westminster. Helen is the first black female MP for the Conservative Party and Rushanara Ali is the first Bangladeshi MP.

They are two of the 142 women MPs in Westminster, an increase of 16, just 22 per cent of the total, and both have already compiled a "list" of the issues they will champion on behalf of other women and their constituencies. Boni Sones OBE, Executive Producer, spoke to them shortly after they attended a photocall in Westminster Hall of all the new faces.

Four women PPCs fighting for one seat - Brighton Pavilion!
There's one seat that in all likelihood is going to return a woman MP. Brighton Pavilion has four women PPCs contesting the seat and one man.

Linda Fairbrother our www.wpradio.co.uk reporter cycled off in search of these four women Prospective Parliamentary Candidates. First she stood by the sea and talked to LD Bernadette Millam and then Nancy Platts for Labour, who is fighting to retain the seat for her Party.

Linda then cycled up the hill to talk to Charlotte Vere Conservative, and Caroline Lucas, the Green Party Candidate and the Leader of her party, standing in a seat the Greens hope to win.

Nigel Carter is also standing for UKIP.

Nancy Hot Quote: "Labour has done a lot for women, affordable child care, extended maternity leave, we have made a lot of difference to people's lives. People do forget what we have done, and when they complain about MPs' expenses, I remind them about what Labour has achieved.

"I am very proud of the four women standing, I was a board member of Fawcett and the fact Millicent Fawcett used to live here; it is quite interesting that this is the place we have an all women line-up. The fact Labour had all women short-lists and got more women in has meant we have had more policies for women and these have made a big difference to a lot of women's lives."

Charlotte Hot Quote: "I don't think anybody can claim they are winning Brighton Pavilion, who knows? On the door people still hold loyalties from previous times and I would say it is a three way marginal, Labour, Conservative and perhaps Green, but I would put them the least likely of the three."

Bernadette Hot Quote: "I don't think the voters are thinking we have all female candidates here, they are just thinking who can do the best for them? Campaigning at the weekend the amount of support we are getting with whistles and car horns, we have never seen that before."

Caroline Lucas Hot Quote: "A win for the Greens is very realistic. In the local elections of 2007 we had more councillors than any other party, and in the European Elections of 2009 we got double the vote of Labour and 6,000 ahead of the Tories. An ICN poll in December put the Greens 8 per cent ahead of the Conservatives and 10 per cent ahead of Labour. We have more councillors, people know our policies and they want to vote for them.....

"I think the current political system is deeply off-putting for women, the leader debates with the three men wearing those dark suits and the primary difference being the colour of their ties! It is important to me as a woman at Westminster to stand up for some of the women's issues, like childcare, public transport, the pay gap and more women in the boardrooms. Being more co-operative and less competitive is important."

"The Hustings" Exclusive – The Cambridge Liberal Democrat Hustings

Women's Parliamentary Radio wants to thank the Cambridge Liberal Democrat Party for allowing us to watch its "Hustings" where three men and three women competed to be the next Prospective Parliamentary Candidate. The popular sitting MP David Howarth is standing down. Here we interviewed the six candidates but you will have to listen in to find out who won (don't cheat!). And it seems the winner wanted to thank "the cat" for all the help it had given! It's rare to be allowed into a "Hustings".

The candidates were: Julian Huppert, Belinda Brooks-Gordon, Julie Smith, Rod Cantrill, Sian Reid, Tim Bick.

Boni Sones, Executive Producer, asked how they had each prepared for "The Hustings" and what issues they were choosing to focus on. The Party's Gender Balance Taskforce wants to select more women MPs.

The year: 2009
Penny and Helen and the Women2Win Campaign for the Conservative Party

Penny Mordaunt, is the Conservative's prospective parliamentary candidate for Portsmouth North at the next general election. Helen Whately is the Conservative's prospective parliamentary candidate for Kingston and Surbiton. It's the first time Helen, a consultant in healthcare, telecoms and the media, and a mother of a young son, has stood as a candidate, and she has to defeat a Liberal Democrat. Whereas Penny, a media consultant, stood before for the same seat in the 2005 election which was won by Labour.

Penny and Helen say they are getting a warm reception on the doorstep and that so called "door knocking" to get the vote out is fun. But it's the recession that is top of people's priorities alongside schools and hospitals. They both say they have little time to go shopping for those "colourful" jackets women politicians wear to get spotted. Boni Sones spoke to them at the Conservative Party Conference in Manchester where they sung the praises of the Women2Win campaign and the Rt Hon Theresa May MP.

Penny Hot Quote: "When we go door knocking I am getting a really positive reception, people are in a difficult place and you hear some really sad stories. Over the summer we surveyed 10,000 people and we didn't speak to anyone who hasn't been affected by the recession. What you hear on the doorstep can be quite worrying, but Cameron is keen that we offer practical help too, as well as developing our policies for when we are in government."

Helen Hot Quote: "It seems a strange thing to do to go door knocking for votes, but we get a pretty good reception and people are really glad you have made the effort to find out what their concerns are."

Both agreed the Women2Win campaign had supported them. Penny said: "Women2Win has been tremendously successful, and the Conservative Women's Association has helped too. If we do win at the next election I hope I will be part of a powerful group of women advocates in the House who will work together as the Labour women did, to get behind particular issues of importance to women in the Country. "

Antonia Cox PPC for the Conservative Party for Islington South and Finsbury

Antonia Cox is the official Conservative Party candidate for Islington South & Finsbury at the next General Election.

Antonia is a school governor, local campaigner and mother of three from central London. She is a leader writer for the London Evening Standard and author of the Policy Exchange publication, "The Best Kit", which makes the case for better support of our armed forces.

Antonia recently went to Tunisia with the Conservative Women's Organisation, one of the most advanced Muslin countries in the World in respect of women's rights to look at what women bring to political and economic development there.

Antonia tells our journalist Daisy Ayliffe, how she has been juggling her career, her political life here and abroad, and her family.

Antonia Hot Quote: "Tunisia has a higher percentage of women in Parliament than we do, and they have also got very high levels of participation in the economy, in teaching and in the police. I think a lot of people would say about Muslim countries that there are few opportunities for women but Tunisia is different.

"We are going to have to look at institution building in Afghanistan and it is helpful to look at the civil society institutions like they have in Tunisia, which has some interesting examples of how you can increase women's participation in politics."

Anne Begg MP, Vice Chair of the Speakers' Conference
Parliamentary reform and MPs' expenses

The Labour MP for Aberdeen South, Anne Begg, says she'll be out campaigning in her Constituency over the coming weeks to advise people that if Parliament needs reforming then they need to sign up to a political party to do just that! Anne says the way to overcome the dismay about politicians and their expenses is to get involved in a political party yourself and begin the process of change that is needed.

Anne is a formidable politician herself, being the first wheelchair user in Westminster, and the Vice Chair of the recently instituted Speaker's Conference which is looking at the under representation of women, ethnic minorities and disabled people in the House of Commons. She is also a member of the House of Commons Chairmen's Panel, and stands in for the Speaker in the Westminster Hall debates.

Boni Sones asked her if she agreed that Parliament needed better scrutiny?

Anne Begg MP Hot Quote: She said: "The fees office was not checking

MPs' expenses in the way that we thought it was doing. We thought there was a checking mechanism there but there clearly wasn't.

"We now need proper professional accounting, proper professional scrutiny and I think we need external scrutiny. The irony in all of this is that whenever anybody from the outside has looked at the wages and conditions of MPs they have always come up with a more generous settlement not a worse settlement."

Anne says the way to overcome the dismay about politicians and their expenses is to get involved in a political party yourself and begin the process of change that is needed.

Ms Begg MP said she would be out campaigning in her constituency:

"The only way I know how to react is to get out there and knock on doors and speak to people one by one and I will carry on with my case work doing each case individually. I can't deal with the deluge happening above my head, so I can only carry on doing the job that I thought I was elected to do. I will be knocking on doors next week because it is Whit week."

Dawn Butler MP one of only two black women MPs

The President of the United States, Barack Obama, is soon to visit Britain. The MP for Brent East, Dawn Butler, will be sure to meet him.

As one of only two black women MPs in Westminster and the first black woman Minister, Dawn is at the forefront of championing equal rights in Britain and has just launched "Bernie's List" an initiative to get more Black and Ethnic Minority MPs into Westminster. In this special 30 minute documentary podcast, Boni Sones spent a day with Dawn and other Parliamentarians on the very day that Barack Obama was sworn in as the 44th President of the United States of America.

Thanks to our sound engineer Pete Cook for this brilliant interpretation of the material in this documentary.

The year: 2008
Caroline Lucas MEP – Leader of the Green Party

Caroline Lucas, MEP is the leader of the Green Party and the only woman in Britain to head a major political party. She is the MEP for South East

England, and is standing as an MP in the next General Election for Brighton Pavilion. The Green Party has significant pockets of support across Britain now, with an increasing number of councillors and is hoping for renewed success in next year's European Elections. They also count Lewisham and Norwich South as winnable seats in a General Election.

In this two part interview, wpradio journalist Anne Garvey asked Caroline to spell out her hopes for a new global green agenda and women following Barack Obama's success as President Elect in the USA, and Executive Producer of wpradio Boni Sones, talked to Caroline about the specific policies of the Green Party.

Peace on the Streets Summit in Westminster
Labour's Vice-Chair of Youth, Dawn Butler the MP for Brent, has hosted a "Peace on the Streets" summit in Westminster with Choice FM. She wants to involve Black and ethnic minority communities in finding public solutions to guns, gangs and knife crime. A number of London MPs from all parties listened to the panellists speaking including Simon Hughes, the President of the Liberal Democrat Party. Boni Sones spoke to him, Choice FM, and Dawn as the summit ended.

Dawn Hot Quote: "I think young people have had enough and I am very optimistic for the future. Young people can emancipate themselves as Bob Marley says in his song. The media needs to promote more positive messages of young people it shouldn't be all about knife crime".

Lynne Featherstone MP, knife crime.
Women's Parliamentary Radio recommends you read the blog of the Liberal Democrat's youth and equalities spokesperson, Lynne Featherstone MP. It's one of the best on the block and you'll learn loads about the daily life of a leading politician. She knows how to blog.www.lynnefeatherstone.org.

You can listen to our audio report of Lynne defending young people here. It's not all knife crime... there's much more to being young.

Dawn Butler MP visits "Playbuilders" in her constituency

The Labour MP for Brent, Dawn Butler, has been visiting play facilities in her constituency with local councillors to see what a difference £1 million of new funding will make to the area. Brent was given the £1 million by the government as one of 43 new "playbuilder" authorities. It's part of a £235 million government investment on children's play. Boni Sones spoke to her at the Villiers Road site, with local councillors Lesley Jones, Mary Arnold and Harry Singh.

Dawn Hot Quote: Dawn Butler MP for Brent, is standing in the middle of a group of teenagers and mums with young children. The location is Willesden Green Library on the tiniest of play areas. She turns her head to answer the question: "You read in the papers there's unquiet but I'm not involved in it. Brown's just getting on with the job, he's met my young people in the Constituency, and I've taken them to number 10."

Then comes the proudest line of all: "Without Gordon we wouldn't have had this £235 million pound redirection of funds."

She admits the government is going through "rocky times" but says Brown is a "stable" person who doesn't go in for gimmicks. "I can see the change Brown's policies have made in my constituency. You can see the change in the young people, the difference the policies have made and now we have another £1 million for play facilities under the "playbuilder" scheme. "There are 43 "playbuilder" areas and Brent is one."

And then she thanks her boss again. "It was Gordon who did this, we would never have had YOP – Youth Opportunity Fund - I will always be grateful to him for taking young people seriously."

Charlotte Leslie a Conservative PPC!

Charlotte Leslie, is the Conservative Party's Prospective Parliamentary Candidate for Bristol North West. She has already established a name for herself as a Guardian young blogger, and for speaking up on the under achievement of boys at school and the feminisation of Society. So is blogging or old fashioned 'door knocking' the best way to engage young voters? Boni Sones spoke to her.

The year: 2007
Dawn Butler MP

Dawn Butler, the MP for Brent has just been given a new job by the Prime Minister Gordon Brown as one of six Vice-Chairs of the Labour Party. She will work directly to Deputy Leader, Harriet Harman on youth issues and be involved with the new ministerial team at the Department for Children, Schools and Families. Dawn's enthusiasm for campaigning is infectious. Boni Sones talked to her about her new role and her parliamentary career.

A Day In The Life of Emily Thornberry MP

The Labour MP for Islington South and Finsbury, Emily Thornberry, has a tough job balancing work and family life, but she says she wouldn't swap being a backbench MP for the world. She, like other women MPs, believes the real life experiences of their constituents are helping to enhance and inform government policy. WP Radio journalist Anne Garvey asked her to talk about a "Day in her life".

ELEVEN
Speaking in the Chamber and Westminster Hall

MPs begin their Parliamentary Careers by giving a Maiden Speech. Convention has it that Maiden Speeches have to be about issues of concern to their constituencies, and most draw a portrait in words of the places they come to Westminster to represent. Many confess to being terrified the first time they are called to stand up in the Chamber and speak to their colleagues on their side of the party political divide and the opposition parties a swords length apart on the opposite side of the green benches. The former Speaker of the House, the popular Labour politician Betty Boothroyd, has commented on how snug the Chamber is, and how easy it is to feel at home there. This might seem unbelievable to those who witness the weekly barracking at PMQs. Maiden speeches are indeed terrifying, and colleagues have been known to sit with notes on their laps just in front of those speaking so that they can have a "crib" sheet if need be. When the Labour women of 1997 came to power, they found the traditions of the Chamber, the need to call MPs by their constituency names, with the Rt Hon prefacing all names, bemusing, if not, confusing. They wanted to modernise the House, its traditions and what they saw to be the same old ways of the House. Sexist behaviour was frequently displayed when they rose to speak in the Chamber, with the famous "melons gesture" being made towards them as male conservative MPs wiggled imaginary breasts in front of their bodies as the women rose to speak. The women MPs in particular asked for an alternative debating chamber, one where they would feel more at home. Eventually they and all their colleagues were given another additional debating chamber off Westminster Hall. The House of Commons website says that Westminster Hall debates give more time for individual MPs to raise issues of importance to them with a series of Private Members' adjournment debates on Tuesdays and Wednesdays. This is true, but it also allows MPs who might feel intimidated by the Chamber to feel more at home speaking publicly in a smaller debating hall. Speaking in the Chamber is a powerful tool for bringing about change.

The year: 2014
Speaking in the Chamber – two issues under the spotlight
Protecting children's health – a ban on smoking in cars
Labour's Shadow Public Health Spokeswoman and MP for Liverpool Wavetree Luciana Berger this week steered through Parliament an important amendment to the Children and Families Bill that will in due course make it illegal for adults to smoke in a car in which children are passengers.

The amendment had met with opposition from opponents who claimed it would be unenforceable but in a free vote she won the support of Labour MPs, the Liberal Democrats and Peers in the Upper House too while most Conservatives voted against. Luciana argued that children had smaller lungs, a faster breathing rate and that smoking in cars produced toxic fumes that were far more dangerous than when someone smoked at home leading to illnesses such as cancer, asthma and emphysema.

Luciana Hot Quote: "It was a larger majority than the one which passed the smoking act in 2006. We don't allow smoking in bars, and public places and clubs, why should it be ok for children to travel in that toxic concentrated space in the back of a car and we can look at other countries where bans have been enforced very successfully and they have never looked back."

The Home Secretary Theresa May MP tells Hillsborough families she will see justice is done
The Home Secretary Theresa May MP received praise for her statement on the reopening of the Hillsborough inquest next month from both her own Conservative benches and MPs sitting across the Chamber in the Labour camp. The former Home Secretary David Blunkett, the MP for Hillsborough and Andy Burnham the MP for Leigh, said Mrs May had handled the new investigations into Hillsborough well.

The revelation that some of the families of the dead 96 Liverpool FC fans may have been spied on, and that some police note books had still not been handed over, while some officers were still refusing to give evidence to the new Inquest were ongoing issues with both families and MPs.

Mrs May revealed that 242 police statements from the day of the disaster 25 years ago are now known to have been altered. The Hillsborough Independent Panel found that alcohol did not play a major part in the disaster as was alleged. Margot James the Conservative MP for Stourbridge, told our Executive Producer, Boni Sones of her reaction to The Home Secretary's Statement.

Margot Hot Quote: "David Blunkett and also Andy Burnham were very fulsome in their praise of the Home Secretary's leadership on this issue over the last few years. I think the Home Secretary has really dedicated a lot of her own personal time to talking to the families and giving the police some direction as well as liaising closely with the chair of the inquiry the Bishop of Liverpool."

The year: 2013
Is today's PMQs a "disgrace" or a "passionate discussion of important issues"?
Andrew Lansley MP – The Leader of the House of Commons in conversation with Gisela Stuart MP, Editor of House Magazine

MPs often comment on how when they knock on doors at the weekend, their constituents frequently talk about how much they dislike the weekly Wednesday PMQs "shouting match" in the House of Commons.

So is the "shouting match" at PMQs when the Prime Minster, David Cameron answers questions from the Leader of the opposition, Labour's Ed Miliband a disgrace, or is it healthy democratic "passionate" debate?

Here as Parliament ends its 2013 term of debates, we asked Gisela Stuart, the Labour MP for Birmingham Edgbaston, who sits on our Advisory Board and is Editor of The House Magazine to interview The Rt Hon Andrew Lansley, the Leader of the House of Commons, and the Conservative MP for South Cambridgeshire since 1997.

Gisela also asked Andrew about the power of Parliament over a "weak" Executive, whether "the usual channels" can still influence what is debated, the increasing use of Twitter by Parliamentarians when they are in the Chamber, the new Role of the Backbench Business Committee, the important role Select Committees who now elect their Chairs play, and the difference between "urgent questions" and "ministerial statements"? She then asked him to elaborate on his own "needle" exchanges with the Speaker John Bercow, what he wanted to be remembered for as Leader, and who of his predecessors he most admired?

Surprisingly Andrew chose both his Conservative predecessor, The Rt Hon Sir George Young, and the late Labour politician, The Rt Hon Robin Cook as his "heroes" and enthusiastically supported the new "petitioning system" being introduced.

Rt Hon Andrew Lansley Hot Quote Parliament: "Parliament is clearly both more powerful and more influential. To be fair observers would say "a great deal more influential and to some extent more powerful….. I think the influence of Parliament has risen dramatically and there are a number of ways in which that is true."

Andrew Hot Quote on PMQS: "I maybe slightly at odds with the Speaker's view about PMQs, the Speaker (John Bercow) would like PMQs principally to be an issue where light is shed on issues, in a structured and calm way, whereas I am a realist. PMQs is about demonstrating to a large audience in this country and beyond where the point of debate is and it is heated debate, it is often passionate debate. I think we shouldn't try to diminish the sense in which that passion is demonstrated in a drama at PMQs, I think it is right, it is inevitable and I think we should rather revel in it rather than simply to castigate it".

Standing up for a multicultural society and community cohesion - the New Immigration Bill 2013

Heidi Alexander the Labour MP for Lewisham East has spoken of her concern at elements of the Conservative Lib Dem Coalition government's new Immigration Bill now going through Parliament. When the Bill had its second reading in the Commons this month Heidi said she would not be voting "for or against" the Bill at this stage but that like others she shared concerns about some of its provisions. She said that making private landlords responsible for checking the immigration status of their tenants was "unrealistic".

She called the Bill "The good, the bad and the ugly" and said how much she liked representing and living in a multi-cultural constituency. Our Executive Producer Boni Sones, asked Heidi to explain what was "good" about the Bill and what was "ugly".

Heidi Hot Quote: "This is a very complicated area, and ultimately landlords and estate agents should not be doing the job of immigration officials. We need to find a way to improve the system as a whole and not to focus on these things which may give the Government a headline but also could have very significant implications especially in areas where we have a very diverse population community cohesion could really be threatened by some of these ideas and proposals."

Eleanor Laing begins work as the new Deputy Speaker of the House of Commons

Congratulations to Eleanor Laing the new Deputy Speaker of the House of Commons. Eleanor, the Conservative MP for Epping Forest, has supported us for nearly a decade now, so our congratulations are heartfelt and we join with The Speaker, John Bercow who warmly welcomed her to his team. She beat six other Tory hopefuls to the role, and won 273 out of 551 votes cast in the final round.

Thanks to Eleanor for this Saturday interview from her Constituency Office, when she had already sat in that rather large Speaker's Chair. Not only will she have to remember all 650 MPs constituencies and names, but she will now have to "conform" and go back to wearing black. She is a supporter of family friendly hours in the House and considers herself a real Parliamentarian standing up impartially for all who speak. Eleanor spoke to our Executive Producer, Boni Sones.

Eleanor Hot Quote: "Since my son was born, I have changed my attitude to the Commons Hours, you have to make it possible for people who have families to look after them and to sit in the House and therefore we have to have hours which are realistic and fit in. I care passionately about Parliament. I care enormously about the position of the House of Commons and therefore I don't find it difficult to put my passion for the democratic process ahead of my passion for any particular policy or value."

Standing up for the ambulance service locally with a question to the Prime Minister

Lorely Burt, the Liberal Democrat MP for Solihull, asked David Cameron a question on the future of the West Midlands ambulance service at Prime Minister's Questions today. Her local Solihull Ambulance Station is to close, and campaigners say the level of coverage to replace it will be inadequate, they want the plans delayed until proper coverage has been put in place.

Lorely's question to David Cameron will not only help to raise the profile of this important local campaign it will also ensure the plans now come under more scrutiny at a national level too when she meets the Prime Minister.

She has already written to the West Midland's Ambulance Service, and protested to her local Conservative run Council. The old station is to be sold off, but the full temporary replacement cover for the locally based two-man ambulances is not yet in place.

Lorely Hot Quote: "It's like a dialogue of the death talking to local ambulance service providers, they are not listening to what the residents of Solihull are saying. David Cameron has agreed to meet with me and Ministers and health chiefs to see what can be done. I am absolutely delighted with that outcome."

MPs across party also asked PMQs on a pardon for gay World War 11 Security expert Alan Turing, biofuels and food productivity, contaminated blood products, Atos's welfare assessment processes, the Greenpeace protestors held in Russia, Married couples tax allowance, Prisoner's Rights, Food banks, and the so called Andrew Mitchell Plebgate affair. The spat between the party leaders, David Cameron and Ed Miliband was dominated by the so called "Cost of Living Crisis" and the good news of falling unemployment figures but Plebgate dominated the headlines of today's PMQs.

The Labour Fringe 2013 – "Falling through the Gap"!
Special Needs Education

Sharon Hodgson the Labour MP for Washington and Sunderland West, attended a "Family" fringe event at the Labour Party Conference, speaking on the need to improve the Children and Families Bill, now going through the Lords which seeks to join up services for those with special needs education across providers. It will also reform the systems for adoption, looked after children, and family justice. It will introduce a new system of shared parental leave and ensure children have a strong advocate for their rights with a new Children's Commissioner.

Sharon welcomes the new Bill and is hopeful that further concessions can be achieved in order to improve provision for young offenders, with special needs education.

Sharon Hot Quote: "Education, health and care plans won't apply to children in custody when they go into young offenders institutions, and that is the very place where they should be supported. It maybe that their special needs has led them down that road to end up in a young offenders institution."

Foodbanks – The Prime Minister is challenged on the huge growth in foodbanks across the UK

The Labour MP Kerry McCarthy asked David Cameron a PMQ on the increasing use of foodbanks by people in and out of work. In her own constituency of Bristol East she has seen a growth in the use of foodbanks, which she attributes to the delays in paying benefits, the bedroom tax, food price increase, fuel bills and fare rises too. Our Executive Producer, Boni Sones, asked her why she thought people were finding it so hard to make ends meet and if David Cameron in his reply, had a point that foodbank use increased under Labour too?

Kerry Hot Quote: "Under Labour yes, in the last few years the use of food banks went up, because the economic recession struck and people were finding it harder to make ends meet. But there has been an exponential increase under this government. As the welfare cuts and policy changes have come in it has reached half a million already, which is a huge number of people. I get people coming to me and they are almost shamed faced about saying to me we don't drink, we don't smoke, we don't have Sky TV, they think they are going to be accused of being profligate, and it affects people in work too, there is a lot of in work poverty too!"

A humanitarian catastrophe – Action on Syria?

Why three women MPs voted in three different ways in an extraordinary Commons Debate

MPs were recalled to Westminster this week to debate a special motion to give the coalition Conservative Liberal Democrat government a mandate to take military action against President Bashar al-Assad regime following the use of Chemical weapons in Syria. The Prime Minister, David Cameron, announced the recall on Twitter.

First MPs voted on an amendment put down by the Labour Leader Ed Miliband who wanted to wait until the UN had officially confirmed who used the weapons Assad or the rebels? It called for: "steps to provide humanitarian protection only when compelling evidence that the Syrian regime was responsible for the use of weapons has been provided". The Commons voted against this motion by 332 votes to 220.

The Government motion called for: "a response form the international community that may, if necessary, require military action". However during the debate the government promised to give a second vote if any military action was to be taken. But even so the motion was defeated by 285 to 272.

Here we talk to three MPs who voted in different ways.

Tracey Crouch, the Conservative MP for Chatham and Aylesford who voted against her own government motion after reading 400 emails from her constituents that overwhelming opposed any action.

Penny Mordaunt the Conservative MP for Portsmouth North who strongly supported her government's motion, and sits on the Defence Select Committee as well as being a Royal Navy reservist.

While the veteran Labour MP The Rt Hon Dame Tessa Jowell, who was part of the Tony Blair government when it voted to go into Iraq, voted for the Labour amendment.

Critics later blamed the defeat of both motions on Labour's decision ten years ago to go into Iraq on the basis of what subsequently turned out to be false evidence.

The Americans have already put the blame for the use of chemical weapons on the Assad regime. Hundreds of people died in the attack on the Ghouta area on the outskirts of Damascus on August 21s, and many more were injured. The horrific film footage of the incident showed many children had died.

Jo Swinson MP, Minister and Body Image Campaigner - Twitter trolls, Page 3 Girls, and Kate's "baby" bulge

Jo Swinson, the Liberal Democrat MP for East Dunbartonshire, is the Minister for Employment Relations and Consumer Affairs in the Department for Business, Innovation and Skills and Women and Equalities Minister in the Department of Culture, Media and Sport.

She has championed the Body Image Campaign, praising the new Editor of the Sun, David Dinsmore, for wanting to reinvent Page 3, and also giving Beyonce a pat on the back for not wanting their images "air brushed". However, her praise is tempered with robust condemnation of those who do still judge people on their image, including criticisms of the way the Duchess of Cambridge's post-birth weight "bulge" was commented on as she left Hospital with Prince George, and those Twitter Trolls who send abusive Tweets to women.

In her private life she has a political marriage and is expecting her first child on Christmas Day this year. Gisela Stuart, MP, Editor of House Magazine recently voted Jo our Liberal Democrat MP of the year, so we asked Jo to spell out her achievements herself and what is in store in the coming months for her.

Jo Hot Quote: "You just need to look at Twitter during an episode of Question Time and it is the women panellists who will receive much more abuse and often much more misogynistic abuse, so it is interesting that there is a movement to say enough is enough." Jo is interviewed by Our Executive Producer, Boni Sones.

Our "Tribute" interviews to women MPs Summer Recess 2013

As this 2013 Parliamentary year comes to a conclusion we ask Gisela Stuart, Editor of the influential House Magazine, for MPs, and the Labour MP for Birmingham Edgbaston, to pay tribute to the work of one woman MP and a Peer from each of the political parties.

Here Gisela pays "Tribute" to Anne MacIntosh for the Conservatives, Margaret Hodge for Labour, Jo Swinson for the Liberal Democrats and Baroness Frances d'Souza, a life peer and cross bencher.

Anne is the Conservative Member of Parliament for Thirsk, Malton and Filey who has also been a Euro MEP. She is also Chair of the Environment, Food and Rural Affairs Select Committee. Margaret Hodge has been the Labour MP for Barking since 1994. She is well known now for her work as chair of the Public Accounts Select Committee and for her razor sharp questioning on issues like Google and Starbucks tax avoidance, and more recently on the BBC pay-offs too.

Jo Swinson is the Parliamentary Under Secretary of State for Employment relations, consumer and postal affairs and the Liberal Democrat MP for East Dunbartonshire since 2005. She is well known for co-founding the Campaign for Body Confidence. Frances D'Souza is a life peer, who trained as a scientist, and is currently Lord Speaker.

Tough Choices: Two women MPs Two tough topics
Harriett Baldwin MP, West Worcestershire - Why Welfare Benefit Reform is needed

Will welfare benefit reforms further weaken already poor areas of Britain's economy or will they help people find jobs, and get back into work?

Our Executive Producer, Boni Sones, asked Harriett Baldwin, the

Conservative MP for West Worcestershire to defend her own government's welfare reforms.

Harriett also told Boni why she was supporting the Women and Equalities Minister Maria Miller's campaign to boost women in the workplace. A new report by the Women's Business Council, set up by the government, wants to tap the untapped potential of getting more women into prominent positions.

Harriett Hot Quote: "If you look at womens' pay, for similar jobs now women earn pretty much the same as men, there is still a difference and we need to work on that. But women do not rise up the career ladder as much as men, women paid 60 per cent less income tax then men, suggesting there is a big gap in the types of jobs and seniority they are occupying."

Hazel Blears MP – Helping communities to live together peacefully
Hazel Blears, the Labour MP for Salford and Eccles, is a member of the government's Intelligence and Security Committee. When she was Labour's Communities Secretary she helped set up the "Prevent" Strategy to assist ethnic minority youths to integrate into their communities.

Following the Woolwich attack and murder of Lee Rigby, she has criticised the coalition Conservative Liberal Democrat government for not doing enough to prevent the radicalisation of young Muslims and concentrating policy too much on security rather than integration. Boni Sones asked her what measures were needed to ensure young people were helped rather than deamonised?

Hazel Hot Quote: "I don't think there is any substitute for hearing the difficult things, I met lots of young people who had terrible issues about our foreign policy but I set up advisory groups for young people and women, you have to take it head on that is what politics is about."

Iain Stewart MP on the Same Sex Marriage Bill – David Cameron "cherishes marriage"
When in the Second Reading of the Same Sex Marriage Bill, the

Conservative MP for Milton Keynes South, Iain Stewart spoke about his announcement to his parents that he was gay and would "never be married" he trended on Twitter. He also won others over to support the Bill too.

As MPs continue to debate plans to legalise same-sex marriage in England and Wales after surviving a so called "wrecking amendment", Iain told us why he believes that in five years' time we will all wonder what the fuss was about, not to mention the "swivel-eyed loons" jibe the Tory leadership supposedly made about its rank and file members who opposed the Bill.

Iain Hot Quote: "It is very controversial, and I am glad to back David Cameron. He is a great family man, who cherishes his own marriage and he wants that great thing of marriage to be available to everyone."

Glenda Jackson MP for Hampstead and Kilburn on the legacy of Lady Thatcher

The Independent said she "stole the show" while the Daily Mail said she had launched "an astonishing assault" on the memory of Lady Thatcher.

Glenda Jackson, the Labour MP for Hampstead and Kilburn since 1992 tells www.parliamentaryradio.com for women why she decided to provide an alternative version of the achievements of Margaret Thatcher, during the special commons debate called to commemorate her life. Boni Sones asked Glenda Jackson – a former Oscar winning actress – if she had written her speech or whether she spoke from the heart?

Glenda Hot Quote: "There were thousands and thousands of emails immediately afterwards, I don't know how many letters we got, the telephone got blocked and we did a slight analysis and the division seemed to be about 10 to one in support of what I had said. The thing I found most touching was when people wrote and said "You spoke for England", which I found very moving. And there were a great many women, and I was surprised at this across the whole age range – who had picked up on the comments I made about what I regard as being womanly and a woman!

"The word I still take issue with was that her policies were "divisive" they weren't simply divisive they were actively and desperately destructive – we are all essentially human beings and we are all standing on the shoulders of someone who went before us and those who come after us should be given a fair platform by us to stand on now."

Lady Margaret Thatcher – Tributes in the Commons

The Death of Margaret Thatcher the first woman Prime Minister in Europe has shed new light on the woman her values and her time in power. She was the British Prime Minister from 1979 to 1990 and the Leader of the Conservative Party from 1975 to 1990.

A Soviet journalist called her the "Iron Lady" and among her memorable phrases was "The Lady's not for turning"! As tributes were paid to her in the Commons in a special debate two days after her death, new stories emerged of her kindness, her generosity, and her beliefs from former Cabinet colleagues, and friends.

Opposition parties also paid their respects but they recalled the lasting impact of her policies on some areas of the Country still.

Our Executive Producer, Boni Sones OBE, spoke to three women MPs and asked what the Thatcher legacy would be for women. Eleanor Laing MP(Cons) for Epping Forest, Penny Mordaunt MP (Cons) for Portsmouth North, and Angela Eagle the Labour MP for Wallasey.

Eleanor Laing Hot Quote: "What she told me was how difficult it was to get the balance right between your constituency your duties at Westminster and your husband, your family and your home. She knew that she had lived through it, and personally she gave me some very good advice."

Penny Mordaunt Hot Quote "When in 2005 I fought my seat and lost against Labour, the very next day I had a hand written letter from her, and she did that for others as well. She was someone who was genuinely interested in people. I felt genuinely encouraged when in 2005 she said get back on the horse."

Angela Eagle Hot Quote: "From the point of view of the area I represent in the NW she was certainly a very polarising figure. While I can admire the achievement of Margaret Thatcher for getting there, to be the first woman Prime Minister, I didn't agree with anything she stood for. Mrs Thatcher's model of leadership was more the male one, she presented herself as the exception to the rule and she didn't like other women around her. She filled her Cabinet with men. You don't break the rule by being the exception to it!"

How David Cameron can get more women into politics – let them job share!

Dr Sarah Wollaston the Conservative MP for Totnes has this week spoken up in favour of job share MPs. As the Liberal Demorcat Party has to contend with allegations of sexual misconduct against one of its senior figures, Lord Rennard, Dr Wollaston has written in the Guardian that there is no place for a "casting couch" approach to appointments in political parties today. She has likened Westminster to a "boys boarding school" with just 22 per cent of MPs in the House being women!

Our Executive Producer, Boni Sones spoke to Dr Wollaston in Central Lobby Westminster, after a noisy cat-calling Prime Minister's Questions and asked her if MPs could really job share, or would there be ethical issues to address, if both had different views on certain subjects?

Dr Wollaston Hot Quote: "I find it tiresome how people look at the barriers to job sharing as an MP rather than how they can make it work. I job shared for 11 years in medicine, where you could argue that if you get things wrong, people could be at risk. This works very well across many professions, you apply as a pair, and you have to work together and have a similar ethical framework."

Gay Marriage and Gay Pride!
Iain Stewart MP – Speaking from the heart in the Chamber on The Marriage (Same Sex Couples) Bill

It was one of those defining moments in Parliamentary History. The

Marriage and (Same Sex Couples) Bill has caused division within the Conservative Party, but it was the House of Commons at its best as MPs searched their own moral consciences to speak of why they were voting for or against David Cameron's controversial Bill. Many of the speeches were from the heart and memorable.

One of the most moving moments in that debate came when Iain Stewart the Conservative MP for Milton Keynes South, told of how he "came out" to his parents as a 25 year old gay man in Scotland saying: "Mum, you know I'm never going to be able to marry." He later trended on Twitter. The Bill passed its Second Reading by 400 votes to 175 against. Iain told our Executive Producer, Boni Sones, that his speech had not been planned.

Iain's Hot Quote from his Speech: "I began the conversation with the line, "Mum, you know I'm never going to be able to marry." I used that form of words as a way of broaching an awkward conversation and I did not really think much about it at the time, but I often reflect on those words and it makes me very sad that for so long that was a factually correct statement. I look at the marriage that my parents have – 45 years and going strong – and I aspire to the same thing."

Boni also spoke to Dr Julian Huppert, the Liberal Democrat MP for Cambridge and his Party's Equalities Spokesperson. Julian had spoken up for the Bill before its passing.

Julian's Hot Quote: "Civil Marriages are a step forward but they are still discriminatory. Why has it taken us so long to allow Gay marriage? That is why I am so pleased that we are actually going to do it, we will see this Bill become a reality. But there are still a number of details I would like to work on. I would like to see equal civil partnerships so that opposite sex couples can have civil partnerships. I would like to see humanist weddings legalised in England as they are in Scotland. And there needs to be change on transgender issues where people forefit their marriages. I am so proud the principle was established and that the "yes" vote won."

Meg Hillier MP warns of "long form filling" for parents claiming child benefit

At Prime Minister's Questions this week, Meg Hillier the Labour MP for Hackney South and Shoreditch quizzed the Prime Minister, David Cameron, about the removal of child benefit and the need for parents to fill in "long forms" in order to receive it in the future.

The government hopes to save £1.5bn a year to help reduce the deficit by taking away some of the child benefit from families with one parent with a taxable income of more than £50,000 and if one parent earns more than £60,000 it will be withdrawn entirely.

Child benefit is paid at the rate of £20.30 a week for the first child, and then £13.40 a week for each child after that until each child reaches 16, or 18 if they are still in full-time education, and in some cases until they are 20.

Our Executive Producer, Boni Sones, caught up with Meg after PMQs, in a rather noisy corridor in Westminster.

Meg Hillier Hot Quote: "When people see their first tax return, in the Autumn of this year, I am aware that to fill in these returns you sweat over them, and for people who have never had to do it before, those earning just above the threshold it is going to be a bit of a shock to the system. We need to make sure that government is administered well."

The year: 2012
Head to Head: Emily Thornberry MP - No change needed!

Emily Thornberry, the Labour MP for Islington and South Finsbury voted in favour of not lowering the Abortion limit from 24 to 20 weeks when it was last debated in the Commons in 2008, when Labour was in Government. She still believes the "limit" is right and does not need to be lowered in the light of new scientific evidence. However, on the other side of the Abortion Debate stand the new Health Secretary Jeremy Hunt, who does want to see it reduced to 12 weeks, the Home Secretary Theresa May and the new Equalities Minister, and Secretary of State for Culture Media and Sport, Maria Millar, who think it should be lowered from 24 to

20 weeks. Emily tells our Executive Producer Boni Sones why she believes 24 weeks is the right limit.

Emily's One Minute Solution: "I don't accept that the science has changed. If you go to the Royal Societies and ask their advice it is quite clear what their collective view is, although you will always find one or two doctors who will say something different. The medical establishment's view collectively is that the science has not changed and that while there maybe a few remarkable babies who survive quite often they survive with considerable disabilities and that the abortion limits should remain at the limit that it is."

"There's Nothing Like A Dame"

A question to the Prime Minister, David Cameron, from Ann McKechin, the Labour MP for Glasgow North

"There is Nothing Like A Dame", the Rodgers and Hammerstein song from the musical "South Pacific", gave Labour's Ann Mckechin her 'punch line' for a Prime Minister's question this week on why he hadn't given Honours to his redundant female ministers when he had given them to their male colleagues.

Ann McKechin Hot Quote: "I asked why he had recommended five redundant male ministers for knighthoods but not one of his sacked female ministers was to get any Honour at all. 'There's Nothing Like A Dame' is a light hearted remark but there is a serious point behind it because I think people are questioning how seriously the Prime Minister takes the role of women in our Society.

"Cheryl Gillian and Caroline Spelman are formidable politicians in their own right and I am sure they will still contribute in the House of Commons over the next few years and beyond - but they need to have a few private words with the Prime Minister in the next few months to ensure he doesn't forget about them!"

Mental Health and how our MPs are helping!

Nicky Morgan, the Conservative MP for Loughborough and the surrounding villages, talks to us about her Commons debate on Mental Health. It has already succeeded in changing public perceptions of the illness, thanks to MPs across party who spoke frankly and emotionally about their own mental health episodes in the Debate. The stories they told were moving. Nicky spoke to Boni Sones about the debate in Central Lobby, Westminster.

Nicky Morgan Hot Quote: "People spoke from the heart and people watching in the public gallery and on TV could really tell that MPs were talking about things they really knew about and cared about. A lot of the time we talk about political things from a party point of view but we tried to have a debate that was non-partisan, so that MPs could share their experiences. People have said it really was Parliament at its best, and my goodness don't you sometimes need that."

Fiona Mctaggart MP – Buycotting not boycotting goods that use slave labour.

Fiona Mctaggart the Labour MP for Slough has successfully introduced the "Eradication of Slavery (UK Company Supply Chains)" Ten Minute Rule Bill.

Fiona and other MPs across party are asking women as family shoppers to "buycott" not "boycott" goods that are made using slave labour.

Fiona Hot Quote: "I suppose I thought while I was growing up that Slavery had been abolished. That this Parliament had played a big role in getting rid of it two Centuries ago and that it didn't exist anymore. My horror in recent decades was to find that it is quite widespread still and that it exists around the World today and that it can even be found in this Country. It is down to people like to me in Parliament to end that, if we don't then perhaps no-one else will."

Tightening up health and safety legislation – how companies are escaping justice

Luciana Berger, the Labour MP for Liverpool Wavetree, has introduced a Ten Minute Rule Bill to tighten up health and safety legislation in the workplace to prevent companies going into liquidation to avoid paying out personal injury compensation claims.

It follows the death in 2007 of a constituent, Mark Thornton, who died after a mobile crane toppled over and crushed him.

She said her proposal would close a "loophole" which meant some so called "phoenix firms" facing a Health and Safety Executive (HSE) investigation were able to force themselves into liquidation in order to avoid punishment for an employee's death or injury.

Ms Berger claimed 50 people had been killed last year as a result of accidents at work in the construction industry alone.

Luciana Hot Quote: "For me it is an issue of social justice. The companies concerned have set up again, almost the next day, just with a different name. The pain that families go through to know that firms have managed to avoid paying the fines that they should have paid and avoid justice, yet they are still trading but the families have lost their loved ones."

Seema Malholtra MP – and her Maiden Speech

Seema Malholtra the new Labour MP for Feltham and Heston tells www.parliamentaryradio.com for women how delivering your Maiden Speech in the House is an "overwhelming experience"!

Seema, who grew up in the area, paid tribute to Alan Keen who had been the local MP since 1992 until his death in 2011. When our Executive Producer, Boni Sones, caught up with Seema in Central Lobby Westminster, she had just visited Feltham Skills Centre, been to Prime Minister's Questions, attended the Police cuts debate, the Ten Minute Rule Bill debate on Corporate Manslaughter, and met with the Operation Black Vote mentoring scheme. She has just been voted onto the cross-party Justice Select Committee.

Seema, a management consultant, is well known in Westminster as a founder of the Fabian Women's Network. Many a cheer went up as she stood to give her "Maiden"!

Seema Hot Quote: "My Maiden Speech was an overwhelming experience. The first few weeks of being in Westminster were awe inspiring and the warm welcome from all sides of the House, which is probably peculiar to a by-election perhaps, but nothing does prepare you for making that first speech."

The year: 2011
"Dave and Nick, The Year of The Honeymoon"
Copyright to this report belongs to Linda Fairbrother.

The Times sketch writer Ann Treneman has captured the ups and downs of coalition government in her new book: *Dave and Nick, The Year of The Honeymoon*, and admits to our parliamentaryradio.com reporter Linda Fairbrother that although the "love affair" has withstood votes on tuition fees, the AV referendum, and now Europe too, we are into the latter stages of this marriage and into "the beyond!" Linda managed to sneak into the Reporters Gallery of the Commons, where only Lobby journalists are allowed to ask Ann about her witty pithy new book. How does she manage to think up the metaphors and situations into which to slot her characters and make her readers laugh out loud week in and week out as she looks down from The Gallery onto the Chamber itself? Ann is not short of a few laughs herself as she tells Linda a few tricks of her sketch writing trade. Do listen, it's fun!!

Ann Hot Quote: "If I am too ponderous it just doesn't work in sketch writing, you have to have an eye for the absurd and you have to not think of giving your opinion. It is my job to show what is actually happening and the funny side of it all and you have to think that often politics is very humorous, it just is, it is a very strange profession, people standing up and saying the most extraordinary things."

Improving self-confidence in girls and young women – a soft topic or a hot debate?

Can improving the self-confidence of women and girls be a new route to career success and how much can schools and colleges actively do to improve self-esteem and confidence in young women? Esther McVey, the Conservative MP for Wirral West, a mover and shaker in Parliament has held a Westminster Hall debate on this hot topic to support her impressive work on the "If Chloe Can?" career booklet for girls.

Esther also created momentum recently when she and a number of other Conservative women MPs signed a letter in support of women's rights to all Newspapers saying: "We don't support all of this despite being Conservative. We support it because we are Conservative and believe in equality of opportunity for all."

Here our Executive Producer, Boni Sones, met up with Esther and her Conservative "mates" in Central Lobby Westminster to talk about Self-Confidence in girls and women, the work they have been doing in Parliament and for their Constituents, and their hopes and ambitions for 2012.

Boni first spoke to Esther, then Amber Rudd, the MP for Hastings and Rye, and Harriet Baldwin, MP West Worcestershire. They then walked across to the scarf of the suffragette Emily Wilding Davison and also chatted to Tracey Crouch, MP for Chatham and Aylesford and Caroline Dinenage, the MP for Gosport.

Caroline and the others are determined in 2012 to push the issue of tax free child care forward and helping with the costs of childcare to get more women into work.

Harriett Baldwin Hot Quote: "It's about aiming high, and it starts with girls at school and I remember my teacher saying to me remember Harriett you are a very bright girl but have you thought about becoming a glove buyer at Harrods!"

Amber Rudd Hot Quote: "I am a committed feminist and it's because I a feminist that I am a Conservative not despite it. Conservatives and feminism go together. We believe in enabling women."

How government ministers could help save a life...
Tricky Issue! "I want every child to be a life saver"

Should Emergency Life Skills become part of the National Curriculum? Labour's Bolton West MP, Julie Hilling, says Yes! Her Ten Minute Rule Bill – "National Curriculum (Emergency Life Support Skills) Bill" will get a Second Reading in the Commons in January 2012 but she is mystified as to why more government ministers are not supporting it.

Her modest attempt to save thousands of lives by teaching secondary school children just two hours a year of life saving skills could become a reality if Education Ministers, including Michael Gove, had the energy and will to make it happen. She says the costs would be small and that it also increases confidence and makes children feel better citizens.

Julie is supported in her campaign by The British Heart Foundation. Her Private Member's Bill would require Michael Gove, the Secretary of State for Education, to include the teaching of emergency life support skills in schools as a compulsory part of the National Curriculum, and for connected purposes.

Every year 150,000 people die in situations where first aid could have made a difference. Every year 30,000 people have a cardiac arrest outside of a hospital environment but less than 10 per cent of these survive to be discharged from hospital. Often children are present when these events happen.

Julie told our reporter Amy Lee how she wants "every child to be a life saver"!

In her Constituency 15 year old Patrick Horrock had a heart attack in Hindley Leisure Centre earlier this year but thanks to a member of staff performing CPR and another using a defibrillator he is alive today. In France, Denmark and Norway and some states in the USA, ELS is already a compulsory part of the National Curriculum. Why not here too? Come on Mr Gove you can make such a difference if you want to! The Bill is scheduled for a second reading in the House on 20th January 2012.

Julie Hot Quote: "This government is keen not to prescribe things and say educationalists should prescribe, but they are prescribing other parts of the curriculum. I don't think it is putting a burden on educationalists, if you are saying children should learn about the Kings and Queens of England I think they should learn how to save a life. Minsters could go down in history as a Government who saves lives. I don't understand why they don't want to do this.

"As a Ten Minute Rule Bill it is not going to become an Act, so I am working with others to try and make it happen and promote it, and to make sure that all my schools in my Constituency are life saving schools and I am working with the Fire Service locally too on it.

"In 2011 Everybody has an opportunity to save a life just imagine how awful it is to see an accident and stand back and not be able to do anything. There are courses all over the place go and learn basic lifesaving skills."

A woman in the Commons breast feeding – never!

Guardian journalist Jackie Ashley talks to Baroness Helene Hayman for the Women's Library Fawcett Lecture. We hear how Baroness Hayman, was supposedly breast feeding in the Commons in the mid-1970s when there were just 27 women MPs, and what she thinks of gender balance in the Upper Chamber today, equality and women's portfolio careers. But an elected chamber? Perhaps not.

Jackie, too, chuckles with laughter when Baroness Hayman recalls that she never actually breastfed although her male colleagues to this day claim to have witnessed it! Oh well, that is life, but these same issues of work home-life balance will never fade away, they just keep repeating themselves it seems. Over to Jackie now for this very special report. Thanks to the Women's Library.

Helene Hot Quote: "Women's different career experiences do allow them to bring back a lot into politics later in their lives. These female experiences of doing 'other things' rather than just the traditional career paths in life should be valued."

The year: 2010
Voting reform and more women in Westminster

MPs will vote on the government's plans for a referendum on AV the first day back after their summer break. Critics say our "First-Past-The-Post" voting system lets down female candidates because of the advantages it hands to incumbents. In the UK just one in five of our MPs is female. So will the new AV ("alternative vote") system be any better?

Our Executive Producer Boni Sones OBE, asked three women MPs if changing the voting system would help further women's representation.

Here Jo Swinson LD MP East Dunbartonshire, Angela Eagle Labour MP for Wallasey, and Margot James Conservative MP for Stourbridge give you their verdict.

AV allows voters to rank candidates in their constituency in order of preference.

Read more in Chapter 13.

Esther McVey MP for Wirral West launches "If Chloe Can"

The new Conservative MP for Wirral West, Esther McVey, has just written an inspirational careers "bookazine" aimed at 11-13 year olds on Merseyside. We asked her why and caught up with the "real Chloe" from her local Belvedere Academy. But first the www.wpradio.co.uk round table debate also spoke to: Debbie Moore – First Female to set up a PLC Pineapple; Lucinda Ellery – Inspirational Businesswoman; Rona Cant – Adventurer; Gillian McDonald – First UK Female Whisky Distiller; Lisa Pover – Cabbie turned Yachtsman and founder of the Lisa Pover Charitable Trust; Louise Greenhalgh – First UK Female Bomb Disposal Officer in Afghanistan.

The Secretary of State for Work and Pensions, Rt Hon Iain Duncan Smith MP founder of the Centre for Social Justice, was also at the launch. He told Boni Sones OBE, Executive Producer of Women's Parliamentary Radio that young women needed new role models to help them form successful careers. We then spoke to The RT Hon John Hayes MP – Minister for State for Further Education, Skills and Lifelong Learning who will soon be launching more apprenticeships for young women.

Esther Hot Quote: Esther McVey MP told www.wpradio.co.uk: "I was concerned about the alarming job stats to come out of Merseyside because girls didn't have role models so I set about collecting the stories of friends and others I thought were inspirational. Every lady I approached said I will do that because we have messages and stories to tell. You maybe issued a bad set of cards to play with but it is what you do and how you overcome it, and nothing good comes easy you have to keep going. People are told things are going to be so easy and they aren't.

"I wanted to be an MP to address unfairness and that is really my motivational force and that is across the board. From Merseyside we want to extend it right across the UK and "If Chloe can" anyone can. There are tips on how people achieved and what they did and you can see how much time and hard work went into it, it is realistic expectations."

Iain Duncan Smith Hot Quote: "I think it is an excellent idea. I have two daughters I hope they will be able to go on and achieve in their own right, this helps people like them realise others have gone before them and also it is a chance for people who don't have a supportive family like mine do to read this and realise they are just as good as anybody else. They can go on to achieve and that is one of the big problems to get young girls born into a broken home and difficulties to get a sense of self worth and self esteem that values them as human beings rather than as the goods and chattels of somebody else."

Speaking out and speaking up: The class of May 2010 – the new Conservative women MPs

The Queen's speech – Flexible working, equal pay and changes to the rape laws. Esther McVey the Conservative MP for or Wirral West, television presenter and businesswoman and Karen Lumley the Conservative MP for Redditch, an accountant and businesswoman who was the youngest Tory group leader in Wrexham, say what they thought of David Cameron's Queen's Speech.

Their Maiden Speeches and the issues to be fought for - the local economy and protecting local business.

Priti Patel the Conservative MP for Witham a former press and PR advisor and an economics graduate and Lorraine Fullbrook the Conservative MP for South Ribble, the former Executive Director of the Women2Win campaign and a former local councillor and businesswoman talk about the issues they will be speaking up for in their forthcoming Maiden Speeches.

The year: 2009
WP Radio interview of 2009!
Fiona Mactaggart MP - changes the laws on prostitution and wins an Emma Humphreys Memorial Prize

Fiona Mactaggart, the Labour MP for Slough, has campaigned and succeeded in changing the laws on prostitution.

It was at 11pm on 3rd November 2009 that Fiona watched the House of Lords pass Clause 14 of the Policing and Crime Bill. It begins to put the responsibility for prostitution onto the purchaser, who has a choice, instead of a seller who often does not. It was one of the most significant changes in politics of 2009 and was in danger of being voted down.

She has won a special prize in the Emma Humphreys Memorial Prize for her work and is Chair of the All-Party Parliamentary Group on Prostitution and the Global Sex Trade and co-Chair of the Parliamentary Labour Party Women's Committee.

Here Fiona tells how she worked with others in her party, Harriet Harman MP, Jacqui Smith MP, and men too as well as women across party to achieve this change. It was first spoken of by Mary Wollstonecraft in "A Vindication of the Rights of Woman" in 1792. Fiona told Boni Sones how she "reached for the stars" and succeeded.

Fiona Hot Quote: "I remember telephoning Jacqui Smith MP, the then Homer Secretary, and said I am planning this campaign is it alright with you? She said she was on the beach. I always imagined she was on an exotic beach, in fact she was in North Wales, and she said "OK go ahead" and that was the trigger for me to get a law similar to the Swedish law passed."

"Finding people to stick up against their party line was important. For the fist time I met a member of the Conservative Party, a Baroness, who did realise it was an issue of conscience and this Baroness went and told her whips this. This was critical. There just wasn't enough people to back the LD amendment so it went through."

"At the time I thought this amendment was a step beyond what we could achieve right now, but you have to reach for the stars because then you get them. Change never happens by accident, change happens when you try to reach for the stars."

The Ann Treneman Diaries – Annus Horribilis: The Worst Year in British Politics

Matthew Parris has called it "brilliant" and Women's Parliamentary Radio wholeheartedly agrees. Here Ann Treneman, the sketch writer for The Times, reads from and reviews her new book. Boni Sones, Executive Producer of www.wpradio.co.uk joins in. The book puts the year's most turbulent events in politics into Ann's very own side-splitting perspective.

Thanks to Ann for allowing us to broadcast these special readings.

Ann Hot Quote: "It was the publisher's idea. It is actually a portrait of the year. I picked the sketches that told the story of the year, not the ones I liked the most. I picked the ones that I feel created a picture of what it was really like. I think people will want to know how bad it really was!"

"Looking back at the sketches I loved it when Gordon thought he was leader of the World, but I remember thinking when Joanna Lumley seemed to be in charge, that the government had lost it. Then there was the stuff about MPs' expenses, it was all too good to be true; I felt so lucky it was true!"

"There is such an organisation as the "Volupts". It's a real group of Labour woman, part of the sisterhood in the Commons led by Harriet. I don't know what they do, probably they have shadowy meetings and cups of tea at which they plot sometimes."

Sally Keeble MP, Vulture Funds

The Labour MP for Northampton North, Sally Keeble, is pushing through a new ten-minute rule Bill, to get the UK to crack down on the excesses of the so called "Vulture funds" that profit out of developing countries debt by buying it up and then demanding excessive repayments. "The developing country debt (restriction of recovery) Bill" aims to tackle the secrecy and profiteering of the vulture funds.

Jubilee Debt, which has led the campaign against the vulture funds, records 54 lawsuits by commercial creditors against some of the poorest countries, some still in process. The vulture funds buy up the defaulted sovereign debt of developing countries at knockdown prices, and then sue, often through the UK courts, for the full face value of the debt, plus compound interest and charges. They're secretive institutions, often based in tax havens, and pursue their claims through jurisdictions around the world. Boni Sones asked Sally, what she thought her Bill could achieve.

Cheryl Gillan MP – The Autism Bill

The Conservative MP, Cheryl Gillan, is successfully pushing through a Private Member's Bill on Autism in The House. It will ensure local authorities and NHS service providers give adequate support for adults with this learning difficulty. It will champion new pathways for diagnosis, assessment and support for those with Autism.

The MP for Chesham and Amersham says she was fortunate, after many years, to come top of the Private Member's Bill ballot. She talked to colleagues and charities before deciding that the gap in existing provision for Autism sufferers needed addressing. As a result of attracting cross-party support for her pioneering Bill, it has successfully passed its third reading in the House and has now gone to the Lords.

This is England's first ever piece of Autism legislation, and Cheryl says she thinks it shows how politicians across party work to bring about change in society and that in the wake of the MPs' expenses scandal, it highlights, the good work that politicians do in Parliament. W P Radio reporter Linda Fairbrother spoke to her.

Sally Keeble MP – How the budget is helping grandparents

The Chancellor, Alistair Darling, has announced in his budget that from April 2011 grandparents who obtain a certificate, will be able to get a National Insurance credit towards the basic state pension for caring for their grandchildren or members of their family aged 12 or younger for 20 hours or more a week.

Boni Sones, asked Labour's Northampton North MP, Sally Keeble, if this was at long last a welcome acknowledgement of the years of informal help grandparents have given families and if it would help to ease the gender pay gap between men and women and progress the government's equality agenda on the eve of a new Equality Bill being published?

International Women's Day Women and the Recession:

Women across party celebrated International Women's Day 09 with a heartfelt debate in the Chamber on Women and the Recession. The debate had been arranged by Labour's Harriet Harman MP, deputy leader of the Labour Party and Vera Baird MP, the Solicitor General. It came a day after women from all parties had been invited to number 11 to discuss how to support women during the recession.

All parties, including the Liberal Democrat's Lynne Featherstone, talked of the importance of the government's forthcoming Equalities Bill becoming law sooner rather than later and not being side-lined because of the recession.

Theresa May MP, Shadow Secretary of State for Work and Pensions and Shadow Minister for Women spoke of the need to help older women and families and her Facebook campaign "Theresa May for Equal Pay". And THANKS Theresa for the mention of WP Radio's women MPs photographs in the debate which are to be promoted to schools.

The year: 2008
Fiona Mactaggart MP

Fiona Mactaggart the Labour MP for Slough, and former Home Office Minister, is an advocate for the reform of the Prostitution laws in this Country. She would like to see Britain adopt a model based on Sweden, where all paid prostitution is outlawed. In countries such as New Zealand, they have actually legalised prostitution, but Fiona says that won't work here. She believes we need a total ban on buying sex to protect women and to stop the trade in prostituion and trafficking. In this extended interview, Boni Sones asked her why?

Ann Treneman

She needs no introduction as a Parliamentary sketch writer. Ann Treneman's columns in the Times newspaper are much admired. She was nominated for the Dods Scottish Widows female political journalist of the year this year. She likes to describe what she witnesses in the Chamber as a playground spat. No more so then when the women MPs collide and she witnesses "a catfight". Here she reads from three of her sketches and talks to Boni Sones.

The Oona King Diaries

Oona King, is credited with writing a frank, authentic and genuinely humorous book on her time as an MP in Westminster. She was elected as the MP for Bethnal Green and Bow in 1997 along with 100 other Labour women, one of only 239 women ever to be elected to Parliament. She achieved significant change while she was there on issues such as housing, landmines and the prevention of genocide.

Oona's remarkable social values were given her by her Jewish mother Hazel and her father Preston. She lost her seat to George Galloway, of the Respect Party, in 2005. As part of the wpradio.co.uk celebration of 90 years since women got the vote, Oona reads from her diaries and is interviewed by Boni Sones. Sound engineer is Pete Cook of Screenspace.

The Oona King Diaries – House Music is published by Bloomsbury, £12.99. Copyright Oona King.

Nadine Dorries MP – Conservative

Nadine Dorries the Conservative MP for Mid Bedfordshire is at the forefront of a campaign to reduce the time limit on abortions. As a former nurse, she is a passionate advocate of a 20 week limit. She is interviewed by Brian Shallcross of GCap media.

Theresa May MP – Conservative
The Shadow Leader of the House of Commons, Theresa May, has told wpradio.co.uk that she thinks debate in the Chamber is sometimes too confrontational. While she supported her leader, David Cameron, for being robust in Prime Ministers Questions, she said she was disappointed that The Leader of the House, Harriet Harman, chose to be confrontational in the recent International Women's Day debate. Boni Sones spoke to her.

Lynne Featherstone MP
Lynne Featherstone, the Liberal Democrat MP for Hornsey and Wood Green is her Party's spokesperson for young people and equalities. She is said to be a tough politician, and has established a reputation as a national blogger of note. Lynne also uses Facebook and Flickr on her website www.lynnefeatherstone.org. Boni Sones spoke to Lynne about her new brief and her formidable campaigning instincts.

Women MPs celebrate International Women's Day
Barbara Follett MP and David Davis MP
Women and men MPs across party sung marching songs and Jerusalem to celebrate International Women's Day and 90 years of women and the vote. They laid flowers at the statue of the suffragette Emily Pankhurst, which is still outside Parliament, and then walked into the Commons to commemorate the life of Emily Wilding Davison, the suffragette who died trying to get votes for women. Boni Sones joined them.

Barbara Keeley MP – Labour
Barbara Keeley the Labour MP for Worsley spoke of her concern for women to be better represented in Parliament.

TWELVE
Campaigning in Parliamentary Groups

There is much that goes on in Westminster that cuts across the party political divide. The All-Party Parliamentary Groups allow the pressure groups, charities and business interests to take into Parliament issues of concern to them. Political friendships and allegiances can be formed across party. There are hundreds of All-Party groups covering every policy area possible. In terms of women, they are influential in devising strategies to form policy and point out the loopholes in the current legislation. These APPGs are informal groupings of MPs and Peers, and maybe country based for instance the APPG on Zimbabwe, or on an issue of concern nationally or internationally. Oona King, the Labour MP and now Peer, set up an APPG on Genocide Prevention, while others are issue based, like the APPG on Breast Cancer, or the All-Party Parliamentary Group against Trafficking of Women and Children chaired by the Labour politician Fiona Mactaggart, which says that: "Human Trafficking is one of the top three most lucrative manifestations of organised crime – along with drug dealing and the arms trade. Sadly it takes place throughout the UK". These groups allow women's issues to be better represented across party. Select Committees are the formal groupings of MPs across party, men and women, which scrutinise the work of the various government departments and the Secretary of State who make up the members of the government's Cabinet. They look into how each department is spending its budget, how that department is administered and what policies they are pursuing. Some such as the Environment Select, cut across government departments, as does the Public Accounts Committee. Following the Wright reforms, the Chairs of these Select Committees are now elected, not appointed by the government, and they are gaining a reputation for holding people to account. The Labour politician, Margaret Hodge, is the elected Chair of the Public Accounts Committee, and has been instrumental in tackling issues such as Starbuck's claimed tax evasion and the huge public sector pay-offs at the BBC. Meanwhile the Conservative MP, Sarah

Wollaston, a former GP selected on an open primary by her party in Totnes, has been speaking up for further health reforms as a member of the Select Committee on Health. She is particularly keen on a new method of assessing mental illness for benefit claimants and carried out some razor sharp questioning when the Committee looked into the Mid Staffs hospital deaths brought about by neglect and abuse. The women have certainly made a name for themselves in these Committees. Even though the Conservative MP Anne McIntosh has recently been deselected from her Thirsk and Malton constituency she is still the elected Chair of the powerful Environment, Food and Rural Affairs Committee and recently our Advisory Board member Gisela Stuart, Editor of House Magazine, nominated Anne as her Conservative women MP of the year.

The year: 2013
Growing Points – encouraging others to take a step up the ladder!

In the Lords this week a new charity Growing Points launched its ambitious action plan to recruit "Ambassadors" to mentor others from excluded communities to help them achieve "great things". The idea is the brainchild of two Growing Point trustees the Chair Dick Stockford and Steph Palmerone and others. There helping to launch them was Lord Philip Hunt and the Coalitions Social Mobility Tsar Alan Milburn. Our Executive producer, Boni Sones, spoke first to Alan Milburn who told her of his own "mentors" his Mother and his teachers who helped him climb up in life and then Steph and Dick.

Alan Milburn Hot Quote: "Although we have become a wealthy Country we have struggled to become a fairer one. That is why we have pretty low levels of social mobility in this Country compared to many others. The really welcome thing is that now across the political spectrum there is a desire to change that. It's important that initiatives like Growing Points are launched and they will play their part. Many of us in our lives progress because we are lucky and sometimes as in my case it is your Mum or your teacher."

The Youth Parliament at its very best!

The recent UK Youth Parliament debate is an excellent 'watch'. The debate was refreshingly good and robust, and allowed a proper exchange of ideas and speeches putting the weekly Wednesday shouting match at PMQs to shame! http://www.parliamentweek.org/whats-new/uk-youth-parliament-15-november-2013-/

UK Youth Parliament members are the only group, other than MPs, allowed to sit on the green benches. Nearly half-a-million 11 to 18 years olds from across the UK voted for the issues that they debated with regional representatives being called to speak by the Speaker, John Bercow.

MYPs voted to decide on their new national campaigns. Votes for 16 and 17 year olds in all public elections' received 217 of the 233 votes cast. The 'A curriculum to provide us for life' received the 136 of the 293 votes cast.

Three other motions were debated: 'Zero tolerance towards bullying in schools', 'Combating youth unemployment' and 'Better work experience and careers advice'.

"Place and Train" – supporting a new system for helping those with mental illness back to work

Dr Sarah Wollaston, the Conservative MP for Totnes and a member of the Health Select Committee has written this week of her own problems with mental illness and postal natal depression and used this personal experience to better inform the public policy debate over how people are assessed for disability welfare benefits.

Dr Wollaston is asking the Works and Pensions Minister, Iain Duncan Smith, to use the recently announced delay in bringing in a new system of personal independence payments to look at a totally new system so called "Place and Train". There had been concerns about the ability to carry out the necessary assessments in time. Dr Wollaston wants the Department to trial an "Individual Placement and Support scheme" to help those with mental illness receive support when they are back at work, not before they return. When ill she says the discipline of going to work helped her recover quicker.

Dr Wollaston Hot Quote: "There is nothing wrong with having a functional assessment, but where someone flags themselves up on the forms as having a mental health issue at that point there should be a system for getting more background information and giving them more support. We need some pilots in this Country of "Place and Train", so that you look for a work placement and you support someone through it. In my case I was fortunate, I had a supportive family, but where that family support isn't there let's help those people particularly through the first few weeks."

Our Original Thinkers Series!
Full number Portability for all Bank Accounts

Andrea Leadsom, the Conservative MP for South Northamptonshire, wants the government to introduce full number portability for all our bank accounts.

A group of major high street Banks this week announced they would be introducing Seven-day switching to make changing bank accounts with all your direct debit details from one to the other faster and easier, but Andrea wants the changes to go further.

At the moment consumers stay with one Bank for most of their lifetimes and there is little variability in what we are charged for the service. But even Seven day switching will still mean the bank holds and controls our bank account numbers and details.

With full number portability our details would sit on a Vocalink system, independent of the banks, and we would then give permission for whatever bank we choose or banks to access it. We would control who our bank details sit with, rather like our own portable mobile phone number system, where we can switch providers.

Andrea Hot Quote: "Seven day switching is an improvement, but Greg Clarke, the City Manager, has been incredibly supportive of full number portability. I hope the new Independent Payments Regulator which is to be set up as part of the new Banking Reform Bill, will look at full number portability, and if it is beneficial, I hope the government will bring it in."

Modern Slavery – Fiona Mctaggart wants tough new measures to help trafficked people

Fiona Mctaggart, the Labour MP for Slough and the new chair of the All-Party Parliamentary Group on Trafficking has been a long standing campaigner against human trafficking and the sexual exploitation of young children. She introduced her own Private Member's Bill on the use of trafficked labour in the Supply Chain to supermarkets.

Now she is waiting to see the full details of the Government's proposed new Modern Slavery Bill, details of which are not yet known. In Scotland this week a Labour MSP Jenny Marra, has introduced her own Human Trafficking Bill calling for it to be made illegal to punish people forced to commit a crime as a result of trafficking. Here Fiona tells our Executive Producer, Boni Sones, what measures she would like to see in the new UK Bill.

Fiona Hot Quote: "I think that a critical thing, which I hope the government will do, is to make sure that within the legislation there is a mechanism to make sure that the data about who is trafficked, how and where to, is much better than it currently is. Until we know who is affected we won't get solutions to this evil problems."

Andrea Leadsom MP – How a vision of a "Fresh Start" for Europe became a reality!

Andrea Leadsom, the Conservative MP for South Northamptonshire, began her Parliamentary career in 2010 with a clear view of re-negotiating our relationship with Europe. She set up the Conservative "Fresh Start Group" and is Co-Chair of the All-Party Parliamentary Group for European Reform. Our Executive Producer Boni Sones, caught up with her in Westminster to get her reaction to the Prime Minister David Cameron's pledge this week for an in/out referendum on Europe. Won't the uncertainty be bad for business?

Andrea's Hot Quote: "I've wanted to be an MP forever and it's always seemed to me that actually understanding the facts – because the EU is like a massive bowl of spaghetti – it is so interlinked, everything leads to everything else, so it is actually difficult to unravel it. So actually doing some of the core research, investigating what actually would work better, which directives, which bits of EU policy should we change, has been worthwhile. I am delighted that we have got so much support."

The year: 2012
The Cross-Party Unplanned Pregnancy Inquiry - birth control can reduce abortion

Three women MPs are working across Party to ask serious questions about the number of unplanned pregnancies in the UK. Although teenage pregnancy in the UK has declined over the past decade, it remains the highest in Western Europe. There is also concern about the number of abortions for women in their 30s and the number of repeat abortions in all age groups. So do women need better birth control advice, and if so, how should it be given, should the UK follow the example of India and take advice free into workplaces?

Our Executive Producer, Boni Sones, spoke to the Inquiry's Chair, Amber Rudd, Conservative MP for Hastings and Rye, Sandra Osborne, Labour MP for Ayr, Carrick & Cumnock, Lorely Burt - Liberal Democrat MP for Solihull. They have already conducted two oral evidence sessions, alongside Julia Manning from 2020health.

One Minute Solution – Amber: "Certainly there are too many abortions and the way to reduce that is to have less unwanted conceptions. We are trying to change the framework of the debate so that we talk about contraception rather than abortion!"

Sandra: "There are still far too many unplanned pregnancies among teenagers, and amongst older women where the abortion rate is on the rise. We do need to look into it to make practical recommendations on the progress that has already been made."

Lorely: "The young women who came in were absolutely wonderful, I think we learnt so much from them. One of the early witnesses was talking about India, and in India they actually took the contraceptive advice out into the factories and out into the business places. I thought what a wonderful idea. We need to look at where we deliver contraceptive advice."

Head to Head: Declan Duggan's new book In the Name of the Son

Former Dunstable publican Declan Duggan, has written about how he worked with Ministers, MPs and Peers to change the law after his much loved 19-year-old son Kevin was killed by a drunken driver. The changes allowed blood samples to be taken from suspected drunk drivers, even if they were unconscious. It is estimated to have saved more than 500 lives in the past decade. But he spent years fighting the system to get the police and the authorities to take notice of his concerns. His account in this new Book *In the Name of the Son*. http://www.filamentpublishing.com/Books_TheSon.asp – is a moving one. The Labour MP the Rt Hon David Blunkett has written the foreword to the Book. He was the Home Secretary in 2002 that enacted what is now called 'Duggan's Law'. Declan talks to Boni Sones, our Executive Producer.

Declan's One Minute Solution: "I had to challenge the police, I had to wait for weeks and months, and I had to employ a detective to work for me, which was very frustrating as you can imagine. I was a grieving father, we had to challenge the police to do an investigation, and we found out that the boy concerned had been drinking all day long, but because he was unconscious they couldn't take a blood sample and there was no evidence so everything was left. The boy who killed my son was getting away scot-free and my son was in a grave in Dunstable. David Blunkett was the Home Secretary and he passed the law – Dugan's Law – in July 2002 and it came onto the Statute books on 17th October, which is the ten year anniversary today."

Head to Head on Youth Justice: Are young people being "failed" by the prejudices of society?
Linda Fairbrother talks to Baroness Cohen of Pimlico, a lawyer and crime fiction writer.

Our Reporter Linda Fairbrother goes "Head to Head" with Labour Peer Baroness Cohen of Pimlico, on why the youth justice system fails young people who get into trouble. The interview took place at a recent High Sheriff's Legal Conference at the Cambridge Union Society from where Linda now reports.

Baroness Cohen one minute solution: "We now know far more about how the child and adolescent brain develops, and short sharp shock (treatments) are being delivered to a brain that just isn't able to receive or process that information in most cases. It either brutalises or terrifies or drives people into crime. The answer that overwhelming came out of the Conference, I thought, was early intervention by the Community and in relation to families too because much Youth Crime, comes out of children who themselves have been badly neglected in one way or other. It requires intervention in families, it requires intervention in the schools, and it requires all of us to take more interest and put some more help in too."

The Jubilee naming of the Clock Tower "The Elizabeth Tower" Angela Eagle, MP, brings you live coverage

A suggestion by Tobias Ellwood, the Conservative MP for Bournemouth East, to rename the East Tower housing "Big Ben" the "Elizabeth Tower" was this week officially launched by The Speaker, John Bercow, and Mr Ellwood himself. But there was no "unveiling", no "champagne" corks popping, just lots of enthusiasm and clapping as MPs and supporters gazed at the new name plate: "The Elizabeth Tower". So what exactly happened? We got Angela Eagle the Labour MP for Wallasey, and Shadow Leader of the House, to narrate the naming ceremony for you.

Angela Eagle Hot Quote: "It's very rare that you have a Monarch who reigns for as long as Queen Elizabeth and does such a fantastic job. I think the Jubilee demonstrated what affection she is held in by the Nation and this is an apt recognition of that. In a year-and-a-half she will be the longest reigning Monarch in British History, she is second behind Victoria."

Why our prisons need reform!

Juliet Lyon, Director of the Prison Reform Trust on why we have just 13 women's prisons leaving families and children unable to visit their mothers, sisters, wives and friends while in jail, sometimes for very short periods of time. Is prison the right solution for women offenders? Juliet also tells us how the number of children in our prisons has been successfully reduced thanks to a PRT campaign "Out of Trouble" – a 37 per cent drop in child custody and a significant drop in youth crime too. Congratulations to those women MPs across party who have campaigned for change including Labour's Jean Corston and members of the present Coalition Government.

Juliet Hot Quote: "We're delighted to see this 37 per cent drop in child custody and a massive drop in youth crime, which has occurred over the last five years, and our programme "Out of Trouble" has been one of the major contributors to that change. We have worked very closely with Government to help effect that change. We are now going to be working with Government, across Party obviously because this isn't a party political issue this is something everybody has signed up to."

Is the book or the film of Harry Potter better?
World Book Day – 1st March 2012 – www.worldbookday.com

Campaigners often bring their campaigns to the heart of Westminster, and World Book Day 2012 set up a colourful display in the Committee Corridors to celebrate books and reading with MPs.

Here we asked the MPs to read extracts of their favourite children's books to our listeners!

You will hear from Joanna Prior, Chair of World Book Day 2012, Stephen Williams, Liberal Democrat MP for Bristol West, Lyn Brown the

Labour MP for West Ham, Alan Hurcombe, Group MD for Scholastic, and Tristram Hunt, the Labour MP for Stoke-on-Trent Central, author and Chair of the All-Party Publishing Group, who launched the campaign.

A World book day £1 token will buy you one of the eight specially-produced World Book day books. Our MPs seemed to like "How to Train Your Dragon", by Cressida Cowell. Are you sitting comfortably? Now they will begin...

Jo Swinson MP on MP on Body Image – Again!
Jo Swinson, The Liberal Democrat MP for East Dunbartonshire, Chair of the All-Party Parliamentary Group on Body Image: The screening of the Jennifer Siebel Newsom film "Miss Representation" looked at how the portrayal of women in the media leads to an under representation of women in public life. It was Jo and the Equalities Minister, Lynne Featherstone, who first kicked off the Body Image campaign in 2009. Their campaign has led directly to air brushed images from advertisements being withdrawn and is now "mainstreamed" as an issue in Parliament itself.

Jo Hot Quote: "The campaign has come a long way since 2009 when Lynne and I first raised this as opposition MPs. The Film has a lot of different people supporting it and even the advertisers are now realising that we need to treat this issue differently. We have seen bare Minerals do an advertising campaign choosing their models on the basis of their stories and their attitude and their inner beauty as much as how they looked. And No 7 have stopped airbrushing in their advertising campaigns, we are seeing a lot of change within Industry and I hope that with the screening of this Film "Miss Representation" we can now look at how to go about the next steps."

The year: 2011
A life story of one woman in the Commons and another about young women starting their working lives: 'If Chloe Can!'
"Aim high and you can succeed" – Esther McVey MP the National Youth Theatre tour "If Chloe Can"!

Esther McVey MP the Conservative MP for the Wirrall West and PPS at the Department of Work and Pensions took her "campaign" to give positive role models of extraordinary success to young women to the National Youth Theatre. They turned her recently launched book into a play 'If Chloe Can'. It will now tour major cities in the UK, Manchester, Liverpool, and Sheffield.

Our new parliamentary reporter Amy Lee and our Executive Producer Boni Sones, spoke to Jo Salter, the first female fighter pilot, Lucinda Ellery, a hair loss specialist, and Debbie Moore of Pineapple Dance Studios. They then chatted to three young women from Fulham Cross School and Esther McVey herself about the production, its ideals, and the future for this imaginative venture.

Debbie Moore Hot Quote: "Guts and hard work lead to success, there is no such thing as a free lunch. Common sense and confidence are essential."

The year: 2010
Eleanor Laing MP for Epping Forest – Constitutional Reform

Eleanor Laing the MP for Epping Forest is Chairman of the Conservative Home Affairs and Constitutional Affairs Committee. She also sits on the Select Committee on Constitutional Affairs and is examining the new "Parliamentary Voting System and Constituencies Bill" currently going through Parliament. Eleanor is against voting reform and the suggested system of AV, thinks the 5th May date for the referendum is flawed, and believes a wholly elected House of Lords would be a mistake, but she does agree with larger constituencies and reducing the number of MPs from 650 to 600. In this special interview Boni Sones, our Executive Producer, begun by asking her why she opposed voting reform at this point in time?

Eleanor Hot Quote: "The coalition agreement provides for voting reform but changing the voting system at this time will cost £100 million at a time when the Country is in serious economic crisis. I personally think it is quite wrong to spend £100 million of tax payers money on this when it could go to schools, hospitals, nurses and other worthwhile causes."

"We should wait until we are in better economic circumstances but we have to have the referendum because it is part of the coalition agreement. I do accept that it is a price worth paying in order to have the stability of the coalition, which then allows the government to tackle the economic crisis."

"To hold the referendum on the same day as local elections in England and the same day as Scotland, Wales and Northern Ireland have national elections is likely to distort the result. It should be held on a day when there are not other important elections. The different turn-outs with other elections are likely to distort the results, I don't know what that distortion will be but it will be distorted."

"I do agree with changing the boundaries and having larger constituencies. I don't think anybody can argue against equalisation of constituencies. We are all having to work harder and MPs should do the same."

Women's Parliamentary Radio at the Conservative Party Conference – The Fringe and women!!

Juliet Lyon CBE, Director of the Prison Reform Trust, spoke at a fringe event at the Conservative Party Conference on "Should there be fewer people in prison"? She believes that the numbers of women in prisons could be cut in half, without risking public safety.

Juliet says the new Women's Centres, set up by the last Labour government after the "Corston review of women in prisons", are "one of the most attractive and cheap solutions" compared to the cost of putting a woman in prison, upwards of £45,000 a year. Boni Sones spoke to her.

The Conservative Women's Organisation teamed up with ActionAid UK to look at the issue of "On the Frontline: Women, Peace and Conflict". They are calling for the Conservative government to appoint an International Violence against Women Minister.

Our reporter Linda Fairbrother first spoke to panellist Nicola Blackwood MP, Chair of the All-Party Parliamentary Group on Women and Conflict, then Bobby Middleton of the European Union Women's Organisation, Matilda Parker, from Liberia, and Dorcas Erskin, of ActionAid. Finally she caught up with Pauline Lucas, Chairman of Conservative Women's Organisation.

The Immigration Minister, Damian Green MP, told a "Big Brother Watch" fringe that the government would not be banning the Burka. He said he thought such a ban would be "Un-British". Our reporter Linda Fairbrother, managed to ask him why as he walked to his next talk?

The Liberal Democrat: "The Body Image Debate"
Two Liberal Democrat MPs, Jo Swinson and Lynne Featherstone have launched a "Real Women: The Body Image Debate" on International Women's Day.

Jo is the MP for East Dunbartonshire and Lynne the MP for Hornsey and Woodgreen. They believe that the constant bombardment of perfect images of women in the media are leading to all kinds of mental health disorders such as depression, anxiety, lack of self-esteem, eating disorders to name but a few. They are campaigning for adverts which have been "air-brushed" to be labelled as such. Their suggestions also include "health certificates" for models, more sport and "image" education in schools. This campaign has won the backing of academics, doctors and clinical psychologists worldwide.

Our wpradio.co.uk reporter Linda Fairbrother brushed up her body image with a bike ride to the train station to interview Lynne. It's a campaign we are supporting.

The Chilcot Inquiry on Iraq
For eight years Oona King was the popular Labour MP for Bethnal Green and Bow in East London until she lost her seat to George Galloway of Respect, her defeat being attributed to the Iraq war.

A year after becoming an MP, in 1998, she founded the All-Party Parliamentary Group (APPG) on the Great Lakes Region and Genocide Prevention. She initially opposed military action but eventually supported going to war in Iraq and while reading from her diaries "House Music" in part 2 she told Boni Sones, why she still thought that decision was right. However, she regrets the lack of post conflict planning. She was appalled by the genocide of children in Iraq.

The year: 2009
Lyn Brown MP Summer holiday reading and her love of Libraries!

Lyn Brown, the Labour MP for West Ham since 2005, is a passionate champion of the library movement. From the time her mother took her to a London library as a child she confesses to having "wolfed down" books of all kinds and to having been "radicalised" by them. She is Chair of the All-Party Parliamentary Group on Libraries, which is due to publish a report on modernising the service in the autumn and an assistant Whip.

The novels which have changed Lyn's life include: *Gone with the Wind* by Margaret Mitchell, *To Kill a Mocking Bird* by Harper Lee, and now she's pouring over her summer holiday reading which will of course include *A view from the Foothills* by her colleague Chris Mullin. Her mother worked as a packer in an icing sugar factory, but she taught Lyn that reading was the best way to "improve" yourself, and that's just what she's done, now as an MP in a neighbourhood near to where she grew up.

The Million Women Rise Coalition

WP Radio joined 6,000 women on a march with The Million Women Rise Coalition through London to celebrate International Women's Day 09.The coalition campaign group www.millionwomenrise.com aims to "End male violence against women". As Seema Malhotra of the Fabian Women's network, walked with the protestors from beginning to end, she heard why women, families and children turned up in such large numbers to stop the violence against women here and in countries like the Congo.

Seema even met four generations of one family as she narrated the progress of the Million Women Rise march and eventually caught up with its Co-ordinator Sabrina Qureshi, to allow her to tell her story too.The march coincided with a new initiative launched by the Home Secretary Jacqui Smith to help prevent Domestic Violence from occurring, particularly during the recession. Producer Boni Sones would like to thank all concerned for this special 30 minute radio documentary podcast and also the women from the North East for their "Nanna was a Suffragette" song. Thanks to our sound engineer Pete Cook of Screenspace.

The year: 2008
All-Party Parliamentary Jazz Appreciation Group

Not every politician is gloomy about youth culture today. The All-Party Parliamentary Jazz Appreciation Group has teamed up with Yamaha, Classic FM, Jazzwise, and PPL to award six jazz scholarships to young muscians who took their jazz direct to MPs in the Commons. Michael Connarty, the Labour MP for Linlithgow & East Falkirk, is co-Chair of the parliamentary group and Mrs Linda Riordan, the Labour MP for Halifax, is a supporter. Boni Sones asked them why

Anne McGuire MP

Anne McGuire, the Labour MP for Stirling and the Minister for Disabled People found time out from her ministerial duties to attend the launch of the Jessops Parliamentary photo competition. She was one of a number of MPs who had taken poignant pictures of people and places on their trips abroad. Anne's picture was called "Flowers for the lost: at Auschwitz Birkenau", which she visited with school children from her constituency. Boni Sones spoke to her as the exhibition was launched.

THIRTEEN

More Talking Points: When public discussion leads to political debate

This selection of topical reports covering our seven years of broadcasting could have been placed in any of the proceeding Chapters. What makes these reports stand out is that these interviews arose out of public discussion outside Westminster before being taken up as political challenges that needed to be confronted. It is more often than not the media itself that highlights an issue as being topical, and the splashes on the front or inside pages of the tabloids and broadsheets immediately give rise to public debate and concern about this so called "topical" issue. Alarm is raised in a certain policy area and politicians of all parties are "told" they must act. But what should or can be done? A famous case study in this area relates to what policy makers now call "dangerous dogs" legislation, where the Minister of the day wakes up to announce the government will do some new initiative because there is such a "hullaballo" in the media about the issue under discussion. John Major's Conservative government introduced the Dangerous Dogs Act 1991 that made it illegal to own certain dogs without them being muzzled or kept on a lead in public after a summer when aggressive dogs had seriously injured and even killed children. But the Act was criticised by some as being an "over reaction" to the public mood of the day driven by the media because it was so difficult to implement. In one BBC Radio 4 poll in 2007 it was included as one of the public's most unpopular pieces of UK legislation. In other cases the media may pick up on a topical issue because charities are pushing for change, and the way in which International Women's Day each year has gone from a fringe event to a mainstream one picked up by all papers across the spectrum shows how campaigning groups can make their particular issue topical by designating set times in the year and special events when issues are discussed. Politicians of all persuasions, Conservative, Labour, Liberal Democrat and Independents are then called into the radio and TV studios to give their parties policy position on the "proactive" issues under the spotlight. These yearly diary events now give rise to much public discussion on issues ranging from FGM, Cancer, Women and violence in other countries, and now men's public health concerns too such as prostate cancer. The Conservative MP Nadine Dorries, introduced a private member's Bill on Sex Education and abstinence in sex, Baroness Ann Jenkin, held a fund raising lunch in the Lords to highlight poverty around the World, while the campaign group, Million Women Rise put the issue of violence in the Congo firmly on the agenda, even though it was far removed from domestic political concerns. "Reactive" issues are also responded to with speed such as when the Labour former Minister, Hazel Blears, had much to say on the issue of communities and terrorism when recent troubles arose. Emma Bonino the Vice President of the Italian Senate, was able to fly into London to join an Iraq vigil, during one important 100 years of International Women's Day celebration. On a lighter note the Labour politician Emily Thornberry was able to highlight the long hours in Westminster after the popular Danish TV drama "Borgen" made the issue of women leaders topical again. The 24/7 fast rolling media news agenda now means comment is needed all day and all night, and as other countries address their parliaments gender balance the UK is increasingly being asked to do the same and to provide panel discussions that at least have "one woman" on them. Dame Anne Begg, the Vice-Chair of the Speaker's Conference which looked at how to get more women into Parliament, now says she regularly asks if there will be another women on the panel when she is requested to join in public debates and discussions. "Why are there so few women in Parliament still?" "Is positive discrimination needed?" "Why do women themselves not like positive measures?" Some might say: "When There's a Woman in the Room", women's issues get discussed. Who knows with more women in Parliament there might even be less "dangerous dog" legislation in the future, and more rounded public discussion on topical issues. Let's all hope so. With better public discussion in mind we asked the Times Columnist Ann Treneman to interview three women politicians on reform of the Commons. The interviews were witty and informative, and show the reforming zeal of women parliamentarians in all parties.

The year: 2012
Emily Thornberry MP: Tricky issue: A woman as Prime Minister - In Film and TV – but who will be next?

A look at the life of Margaret Thatcher with Meryl Streep in "The Iron Lady" and the Danish TV drama "Borgen" – are both giving the chattering classes something to think about in the corridors of power in 2012. Who will be the next woman Prime Minister in the UK? Labour's Yvette Cooper perhaps?

We put our thinking caps on and trod off along those corridors to interview Emily Thornberry the Labour MP for Islington South & Finsbury since 2005 to get her take on it all. Emily, a mother of three, has watched both, and says the real shock is seeing the mythical Danish Prime Minister Birgitte Nyborg (Sidse Babett Knudsen) go home to see her family so often. She also says that far from being just the "The Iron Lady" Margaret Thatcher could be disarmingly flirtatious with those who visited her, including trade union officials.

But behind the humour is a serious issue that never goes away in Westminster. The long hours, its impact on MPs and their families whether men or women, and the need for further reform. Emily tells us the newly honoured Dame Joan Ruddock, will be taking up the issue again soon. Congratulations Joan from all of us! You deserve that Honour. Thanks Emily for the interview.

Emily Hot Quote: "The hours need to change, the hours are mad, the hours make no sense at all. And hopefully the wonderful Dame Joan Ruddock will lead the charge and hopefully hours will finally come back to something which is in some passing way normal, at the moment they are crazy. All of us need some support."

Baroness Kramer of Richmond Park: Welfare Reforms – making the benefits go round but allowing the bonus culture to flourish?

The Coalition Government's Welfare Reform Bill returns to the Commons this week after it has suffered a number of defeats in the Lords. The defeated proposals include plans to charge lone parents to use the Child

Support Agency, changes to disabled benefits for young people and changes to benefits for cancer patients restricting them to one year only. The Bill also introduces a cap on benefits of about £26,000 a year, which is the income of an average family.

But is it "fair" that there should be cut backs in benefits at the same time as bankers, including The RBS Chief Executive, Stephen Hester, are drawing million pound bonus payments? Boni Sones, Executive Producer of www.parliamentaryradio.com for women trundled up the corridors of the Lords to put those questions to the LD peer Baroness Susan Kramer of Richmond Park.

Baroness Kramer Hot Quote: "The Welfare State is not being withdrawn from those who are most vulnerable. We are moving towards the universal credit, which I think is the most significant reform. I give incredible credit to Iain Duncan Smith, The Works and Pensions Minister, for driving that forward."

The year: 2011
Face to Face Encounters: Hazel Blears MP talks to the Political Editor of the People

Nigel Nelson

Hazel Blears, the Labour MP for Salford since 1997, who served as the Secretary of State for Communities and Local Government and Minister of State for Policing and Counter Terrorism has a lot to say on the new Coalition government's "Prevent" strategy to combat terrorism.

It was launched in 2007, when Hazel was a Minister, to stop people becoming terrorists or supporting terrorism. Almost £80 million was spent on 1,000 Prevent schemes, in the battle against Al-Qaeda. But it was dogged with controversy and allegations money went to the wrong groups. So what does Hazel think of the new Coalition government's "re-focused" Prevent strategy? Nigel Nelson the Political Editor of the People asked her in this special wpradio.co.uk "Face to Face Encounters" interview. Read Nigel's blog: www.blogs.people.co.uk/nigel-nelson.

Ann Treneman and Gisela Stuart MP "Face to Face"
Women's Parliamentary Radio hears from The Times sketch writer Ann Treneman in the third of her special "Face to Face Encounters" series on reform of Parliament. This week Ann talks to Gisela Stuart the Labour MP for Birmingham Edgbaston since 1997 and Editor of the House Magazine.

Gisela Hot Quote: "The biggest change I have witnessed in Parliament is that it is no longer unusual to see a woman on either side of the Benches and the age profile has also improved but not the social profile, we need to reach out to people in the real world who have done a real job rather than those who have been special advisors."

Penny Mordaunt MP and her "Special Educational Needs Bill"
Penny Mordaunt the Conservative MP for Portsmouth North has introduced a Private Member's Bill on "Special Educational Needs" provision. Penny wants the money to follow the pupil and even though such Bills rarely become law, her Bill is already attracting the attention of Government Ministers and may be taken up as an issue by them in the future eventually leading to change. Penny talks to Boni Sones our Executive Producer.

Penny Hot Quote: "Provision is one thing, my Bill isn't addressing: Should there be more special needs schools? What we need to do is to increase the power parents have and enshrine in law that their children should have access to the best education to help them for their particular needs."

The story of Queen Mothers in Ashantiland, Ghana – Dilys Kyeiwaa Winterkorn
The role of women in the Arab Spring uprisings and now in Bahrain is highlighting the different cultural values placed on the role of women in today's "global village society". In one African Country, Ghana, Queen Mothers have traditional had a powerful "feminist" role to play in

organising their communities and providing a safety network within them. On issues such as politics, agriculture and education the women speak up and get their voices heard, all thanks to a "golden stool", and a Queen Mother called Yaa Asantewaa the Great. Dilys Kyeiwaa Winterkorn will tell you more. She spoke to Boni Sones.

What are they banging on about? Women MPs putting policy issues on the agenda.

Nadine Dorries Conservative MP for Mid-Beds talks to us about her "Sex Education" Ten Minute Rule Bill to encourage abstinence in sex through incorporating it into sex education in schools.

Rachel Reeves Labour MP for Leeds West tells us about the "Hands Off our pensions" campaign for women who are being affected by public sector cut-backs, particularly some 57-year-old women.

Could you cook a lunch for just 33p? Eating for £1 a day to relieve world poverty.

Baroness Anne Jenkin of Kennington, has a reputation for her work fundraising for charities. It is not surprising then that within weeks of putting on her "Red Robes and Ermine" she could be found in a small kitchen along a corridor several flights of stairs up in the Lords cooking a lunch for her fellow Peers and supporters that cost just 33p.

Baroness Jenkin, was taking up the challenge put down by the "Below the Line" charities fighting poverty around the World: RESULTS UK, Christian Aid, Think Global, Restless Development, and Salvation Army (International Development), to live off just £1 a day for food and drink. 1.4 billion people have no choice but to live their lives below the poverty line.

Anne's "good housekeeping" 33p a day "soup kitchen" in the Lords managed to provide not just a filling soup, but pitta bread, cheese and tomatoes to her "hungry" colleagues too. Baroness Jenkin was joined by Baroness Trish Morris, Baroness Judith Jolly, helper Dorothy Tyson, and four younger supporters Guy Kirkpatrick, Matti Navellou, Ashli Alberty, and Kathryn Llewellyn. Our intrepid www.wpradio.co.uk reporter Linda

Fairbrother went to join them and taste the soup but first she began to smell it as she found her way to that kitchen.

And here is Anne's Soup recipe: Feeds 10 for just over a £1.

> *1 kg frozen veg 65p (Tesco)*
> *Two stock cubes 2p (10 for 10p Tesco)*
> *10gm Lentils 10p*
> *Can baked beans 25p*
> *Half enormous potato 12p (market)*
> *Onion 10p (market)*
>
> *Cook it up and mash with potato masher.*

Anne Hot Quote: "The £ a day is the World Bank's definition of the poverty line, and it is quite a challenge for us but much more of a challenge for those who have to really do it. You spend so much time putting things in and out of your shopping basket and working it out down to the last penny."

The Million Women Rise coalition report on violence in the Congo.
The Million Women Rise coalition went to Westminster recently to present their findings of their recent trip to the Democratic Republic of Congo. There will be Presidential elections in the Congo at the end of this year, and their report on their trip "Congo: The road to Mwenga", which has five tough recommendations, will be presented to Parliament soon by the Chair of that meeting, Jeremy Corbyn MP, Vice Chair of the All-Party Human Rights Group (APPG).

The trip was part of the Third International Action of the World March of Women that involved women from 48 countries. The Million Women Rise coalition report and film of the trip aims to address the realities of sexual and gender-based violence for Congolese women as well as strategies for ensuring that those who commit them are brought to justice. Our Executive Producer, Boni Sones spoke to the speakers and audience. *Fact file:* **"The UK government effectively monitors and evaluates the impact of UK tax** payers' contribution of 1 million dollars a day spent in the DR Congo. But it "does not reach women who have been raped or improve prospects for the future". To sign a petition on the Congo, to be sent to Equalities Minister and International Violence Against Women champion, Lynne Featherstone MP – see http://www.congonow.org.

Jeremy Corbyn Hot Quote: "The rape of women in the Congo is the worst in the World, the largest number of people who have been killed in any conflict since the First World War is in the Congo. This is a catastrophe that has been going on for a very long time and the World needs to know about it."

Ann McKechin MP for Glasgow North and Shadow Secretary of State for Scotland

Ann McKechin has been an MP since June 2001 and the MP for the newly configured constituency of Glasgow North since 2005. She was Scottish Office Minister in the last Labour government and is now the Shadow Secretary of State for Scotland. Ann previously served on the Scottish Affairs Committee and then as a member of the International Development Committee and was Chair of the All-Party Group on Debt, Aid and Trade and Chair of the backbench group of Scottish Labour MPs.

Our intrepid www.wpradio.co.uk reporter Linda Fairbrother spoke to her about how she managed to work as a Westminster MP, with the Holyrood MP, the Regional representatives and the Euro MP. How does "devolved" government work for the people who vote for her?

And what a "swell" party it was – Speaker's House and International Women's Day

On 2nd April 1911 a lone suffragette, Emily Wilding Davison hid herself in the broom cupboard in the Chapel of St Mary Undercroft, in the crypt of St Stephen's Hall, Westminster, on the night of the census so that she could give her address as the House of Commons.

100 years later there was no need to hide. The Speaker John Bercow opened the doors of his State Rooms to the women MPs from all parties

with their friends and special guests from campaigning organisations to mark the Centenary of International Women's Day. Emily who died after pinning a sash to the King's horse at the Epsom races would have been wide-eyed at being allowed into the State Rooms, Speaker's House, House of Commons. The 16th March party was organised by three women MPs Mary Macleod MP, Kate Green MP and Jo Swinson MP from Conservative, Labour and the Liberal Democrats. If walls could have ears? No need – Women's Parliamentary Radio journalists Linda Fairbrother and Boni Sones captured this sound portrait for you in this special three part documentary "**A Message to Emily?**"

In Part One Boni spoke to: Caroline Adams from the women's Parliamentary Labour Party and organiser, Barbara Gorna and Joan Lane, film producer. Vicky Booth, Diversity Officer for the Liberal Democrats, Fiona Mactaggart MP and Lydia Simmons. Barbara Keeley MP, Fawcett acting CEO Anna Bird, Sharon Hodgson MP, Sue Tibballs of the Women's Sports Foundation. Joan Ruddock MP and Councillor Joan Millbank. Maria Eagle MP and Yvette Cooper MP.

In Part Two Boni spoke to: Baroness Elspeth Howe, Baroness Hussein-Ece. Cherie Blair and Sarina Russo. Lorley Burt MP and Helen Berresford, Kealey Hastick from Platform 51. Helen Grant MP and Martha Kearney BBC journalist. Harriet Harman MP, The speaker John Bercow MP and last but not least the most senior woman in the Cabinet, the Home Secretary and Minister for Women Theresa May MP.

In Part Three Linda spoke to: Nan Sloane from the Centre for Women and Democracy, Margaret Beckett MP, Baroness Ramsay, Kate Green MP, Lesley Abdela from Shevolution. John Bercow MP, Caroline Spelman MP, and Lee Chalmers of the Downing Street Project, Liberal Democrat supporter Dinti Batstone, Jo Swinson MP.

John Bercow Hot Quote: "International Women's Day reminds us that we have a duty in whatever our capacity to do something to make a difference for women internationally. These rooms are State Rooms and what better use than to use them to fight the cause for women and equality. We congratulate the trail blazers but there is still a great deal to do and we must get on to do it!"

Theresa May Hot Quote: "I think we have made some very important steps. We are great supporters of the new UN Agency for Women, and we are looking for that agency to be able to promote the needs of women across the World. My message to Emily would be we are not complacent and we are still fighting."

"Face to Face Encounters": Times sketch writer Ann Treneman talks to Natascha Engel MP who is Chair of the new Backbench Business Committee

So what are those "usual channels" that govern the House of Commons? Ann Treneman, sketch writer of the Times, talks to Natascha Engel MP who chairs the new Backbench Business Committee which was set up on the 15th June 2010.

This is the first Business Committee of any kind to be established by the House. Ann Treneman, who watches and reports on the debates in the Chamber from the lofty heights of the "Lobby", is more qualified than most to comment on whether or not it is helping to modernise the Commons and transfer power to the ordinary backbench MPs. Strangely in her "Face to Face Encounters" series Ann agrees that these debates are: "less yarboo and me you"!

Natascha Hot Quote: "People used to talk about the dark forces of the whips offices, and that really has changed. The Backbench Business Committee has made a massive difference to how we work in Parliament. People have to take responsibility for what is being debated and there are no whips to ask anymore and that really has made a big difference."

International Women's Day 2011 – two women MPs campaigning with women MPs across-party for women's rights!

Rachel Reeves MP – "Hands Off our pensions!"

Rachel Reeves MP, the Shadow Minister for Pensions for the Labour Party, is calling on the coalition Conservative Liberal Democrat government to reverse the changes it has announced to delay the pension age for women by two years, in some cases.

The MP for Leeds West, tells Women's Parliamentary Radio, www.wpradio.co.uk that it's about time the Women's Minister, Theresa May MP and the Equalities Minister, Lynne Featherstone MP, stood up for women and called on the Government to announce a "U" turn on this issue as it has done recently on selling off forest lands. She talked to Boni Sones, our Executive Producer.

Rachel Hot Quote: "We have united the Trade Unions, Saga, Age UK and the Daily Mail saying the Government should reverse these changes and I hope the Government, like on forests, will think again because these changes are not fair or proportionate and they will pay the price at the ballot box for this one!"

Fiona Mactaggart MP – why women here and in the Congo need a "Women and Equalities Audit Committee"!

Fiona Mactaggart MP tells Boni Sones OBE our Executive Producer why she will be calling on government ministers to set up a "Women and Equalities Audit Committee" in the International Women's Day Debate in the Commons on March 10th. Fiona the Labour MP for Slough and Shadow Spokeswoman on Women will use the debate to call for the Government to be made accountable on all women's issue through the mechanism of a new Committee. The Committee would audit Government Departments on how they are treating women across the board on issues such as pensions to those such as rape in the Congo and the human rights of women in Afghanistan. Go for it Fiona!

Fiona Hot Quote: "We need to tackle the issue of women's voice, and representation of women and one of the things we don't do well enough in Parliament is to make sure that the Government is held to account on the issues of women and equalities. I have tabled an amendment to make sure we do that, to suggest that we create a "Women and Equalities Audit Committee" so that we can quiz any government department about the impact of their policies on women."

Infant Early Attachment and The Big Society: Andrea Leadsom MP talks to Linda Fairbrother

One in ten mums suffer from post-natal depression. Now Andrea Leadsom the Conservative MP for South Northamptonshire is taking an issue close to her heart to launch a Northampton charitable venture, with patrons, donors and volunteers to provide perinatal mental health care for mothers and their babies. Andrea had a 25 year career in banking and finance, and was a Trustee and Chairman of the children's charity OXPIP (the Oxford Parent-Infant Project), which offers intensive therapeutic help to parents and their babies in the first two years of life.

Andrea, who suffered from post-natal depression herself, believes that many of the problems our society faces can be traced back to poor early attachment. She's already held a Westminster Hall Debate on Early Attachment and says her campaign to mainstream this issue into social policy has cross-party support. Andrea thinks that if her Big Society launch of the new Northamptonshire project is a success it could be a template to "role out" across Britain. She's not contemplating failure despite the public sector cut-backs!

Andrea Hot Quote: "Early infant attachment really is my passion. In 2001 I had two children and was quite depressed after having had my first child. I had worked in a senior role in banking and was experiencing this radical change but I had a supportive family and health visitor and I went back to work and that snapped me out of it."

More Talking Points

Linda Fairbrother meets: "The movers and shakers" – Baroness Shreela Flather, "Woman: Acceptable exploitation for Profit".
Baroness Shreela Flather, the first Asian woman to receive a peerage, and known for wearing a sari, says her book *Woman: Acceptable exploitation for Profit* is meant to "tread" on a few toes by tackling the great taboo of children working for a living and the role of women in India and Africa.

Baroness Flather says the United National Millennium Development Goals will not be met by the target date of 2015 and that only by shifting the focus to women themselves and enabling them through small business, technology and income generation can real progress be made. Family planning and education are key to harnessing their talents. Our www.wpradio.co.uk reporter Linda Fairbrother spoke to her.

Ann Treneman "Face to Face Encounters" series.
Ann Treneman, sketch writer of The Times starts off our new "Face to Face Encounters" series of interviews talking with Caroline Lucas, MP for Brighton Pavilion and Leader of the Green Party on her proposals for the reform of Parliament.

Caroline's report "The Case for Parliamentary Reform" has just been debated in Westminster Hall. It includes measures for "electronic voting", changing "the parliamentary language", ending the "talking out" of Private Members Bills, and publication of the "Speakers' List" so MPs know when they are going to be called to talk in the Chamber. Caroline, an MEP for ten years, estimates that just queuing up to vote accounts for around £30,000 a week in MPs' salary costs, and 250 hours of their time each Parliamentary year. Here Ann – renowned for her portrayals of Westminster as a series of "playground spats" between "bickering children" – finds out if Caroline is a modern day "Mary Poppins" and destined to fail?

Caroline Hot Quote: "The culture is an old boy's club, that is the feel of it. One of the reasons I hold out some hope – because I do appreciate others have tried to reform Westminster – is that there are a lot of new MPs from professional backgrounds who are still reeling in shock about how this place works. I hope these voices get heard, because there really is quite a groundswell for saying there are things we could do, fairly simply, to make this place operate more efficiently."

Emma Bonino – Vice President of the Italian Senate – Iraq Vigil and 100 years of International Women's Day

Emma Bonino, Vice President of the Italian Senate, and a Radical Party member, flew into London to join an all night vigil against the Iraq war, while Tony Blair was giving evidence to the Iraq inquiry. She is known for her work on human and civil rights issues, such as "against hunger in the world" and for her campaigns for women's rights including campaigning against female genital mutilation. She is also a founding member of "No Peace without Justice", supporting the creation of the International Criminal Court. She has received several international awards, including the "2004 Open Society Prize" for her outstanding achievements as a female world leader. Here in this Exclusive interview she tells Boni Sones OBE, Executive Producer of www.wpradio.co.uk why she joined the vigil and why she will be "passionately" supporting 100 years of International Women's day in March 2011!

Emma Hot Quote: "I strongly believe that in many parts of the World, the women are the element for change so I think continuing to be interested in women is not diminishing in a political career I think it is a fantastic tool – I cannot avoid it I am so interested and so passionate. Women's rights can make a better World."

In 2011 www.wpradio.co.uk goes global! Join us on the Bridge.

Our www.wpradio.co.uk reporter Linda Fairbrother started off the New Year by looking at the work of "Women for Women International". She spoke to Director of Policy Britta Schmidt about the role of women in Afghanistan.

Executive Director Kate Nustedt then told Linda about their "Join Me on the Bridge" campaign linked to the 100th anniversary of International Women's Day 8th March 2011. All women MPs and men are being invited to join them. Do listen.

Our Reviews of the political year

Linda Fairbrother asks the Times columnist Ann Treneman to review the political year. Her book *"Annus Horribilis": The Worst Year in British Politics* – is available on Amazon.co.uk. – Here she tells us how she rates the women politicians in the Chamber in 2010 and says she's got a soft spot for Theresa May MP, the Home Secretary but she gives Harriet Harman full marks too! However, Ann can't quite remember who the Lib Dem women are. Oh dear...

The year: 2010
2010 Voting Reform and More Women in Westminster

MPs will vote on the government's plans for a referendum on AV the first day back after their summer break. Critics say our "First-Past-The-Post" voting system lets down female candidates because of the advantages it hands to incumbents. In the UK just one in five of our MPs is female. So will the new AV ("alternative vote") system be any better?

Our Executive Producer Boni Sones, asked three women MPs if changing the voting system would help further women's representation. Here Jo Swinson LD MP East Dunbartonshire, Angela Eagle Labour MP for Wallasey, and Margot James Conservative MP for Stourbridge give you their verdict.

AV allows voters to rank candidates in their constituency in order of preference. Anyone getting more than 50% of first-choice votes in the first round is elected, otherwise the candidate with the fewest votes is eliminated and their backers' second choices allocated to those remaining. This process continues until a winner emerges.

Angela Hot Quote: "It is a red herring to say any particular voting system is better than any other voting system for getting more women selected and elected. There are mechanisms in any system whatever the way that you vote for getting women selected in safer or winnable seats and then ensuring that they are elected. The Labour Party fought for All-women shortlists in safe seats and we had 101 women elected in the landslide victory of 1997, you have to be determined to do it."

Appendices

Our important web links

Our Wikipedia entry tells our history
http://en.wikipedia.org/wiki/Women's_Parliamentary_Radio

The book *Women in Parliament: The New Suffragettes*, by Boni Sones with Professor Joni Lovenduski and Margaret Moran MP captures some similar stories as told by the Blair's Babes and others across Party, 83 women MPs in all.

http://www.amazon.co.uk/Women-Parliament-The-New-Suffragettes/dp/1842751409

The Harman Shephard audio Archive of the 82 interviews from this book can be found at the British Library (It took six years to get permission for all the interviews to be deposited!)

http://museumpublicity.com/2010/09/07/audio-archive-charting-modern-women-mps-opens-at-the-british-library/

It is listed at the British Library here (permission needed to access).

http://cadensa.bl.uk/uhtbin/cgisirsi/x/0/0/5?searchdata1=CKEY7012165&library=ALL

The link to our photographs of women MPs party by party to celebrate 90 years of women and the vote in 2008 – http://www.wpradio.co.uk/photos.php

The audio Archive of all our 350 interviews in the UK Parliament, Africa, Asia and Europe since can be found at the London School of Economics. http://blogs.lse.ac.uk/library/2012/05/28/the-boni-sones-archive/

Previous press articles revealing sexism in the Commons
Media commentator Roy Greenslade's apology to women MPs http://www.theguardian.com/media/2005/aug/29/mondaymediasection

Boni's supporting Guardian article with quotes from women MPs
http://www.theguardian.com/media/2005/aug/29/mondaymediasection3

Jackie Ashley's first article about sexism and women MPs
http://www.theguardian.com/politics/2004/dec/07/uk.gender

The Actual listings for our Archive at LSE and BL Content 20 May 28th 2012 – The Boni Sones Archive by Ellie Robinson – London School of Economics

Some exciting things have been afoot with our digital archives lately. We've just agreed to dispatch some of our oldest physical media (e.g. 5 ¼" floppy) to a company in Cheshire to see if they can extract the data for us, and I'm really excited to see what they can come up with. I've been playing around with some 3 ½" floppies from our collections, and am thrilled to have successfully imaged some disks from our Campbell Transcripts collection, and viewed and migrated the WordPerfect files therein.

Our newest accession of digital archives is the Boni Sones archive, donated to us by Boni earlier this month. The collection is the result of Boni's ambitious Women's Parliamentary Radio project, where British and international female Members of Parliament were interviewed about women's issues and the resulting audio files hosted online. This was quite an undertaking, both in an engineering and organisational sense. As Boni writes,

"My sound engineer Peter Cook, who worked with me at Cambridge University, saw "the future" too and together we created what became www.wpradio.co.uk, helped by the web management company Magstar of Cambridge. We were all innovators ahead of our time. I always saw that you could do interviews "as live" rather than "live" streaming, allowing the audience to tune in when they wanted to listen. This was ahead of what others were doing technically and in broadcasting conventions too.

"We had tremendous and heartfelt support from women in the Cabinet and Shadow Cabinets such as Theresa May, Caroline Spelman and Eleanor

Laing for the Conservative women, and Harriet Harman, Vera Baird, and Barbara Keeley for the Labour women, and for the Liberal Democrats Sandra Gidley, Jo Swinson and Susan Kramer were great supporters of us. Their unconditional support has lasted to this very day. We thank them so much."

Also supporting the project were Jackie Ashley, Linda Fairbrother and Deborah McGurran, quite a collaboration! The collection is of extreme significance, both for its comprehensive and candid representation of women in Parliament and their thoughts on women's rights and issues, but also as an indicator of how journalistic practices are changing with new technology. As such it makes a very welcome addition to our collections, sitting very nicely amongst some of other collections such as our Mary McIntosh, Baroness Summerskill and Baroness Seear collections.

Boni has deposited with us the sound files (WAV and mp3) of the interviews, as well as associated administrative files, and four group MPs photographs, party by party, taken by PA photographer Kieran Doherty (who did the now famous "Blair's Babes" photograph) to celebrate 90 years of women and the Vote in 2008. The four photographs are called: "The Day the Carlton Club Accepted Women", as the Conservative MP Caroline Spelman noted that the day the photographs were taken was the day the Carlton Club let in women, by coincidence! The collection will be available to researchers in our reading room in the new year.

Harman-Shephard collection of interviews with women Members of Parliament at the BL

LIST RECORDINGS: C1182
Collection title: Harman-Shephard collection of interviews with women Members of Parliament
Collection inventory: 94 mini-discs, 1CD-R
Collection description: Interviews with 83 female and 3 male Members of Parliament, most of whom entered the House of Commons at the 1997 general election (Labour 61 women, 1 man; Conservative 12 women, 1 man; Liberal

Democrat 7 women, 1 man; Ulster Unionist 1 woman). The interviews were conducted by Boni Sones, Deborah McGurran, Eva Simmons, Linda Fairbrother and Angela Lawrence as part of the research for the book 'Women in Parliament : the new Suffragettes' by Boni Sones, with Margaret Moran and Joni Lovenduski, London, 2005, and for the BBC Radio 4 broadcast 'A monstrous regiment', 10 Sept. 2005. Interviews were conducted on the basis of a list of standard questions (seen by interviewees beforehand), with further ad hoc discussion in certain cases. Also included is a CD-R recording of the BBC broadcast 'A monstrous regiment'.

Documentation: correspondence with donor, documents on conduct of the project
Product copyright: BL (content copyright); recording copyright retained by donor
Access restrictions: Private research only. For publication or broadcasting of this material refer to curator.
Copy note: Playback CD-R dubbings of mini-discs also s upplied with the donation.
Acquisition date: 2005-08-20

Press Release: Audio Archive Charting Modern Women MP's Opens at the British Library
Submitted by Editor on September 7, 2010 – 3:34 pm

An audio archive charting modern women MP's representation in Westminster opened to the public on 6 September 2010 at the British Library.

In the 82 interviews, women MPs from across all political parties were asked what they thought of changes in the sitting hours of the Commons, all-women short-lists, the Suffragettes, how poorly the media treated them (commenting on their clothes and hair styles) and what they thought of being called 'Blair's Babes'. The archive, totalling 100 hours, allows many women MPs to tell their own story and set the record straight.

Charting the stories of women MPs, most of whom entered the House of Commons at the 1997 general election, the interviews were conducted a year before the 2005 general election. This was a sensitive time for all MPs, whatever party they were in, when Labour was suffering from the consequences of the Iraq war, struggling with contentious issues such as tuition fees and didn't know if it could secure a third-term in government.

The interviews – accessible at the British Library for the first time – were conducted by five senior broadcast journalists (Linda Fairbrother, Angela Lawrence, Deborah McGurran, Dr Eva Simmons and Boni Sones OBE) between May and October 2004, as part of the research for the Orwell Prize nominated book, *Women in Westminster: The New Suffragettes* (published in September 2005 by Boni Sones OBE with Professor Joni Lovenduski and Margaret Moran MP).

Dr Rob Perks, Lead Curator of Oral History at the British Library, commented:

"This archive charts the experiences of women MPs from both sides of the House and is an important corrective to the predominantly male narratives we have of the political process. The 1997 intake of 120 women MPs was the largest ever and this important collection of interviews, now available at the British Library, documents this new political generation in their own words."

Boni Sones OBE, who donated the archive to the British Library, said: "I am extremely grateful to the British Library for finding a home for this important audio archive and to the women MPs themselves across party who signed the permission forms to allow access to their audio to chart women's modern representation in the Commons."

"We discovered that some of the Conservative Party's male MPs in the mid-1980s still called all women 'Betty' and some made gestures across the Chamber that demoralised the Labour women of 1997, but there were heartening stories too. Both Harriet Harman MP and Gillian Shephard warmly greeted other women MPs even if they weren't from the same party. This archive is therefore named after both of them."

The British Library Sound Archive (www.bl.uk/soundarchive) is one of the largest sound archives in the world. It holds over a million discs, 200,000 tapes, and many other sound and video recordings. The collections come from all over the world and cover the entire range of recorded sound from music, drama and literature, to oral history and wildlife sounds. Collection material comes in every conceivable format, from wax cylinder and wire recordings to CD and DVD, and from a wide variety of private, commercial and broadcast sources.

The British Library is the national library of the United Kingdom and one of the world's greatest research libraries. It provides world class information services to the academic, business, research and scientific communities and offers unparalleled access to the world's largest and most comprehensive research collection. The Library's collection has developed over 250 years and exceeds 150 million separate items representing every age of written civilisation. It includes: books, journals, manuscripts, maps, stamps, music, patents, newspapers and sound recordings in all written and spoken languages. www.bl.uk

Previous press articles in full
Comment: Why equality is still out of reach
Roy Greenslade The Guardian, Monday 29 August 2005

I am a man in his late 50s who has lived through the most profound change in the status of women in British society. The lot of women has improved immeasurably when compared with the interwar generation into which my mother was born.

I have been both an eyewitness to and, in an admittedly passive way, a participant in, what should rightly be regarded as a revolution. Women have not yet achieved equality with men, but they have made terrific advances. Men, on the other hand, have been required to relinquish their grip on power, also a profound change in their status.

But, as with all revolutions, it has usually been a case of women taking two steps forward and often being forced to take one backwards. So women have continually needed to apply pressure to ensure that they do not lose their impetus. Men, even some of those who claim to be sympathetic to the women's cause, have tended to misread this pressure as somehow threatening.

Inevitably, it has been newspapers that have provided the arena for debate while also trying to set the agenda. In various ways they have been both progressive and reactionary, often both at the same time. For example, look back to the Sun's output in the early 70s: while encouraging women to be sexually liberated it also portrayed them as sexual playthings for men. There is a similar ambivalence in much of the Daily Mail's supposedly pro-female content.

This situation is obvious to women MPs who form a political vanguard in the gender struggle. What they say and do – not to mention how they look and dress – appears regularly in the press, and they are acutely aware of the different ways in which they are treated, sometimes subtle, sometimes blatant, from their male colleagues in Westminster.

There is more attention paid to their clothing. Ann Widdecombe's remark about Ken Clarke's Hush Puppies entirely misses the point: those mentions are viewed, by both journalists and their audiences, as a humorous aside about a mild eccentricity, not as a contribution to a stereotype. Articles that highlight Theresa May's shoes, Patricia Hewitt's jacket or New Labour women in "synthetic fibres" do the opposite because they imply that the wearer is somehow as trivial as their dress – or even as trivial as the nature of the article itself – and thus reinforce deep-seated prejudices about women lacking sufficient seriousness.

And to show that I'm no goody two-shoes, here is a mea culpa. Last year I wrote an article about Hewitt in which I referred to her former penchant for wearing dungarees which, fortunately, my (male) editor was savvy enough to remove before it went to print. But I don't think I would have included the same comment if she had been a bloke, and it is a sharp reminder that all of us in mid-revolution are subject to unconscious conditioning. Even so, it does help if we strive to mend our ways.

Despite endless complaints about the way women are represented in the media, there are still regular references to them as mothers, wives or grandmothers. Why, in articles which have nothing to do with their role as mothers, do papers so often refer to the number of children that women MPs have? It would never occur to journalists to write the same about MPs who are fathers.

The last election saw a record number of women elected to the Commons – 128 – 10 more than in the previous poll. Running in parallel with the growing number of women politicians has been the advancement of women in the media: there are four female editors of national papers and many, many more senior women executives than when I started in journalism in the 60s.

But I can't deny that the cultures of both politics and journalism remain male-oriented. It is often difficult to define just how this continuing domination operates and therefore, for both the men and women who exist within those cultures, it is tough to devise a strategy to effect change.

Changes have been made though, and more will surely occur as women learn how to overcome the subtle forms of control men, usually unconsciously, continue to exercise.

Confronting how women are portrayed in the media is one sensible way of raising awareness.

It is sobering to realise that the suffragettes' original demand was simply to have the vote. Some saw that as the end in itself, others as the first step on a long road towards genuine equality. Modern women MPs are still travelling down that road and are right to complain that their feet are sore.

Belittled women
The late Mo Mowlam found some press coverage painful and unfair. Many women MPs feel the same, as a new book and BBC Radio 4 programme reveal. By Boni Sones, The Guardian, Monday 29 August 2005

Are the media fair to women politicians? Or do they use stereotypes to describe both their rise and their fall as they climb the slippery pole to power? Do they focus too much on their appearance, their hair, their shoes, the colour of their dress, their low-pitched voices, at the expense of their achievements? The recent death of Mo Mowlam has reignited this debate. Like many other female politicians she found press coverage of her painful and unfair.

I too became tired of jaded media coverage of women MPs and their achievements, so two years ago I set out to interview the 135 women elected to parliament since 1997. I chose the year deliberately, for there was one act that defined the 101 women elected on a Labour ticket in 1997 more than any other. It lives to haunt them today.

On May 7 that year, Tony Blair lined up on the steps of Church House with all but two of Labour's women MPs for a photograph. (Clare Short and Kate Hoey did not take part.) The Mirror had first used the catchphrase "Blair's Babes" a month earlier when it pictured a group of models who had expressed the intention of voting Labour. When on May 8, the Mirror ran the picture of Blair and the new Labour women, its headline read: "Blair's Babes (Sorry ... we mean Labour's brilliant 101 women MPs)".

It is clear now that while some women MPs still object to the "Blair's babes" title, many do not. It probably had more significance for those under the age of 50 than those over. Some think that to be called a Blair Babe is a compliment, and Anne Begg believed that the alliteration could have been worse: "It could have been 'Tony's Tarts'." But others, such as Harriet Harman, felt it "demeaned" them all. To correct that impression, Fiona Mactaggart wrote a Fabian Society paper on Labour women's achievements in 2000.

In the end, a small team of us managed to interview 83 serving and former MPs of all political parties, between May and October last year. The interviews have been placed in the British Library and some will be aired in a BBC Radio 4 programme presented by Jackie Ashley, of the Guardian, next month. Linda Fairbrother and I met Mowlam at her farmhouse in Kent in July last year. It was the last interview that she gave.

We talked to her for 90 minutes during which she was alert and quick-witted. Significantly she deviated from several of the opinions she expressed in her autobiography, *Momentum: The Struggle for Peace, Politics and the People*, most notably on No10 and Tony Blair. She seemed more generous and more circumspect about her career in politics. But the depth of the pain she felt about the spin against her was still evident, a pain many other women politicians share, as our interviews show.

Mo Mowlam Labour, Redcar 1987 – 2001
People played on my ill health, making a story out of it ... I was angry at what they were doing; I was angry that Blair didn't speak out, although he did tell me when I spoke to him about it that he didn't mind me getting

a standing ovation at the party conference, it didn't bother him, and that he didn't know who was doing all this [spin] ... and it was outrageous. So, I didn't like it, but you learn the hard way in politics that you can't – if you react against gossip and threats, all it does is get them covered in more papers in bigger letters, and I wasn't interested in doing that. I wanted to minimise the pain.

I think they used that [being a woman] against me, but it was about power. That I was a woman was secondary, I think. That I was a popular woman was the problem; they didn't quite know how to handle that.

Vera Baird Labour, Redcar Elected 2001
The most notable thing is the incapacity of the media, particularly the red tops, to contemplate a woman who is a complex character. She has to be either a mother, or a hard-nosed career girl, or a tart, or a failure, or an emotional mess. You know, she cannot be as complex as men are.

Tessa Jowell Labour, Dulwich and West Norwood Elected 1992
There are very particular journalists and particular commentators that are absolutely vile about women. I mean, they are misogynist, and I think that you have just got to discount them, and you have to grow a thick skin, not read their stuff. And support friends and colleagues when they feel undermined and hurt by what they write. More generally I think that the tension between Westminster politicians and the media is an occupational hazard.

Angela Eagle Labour, Wallasey Elected 1992
They're nasty to every woman who's ever said anything in the chamber, and, in fact yes, I have been treated to some pretty rancid coverage by those sorts of people. I mean, there was when I came out [as gay], yes, but I expected that. So yes, there has been a bit, and it's nasty when it happens and it's nasty for friends and family as well.

Barbara Follett Labour, Stevenage Elected 1997
I remember the Daily Mail or Mail on Sunday going to South Africa and

going to my 85-year-old ex-mother-in-law, pretending they were going to interview her about her son who was shot dead in South Africa – my husband. So she was really pleased because she always wanted publicity for him. And she said, laughingly, "Oh, Barbara, she was a bit of a man-eater when she was young." She was 85 and they spread that right across the front of the banner headline when I was getting elected in Stevenage. Fortunately, people don't read the Daily Mail in Stevenage, they read the Evening Standard!

Jackie Ballard Liberal Democrat, Taunton 1997 – 2001

My daughter, who's now 25, but when I got into parliament she was 18, was incredibly upset and hurt by some of the things that she read, and she was in some ways quite glad when I lost my seat. I mean, in general she'd have preferred me to win, but there were some reasons why she wasn't sorry about it.

Theresa May Conservative, Maidenhead Elected 1997

I would argue that I tend to do politics differently from a lot of the men, and that's partly about not taking a "ya-boo" approach, it's about not thinking that when you're in the chamber, you're only there to deliver killer blows, whereas from the media point of view, if you do not deliver a killer punch or a killer blow then "you're not up to it dear" and I think that's where there needs to be a different understanding of what the job is actually about.

I don't mind about the shoes, I like buying shoes, I love shoes, so I'm quite happy on the shoe front. I wasn't so happy at being described as an old crone the other day by somebody in the media. Yes, it's frustrating to the extent that there tends to be talk about what you look like, how you dress, rather than what you're saying; and obviously that happens more for the women than it does for the men, so there's a frustration there.

Caroline Spelman Conservative, Meriden Elected 1997

Well, it infuriates me, and I think that there are enough female journalists actually in the lobby as well, who if they wanted to do their sisterhood in politics a good turn would stop writing up all the trivia. I always remember, almost within my first month or so, Patricia Hewitt was given an incredibly hard time in a parliamentary sketch about some multicoloured jacket she was wearing.

Sandra Gidley Liberal Democrat, Romsey Elected 2000

When I first came here, I listened to the women Labour MPs, and I heard them say: "Does the Prime Minister agree that the sun shines out of his bottom, or whatever?" – and it sounded dreadful, and I thought, "Yes, the media's right". When I'd been here a little longer, I listened to what the men were saying. They were asking exactly the same question, but the trick is, because they ask it in a deeper voice, and they stand there being the parliamentarian, it doesn't sound quite so sucky really, and that hasn't got across; it's something to do with the voice.

Ann Widdecombe Conservative, Maidstone and The Weald Elected 1987

People say that they've commented on my looks, which they have, ad nauseam. But on the other hand they have commented on William Hague's bald head, Ken Clarke's Hush Puppies, there's always something to be commented on. Though I think if one were to be absolutely objective about it, I have probably had a lot more comment about my circumference than John Prescott has had about his circumference. So I mean there may be a slight dual standard, but what is that except a reflection of the importance that women attach to their looks.

Baroness Shephard Conservative, South West Norfolk 1987 – 2005

There was an article in the Times by Jane Shilling – I shall never forget it – there was a picture of the New Labour women, and Shilling wrote: "Isn't it awful, they're wearing synthetic fibres and strangely coloured shoes, and somebody should have done this and done that ..." I thought: "How can you so miss the point? And how can you so trivialise all this? ... And I was so moved, I faxed to the Times a letter, and the Times said, "Who are you?" They didn't publish it because they said they didn't believe that I was myself!

© Boni Sones and Politico's. The Archive Hour programme is on Radio 4 on September 10 at 8pm. Interviews by Boni Sones, Linda Fairbrother, Angela Lawrence, Deborah McGurran and Eva Simmons. Women In Parliament: The New Suffragettes, by Boni Sones, with Margaret Moran MP and Professor Joni Lovenduski, is published by Politico's in October.

Bullied, patronised and abused - women MPs reveal the truth about life inside Westminster
Major study reveals catalogue of sexist insults, hostility and boorish behaviour despite influx of women MPs by Jackie Ashley, The Guardian, Tuesday 7 December 2004 12:22 GMT

When Gillian Shephard arrived in the House of Commons as a new Tory MP in 1987 she was confused to find herself and her fellow women MPs being called Betty. "There was a Conservative MP who called us all Betty," she recalls, "and when I said, 'Look, you know my name isn't Betty', he said, 'Ah, but you're all the same, so I call you all Betty, it's easier'."

More than 15 years later, with a big increase in the number of women MPs, life has moved on – but only a little. An academic study of 83 current or recent MPs has chronicled their experiences from the day they entered parliament. The picture they paint is of a mixture of crude sexism, patronising hostility, solidarity and hope.

Today's female MPs may not all be called Betty, but they do complain of constant barracking in the chamber, sexist insults, and a patronising dismissal of female MPs by male politicians and journalists.

Barbara Follett says: "I remember some Conservatives: whenever a Labour woman got up to speak they would take their breasts – their imaginary breasts – in their hands and wiggle them and say 'melons' as we spoke."

Jackie Ballard, a Liberal Democrat who left parliament at the last election, cites a leading Tory MP who kept up a stream of remarks just out of hearing of the Speaker, "maybe about someone's legs or someone being a lesbian... if he worked for me he'd probably be sacked". The same MP is reported as announcing, while drunk in the chamber, that he'd like to "roger" a nearby woman.

The study was overseen by Joni Lovenduski of Birkbeck College. More than 100 hours of tapes of interviews with women MPs will be lodged in the British Library.

The interviews show how even after the great influx of women in 1997 – 120 of them in total – female MPs were expected to stick to traditional "women's issues", such as health and education. Several complain of the put-downs they experienced when stepping on to the male territory of defence. A typical recollection is from Glenda Jackson who says that while she was speaking on defence, a Tory MP called out: "Stick to what you know Glenda." When Labour's Dari Taylor resigned from the defence select committee – one of only two women on it – the chairman, Bruce George, stood up and said: "Well, I have to make this announcement: one down one to go."

The blatant hostility from some male MPs was astonishing. Even those who publicly espoused equality were furious to see women getting promotion. Harriet Harman recalls a male colleague telling her: "Well, you've only succeeded because you're a woman." One current member of the cabinet was asked, when she was promoted: "Oh, you've had a very fast rise, who have you been sleeping with?"

Another, who asked not to be named, tells of physical aggression when women MPs banded together to vote several women on to one of Labour's committees. "A government minister came up to me and literally pinned me by my neck up against the wall in the lobby and screamed at me and said: 'You've done it now, you've done it now'."

From the start, male MPs and officials seemed reluctant to accept the new Labour women, many of them in their 30s and 40s, who looked, talked and acted so differently from the typical MP. Some simply couldn't believe youngish women could be members of parliament.

Early on in her political career, Estelle Morris, the arts minister, was approached by an MP: "He says to me, 'Oh how lovely to see you Estelle, are you working here, are you a researcher or a secretary?' I said, 'No, I'm a member of parliament' and he froze, absolutely froze."

Yvette Cooper had a similar experience with a Commons doorkeeper. She was asking about the geography of Westminster and he clearly did not believe a young woman could be a member: "He finally said to me, 'No, no, no dear, who do you work for?' And I said, 'I don't work for anybody, I'm an MP' and he was so shocked and so apologetic."

But perhaps the new Labour MPs didn't help themselves. The dominant image of them is in that famous "Blair's Babes" photograph where they are standing in a circle around Tony Blair. Many now think it trivialised them and should never have been allowed to happen. Yvette Cooper was one: "It was a big, big mistake, we should never have posed for it."

It reinforced that feeling of being at the edge of a male world which went right to the top. Mo Mowlam recalls waiting outside the door for cabinet meetings, while ministers chatted: "More often than not the women weren't chatted to; they had to chat to each other."

What comes across from many of the interviews is the appalled sense of culture shock when women MPs arrived in the traditionalist culture of the Commons. Labour's Claire Curtis-Thomas made a revealing mistake: "All the coat hangers had these red ribbons on them, and I thought, gosh how progressive – I mean, isn't that extraordinary, not only do they provide you with a coat hanger... but they also pop an Aids ribbon on there for the day... and then somebody turned to me and said, 'Clare, that is for your sword. It's to secure your sword'. And that's when I knew it really was in the dark ages."

Derision

The hours are more family-friendly now, but there are determined attempts from male MPs to have the clock put back - something most of the women will oppose. The Treasury minister Dawn Primarolo says that when she arrived: "You couldn't get time off. I couldn't get time off when I wanted to go down to Bristol if my son was playing in rugby matches for the school, or football... I thought: I've destroyed my life, what have I done?"

Many female MPs say the changes to the hours have improved things, undermining the old male drinking culture. But it isn't perfect yet. Sarah Teather, the new Liberal Democrat MP, says: "Lots of people say it's like an old boy's club. I've always said, to me it feels rather more like a teenage public school – you know, a public school full of teenage boys."

And the Ulster Unionist Lady Sylvia Hermon singles out the most notorious part of the week: "I really dislike prime minister's questions... I sort of sit and grin and bear it, because it is so uncharacteristic of the rest of the business that's done during the week... I hate the rough and tumble of that half hour, I dread it each week."

Still a minority in such an aggressive, male world, it's perhaps not surprising that a degree of solidarity among female MPs has built up – quite often across party boundaries. Harriet Harman and Gillian Shephard are repeatedly singled out as being the two MPs who always go out of their way to help their "sisters", as Labour's Linda Perham confirms: "This wall of derision hit me and I carried on, got to the third sentence and dried up again... and afterwards Gillian Shephard wrote me a little note on A5 paper, handwritten, and she's put 'Nil desperandum'."

Above all, worse than all the sexism and the mockery, women MPs are angry that their achievements are not recognised. They insist they have brought a new feminised agenda to Westminster politics, in particular, the rise of childcare to the top of the domestic agenda, and the measures on domestic violence.

But many other policies are cited too. Marion Roe, a Tory MP, is proud of her bill outlawing female circumcision in 1985 – "when I did that, nobody knew what female circumcision was." Ruth Kelly cites parental leave, while Teresa Gorman says bluntly, "I put menopause on the map."

The women have undoubtedly made a difference to Westminster, but is this a historic moment in our political history, the tipping point from a world of casual parliamentary sexism and a male agenda? Professor Lovenduski fears that if fewer women are returned to parliament at the next election, and if the vote on keeping the modernised hours is lost, the female influence could wane: "I think it's too early to say... I prefer to be optimistic that the culture has changed for good, but I don't feel absolutely certain about it."

Whose secretary are you, Minister? is being written by Joni Lovenduski, Margaret Moran MP and Boni Sones.

Our Wikipedia link
Women's Parliamentary Radio
From Wikipedia, the free encyclopaedia
Women's Parliamentary Radio is a website which broadcasts audio and video interviews with women MPs of all parties.

All the interviews are pre-recorded and put on the website as reports which can be streamed and listened to immediately or downloaded as podcasts so that they can be listened to later. It covers topical current affairs issues which are of interest to women and their families. Where the issues that concern women are also championed by men, male MPs are interviewed too.

Aim[edit]
WPR has stated its aim as being "the Woman's Hour of Westminster, reporting fairly and accurately on policy issues of concern to women and their families". It was the creation of its Executive Producer, former BBC Political Editor Boni Sones OBE who using her broadcast knowledge foresaw the huge technological shift that was taking place in broadcast journalism through the relaxation of broadcasting laws in 2005 and advances in new technology taking place at that time. Boni taught herself sound engineering techniques and pioneered the first "as live" broadcast interviews online encouraged by women MPs at a Cabinet and Shadow Cabinet level including, Theresa May MP, Caroline Spelman MP, Harriet Harman MP, Vera Baird MP, Sandra Gidley MP and Jo Swinson MP.

Boni also took her web broadcasting work into Cambridge University's Judge Business School where she reported on business and economics leading up to, during and after the Financial Crash of 2008 and 2009. The London School of Economics now has an Archive dedicated to her Parliamentary and University work as an early adopter of broadcast web journalism. It is called the "Boni Sones Archive"!

The British Library also has a collection of 82 audio interviews Boni and her team conducted for a book on women in politics – Boni named the Archive "The Harman Shephard" collection.

Boni also used her web skills and modern developments in new technology to self-publish six books about her childhood growing up in Sizewell in Suffolk in the 1950s and being part of a family who lived off "the fat of the land". The books are called, *The Mermaid's Tale, A Portrait of Suffolk, Two Mermaid's Together, Food on the Table – All in One, Dear Alex – All in One, All4Now*, and *Home Fires:20 poems 4 2012* – all are deposited in the British Library, and all are on Amazon.

Audience Reach

From January 2012 to January 2013 www.wpradio.co.uk and www.parliamentaryradio.com got over 2,000 visitors each month. In October 2012 it had 3,697 visits in one month. For the year it had 400,482 hits, 12,650 unique visitors, and 35,518 visits.

History[edit]

The project has grown out of the publication of the book by Methuen in September 2005 *Women in Parliament: The New Suffragettes* by Boni Sones, Margaret Moran and Professor Joni Lovenduski, where women talked frankly about their lives in Parliament and their achievements to date. The project's founders are concerned that, nearly ninety years after women won the right to stand for elections to the House of Commons in 1918, only one in five Members of Parliament is a woman.

The publication of the Book led Roy Greenslade, then media commentator on the Guardian, to offer his own "mea culpa" to women MPs for the descriptions he has used of them previously. His article ended:

"It is sobering to realise that the suffragettes' original demand was simply to have the vote. Some saw that as the end in itself, others as the first step on a long road towards genuine equality. Modern women MPs are still travelling down that road and are right to complain that their feet are sore."

Boni has been helped throughout in her work by journalist colleagues Jackie Ashley of the *Guardian*, Deborah McGurran of BBC East, Linda Fairbrother formerly of Anglia TV, and MPs working at a Senior Level across party including recently Gisela Stuart MP, Eleanor Laing MP, Baroness Susan Kramer, and Penny Mordaunt MP. The Charity campaigner, Boo Armstrong provided much needed encouragement and support as an Advisory Board member in the early days.

Since WP Radio began in Spring 2007 over 250 interviews nationally and internationally and 30 documentaries have been broadcast. It is now celebrating its sixth year of broadcasting and will become an Archive site only from Summer 2013.

In January 2013 Boni's four portraits of women MPS party by pary by Kieran Doherty who took the famous "Blair's Babes" photograph went on display at the National People's History Museum in Manchester as their "Object of the Month"! The United Nations has also collected them.

In October 2009 Boni displayed at the National Portrait Gallery, and later in the Commons itself, these four group portraits to celebrate 90 years of Women and the Vote. She also published a DVD of her and her colleagues interviews and these portraits and sent to all women MPs.

In 2011 a new platform was launched www.parliamentaryradio.com after the London School of Economics took the www.wpradio.co.uk site into its Political Archives to preserve for historians of the future to study.

Earlier in 2011 wpradio also broadcast interviews with women MPs in the UK Parliament interviewing women MPs from other Parliaments using the telephone in place of a so called "line booking"! One of the stated aims of wpradio was to "link in" women in Parliaments all over the World, thereby creating a radio online "World Service" for them reporting parliament by parliament.

In 2010 the broadcasts of wpradio were featured on a wall where audiences using headphones could listen to ten of its interviews at the well received and reviewed Tricycle Theatre's "Women Power and Politics" plays.

In 2008 Women's Parliamentary Radio was shortlisted for Channel 4's Hansard Society Democracy Award and Boni Sones, Executive Producer of the channel, was nominated for the Dods & Scottish Widows female political journalist of the year award. In January 2009 she was awareded an OBE for "Services to Broadcasting and Public Relations".

www.wpradio.co.uk is based partially in the Parliamentary Lobby and was assisted by Muir Morton, the then Deputy Serjeant At Arms in the House, and the late Brian Shallcross, of GCap Media, and a former Chairman of the Lobby who saw the need for a new broadcaster on behalf of women MPs themselves and the potential of new media.

The write-up and press release for our link to our four photographs of women MPs party by party to celebrate 90 years of women and the vote in 2008
http://www.wpradio.co.uk/photos.php
PRESS RELEASE – www.wpradio.co.uk – Women's Parliamentary Radio
Embargoed until 00.01 hours 29th October 2008
Women's Parliamentary Radio in association with the Labour, Conservative, Liberal Democrat and Independent Labour parties launches a national photographic viewing
"The day the Carlton Club accepted women – 90 years after women got the vote."
A viewing of photographic images of 104 of the 125 women MPs in Westminster will be unveiled at a press breakfast launch at the National Portrait Gallery on the 29th October from 8.30 am to 9.30 am to mark 90 years since women were first given the vote.

The original "Blair's Babes" Reuters photographer Kieran Doherty was invited back to Westminster to take the historic group composite photographs by Women's Parliamentary Radio working in association with the Labour, Conservative, and Liberal Democrat Parties and the Independent Labour Party. They will be shown as a framed wall size set, with each party side by side.

Maria Eagle MP, the Deputy Minister for Women, will be launching the viewing with Theresa May MP, the Shadow Minister for Women and Lynne Featherstone, the Liberal Democrat's Equalities spokesperson.

Maria Eagle, Deputy Minister for Women said: "Britain is a more equal society today than it was eleven years ago when 101 Labour women MPs were elected. We had almost trebled the number of Labour women MPs and doubled female representation in the House of Commons in one general election. That increase has been particularly beneficial to women and, over the past decade, the gender pay gap has been reduced; maternity leave has been extended; the number of childcare places has been doubled and parents of children under the age of six have won the right to request flexible working.

"However, still only 20% of the members of the House of Commons are female and we rank a rather shameful 51st on the international women's representation league table. Even more worrying is the fact that we have only 2 Black women MPs and not a single Asian one.

"The Government is committed to correcting this democratic deficit by helping more women get into public life by extending all women shortlists for parliamentary candidates to 2030; setting up a taskforce to help more Black, Asian and minority ethnic women become councillors and introducing a new, 21st century, Equality Bill to make Britain fairer for everyone."

Theresa May MP, The Shadow Leader of the House of Commons and Shadow Minister for Women, said: "This is a wonderful achievement which marks the 90th anniversary of women first getting the vote, but which I hope will have lasting benefit in showing women that politics is for them. We need to show positive images of women in Parliament to encourage others to aspire to stand and be elected. This is the first time that such a positive image of women across all parties in Parliament has been put on public view. Well done to all for achieving this milestone."

Lynne Featherstone MP, Liberal Democrat Equalities Spokesperson, commented: "These great images tell us two things about women in Parliament – one, how far we've come and two, how far we have to go. Sadly a similar photos of the males MPs would still take up four times as much wall space of the National Portrait Gallery.

"In the first 90 years we have certainly made our mark, but it shouldn't take another 90 before the number of male and female MPs are equal. We owe a debt of gratitude to suffragettes who fought so hard for us to get where we are, but we must fight with the same zeal to finish what they started."

Clare Short MP, Independent Labour said: "It is important not to forget the contribution the original suffragettes made to the lives of women in this Country. This year marks 90 years since women over 30 were given the vote and in July, it will be 80 years since the voting age was lowered to 21 for women. I am pleased that women of all parties took part in this photographic portrait, party by party, so that there is a visual image to show just how far women have progressed and how much work there is still to do to get more women MPs in parliament."

The House of Commons has already acquired one of the sets of 25 of the four portraits for its permanent collection. Hugo Swire MP, Chairman, The Speaker's Advisory Committee on Works of Art said:

"The House of Commons Works of Art Collection documents significant moments in Parliamentary history. We are delighted to have added this unique photographic record of women MPs of today, to mark the 90th anniversary of women first being able to take their seats in this House."

Until now the most often used photographic image of women MPs has been the so called "Blair Babes" picture taken on 7th May 1997 shortly after 101 Labour women were elected to Westminster as a result of positive action by the Labour Party. That picture was taken by Reuter's Kieran Doherty, who had climbed up the steps to get the women looking up at him and waving. Many disliked it.

On May 21st 2008 Kieran was invited back to Westminster at the invitation of Boni Sones, founder of Women's Parliamentary Radio, to photograph the women MPs again. The new composite portraits, taken party by party over three photo calls, aim to ensure that a more enduring image of women's participation in the political process survives.

As Caroline Spelman MP, Chairman of the Conservative Party, arrived for the photo call she announced that "The Carlton Club" had just voted to accept women. The display is entitled "The Day the Carlton Club accepted women – 90 years after women first got the vote."

Jackie Ashley, Chair of Women's Parliamentary Radio said: "Kieran Doherty's photographic viewing is a remarkable achievement for all concerned. To be able to take photographs of this many women MPs this quickly shows the true talents of a news photographer at the top of his profession. Kieran remained cool throughout and fully in command of his art as the women leapt in and out of the photographs. He even managed to capture the Dalai Lama as he bid his farewell to Westminster after speaking in Parliament Hall and the tallest and shortest female MPs standing back to back. It was a really historic day on many fronts."

Boni Sones, Executive Producer of wpradio.co.uk said: "When I co-authored the book *Women in Parliament: The New Suffragettes*, with Margaret Moran MP and Professor Joni Lovenduski, in 2005, I stated in the introduction that when you walked around galleries like the National Portrait Gallery all you could see were male MPs waving order papers. A prominent national visual image of our women MPs in Westminster is needed to show all women that politics is a career they can aspire too and to mark the considerable achievements of contemporary female MPs, 90 years since women first got the vote."

Background:

Each party gave its permission for the photograph to be taken to mark 90 years since women first got the vote. In February 1918 women over 30 were first granted the vote and 10 years later in July 1928 the voting age was lowered to 21.

Kieran Doherty assembled the women on the steps at New Palace Yard, under Big Ben in the heart of the Westminster village where the women are well used to assembling to have their photographs taken.

Kieran said: "I was worried about the weather in the days leading up to the photo calls but in the end I was lucky and the rain stopped. The late May, early June light was ideal for photographs of this nature. It is certainly one of the more challenging and significant assignments of my news photography career."

May 21st was also the day after the controversial vote on the Human Embryology and Fertilisation Bill when lowering the legal time limit on abortions from 24 to 22 weeks had been discussed and defeated. It was also the day before the Crewe and Nantwich by-election following the death of the longest serving woman MP, Gwyneth Dunwoody. In America

Hillary Clinton was battling for the Democratic Party's nomination for the presidency which Barack Obama eventually won two weeks later.

The composite photographs are taken party by party with Labour, Conservative, Liberal Democrat and Independent Labour. All three major party's have women as Chairs or Chairmen or Chairwomen.

Harriet Harman MP QC is the Labour Party Chair, Caroline Spelman MP is Chairman of the Conservative Party, and Lorley Burt, is Chair of the Liberal Democrat Parliamentary Party. All three were photographed separately.

Kieran Doherty took advantage of a lighter moment in the schedule when Vera Baird MP, the Solicitor General, arrived and as the tallest woman in Westminster met the shortest woman, Sarah Teather MP, the Liberal Democrats Shadow Secretary of State for Business, Enterprise and Regulatory Reform. They were photographed back to back on the steps of New Palace Yard. Vera is 5ft 11 1/2 inches tall and Sarah is 4ft 10 inches tall.

The photographs can be viewed on www.wpradio.co.uk **photographs. The numbers:**
In all 104 out of a possible 125 women were photographed. Three women MPs had died since 2005.

All the women MPs in the Cabinet and Shadow Cabinets took part. For Labour there are five: Hazel Blears MP, Yvette Cooper MP, Harriet Harman QC MP, Ruth Kelly MP, Jacqui Smith MP.

The Conservatives Shadow Cabinet has four women MPs: Cheryl Gillan MP, Theresa May MP, Caroline Spelman MP, Theresa Villiers MP. The Liberal Democrats have five: Lynne Featherstone MP, Julia Goldsworthy MP, Susan Kramer MP, Sarah Teather MP, Jenny Willott MP. For Labour 83 out of a possible 95 attended, all 9 of the Liberal Democrats, 11 of the 17 Conservative women and one Independent Labour, Clare Short. 3 other women MPs from smaller parties did not take part but were invited. A remarkable achievement for all. Women MPs who died in this parliament since 2005, Patsy Calton, (LD), Rachel Squire, (Lab), Gwyneth Dunwoody, (Lab).

Copyright for the pictures belongs to Boni Sones. You can find out who was photographed by going to www.wpradio.co.uk photographs.

Additional notes:

• Wpradio.co.uk is a web-based broadcaster supported by all parties.

• Wpradio.co.uk now has a number of interviews with women and male politicians of all parties which can be listened to online or downloaded as podcasts.

• Our supporters include Harriet Harman MP, Theresa May MP, Jo Swinson MP and many other female politicians listed on our site.

• For more information contact Boni Sones on 07703 716961.

• Additional information sheet who took part:

INDEX

MPs, former MPs, campaigners and opinion formers by name

Name	Page No
Lesley Abdela	125, 131, 133
Foluke Akinlose MBE	33
Heidi Alexander MP	159
Rushanara Ali MP	146
Lady Nancy Astor	116
Sherry Ayittey MP	132
Vera Baird QC MP	97, 100, 183
Lord Baker	116
Harriett Baldwin MP	165, 175
Anne Begg MP	50, 129, 150
Steve Bell	116
John Bercow MP	20, 105, 106, 188, 208
Luciana Berger MP	18, 156, 173
Lynne Berry	42
Nicola Blackwood MP	197
Hazel Blears MP	84, 101, 165, 204
Emma Bonino	214
Danny Boyle	114
Catherine Briddick	86
Baroness Sal Brinton	40
Dr Belinda Brooks Gordon	86
Lynn Brown MP	194, 199
Chris Bryant MP	54
Lorely Burt MP	24, 72, 160, 192
Dawn Butler MP	151, 152, 153, 154
Alan Campbell MP	87
Dr Rosie Campbell	28
Kay Carberry	65
Barbara Castle MP	62
Lucy Changme MP	133
Katy Clark MP	22, 40
Therese Coffey MP	70, 70
Baroness Janet Cohen	193

When There's a Woman in the Room

Name	***Page No***
Michael Connarty MP	200
Robin Cook MP	102, 158
Yvette Cooper MP	75
Jeremy Corbyn	204
Antonia Cox PPC	150
Elizabeth Crawford	112
Stella Creasy MP	29
Tracey Crouch MP	162, 175
Ann Cryer MP	54, 98
Simon Danczuk MP	79, 81
Davies (Lord)	69
David Davis MP	113
Dame Prof Sandra Dawson	66
Sir Willoughby Hyett Dickinson	107
Caroline Dineage MP	175
Nadine Dorries MP	184, 206
Declan Duggan	192
Gwyneth Dunwoody MP	118
Angela Eagle MP	168, 193, 215
Maria Eagle MP	100
Jane Ellison MP	16, 79, 85
Louise Ellman MP	27
Natascha Engel	210
Lucy Fairbrother	136
Lynne Featherstone MP	36, 64, 95, 152, 185, 198, 211
Prof Nina Fishman	56
Baroness Shreela Flather	207
Caroline Flint MP	96
Barbara Follett MP	53, 113
Cynthia Forde MP	122
Lorraine Fullbrook MP	180
Jane Garvey	112
Sandra Gidley MP	61, 133
Cheryl Gillan MP	182
Paul Goggins MP	109
Vandna Gohil	53

Index by Name

Name	*Page No*
Helen Goodman MP	77, 78, 142
Barbara Gorna	114, 115, 117
Helen Grant MP	38, 146
Joy Greasley	60
Damian Green MP	198
Kate Green MP	15, 17, 83, 113
Dolma Gyari MP	131
Janet Hanson	72
Harriet Harman MP	72, 111, 180, 183
Bridge Harris	27
Dr Evan Harris MP	105, 108
Usama Hassan	82
Baroness Helene Hayman	50, 177
Dr Noreena Hertz	52
Meg Hillier MP	17, 170
Julie Hilling MP	176
Amy Hodge	45
Sharon Hodgson MP	124, 161
Mary Honeyball MEP	51, 134
Chris Huhne MP	56
Tristram Hunt MP	195
Julian Huppert MP	142, 148, 169
Leila Hussein	76
Antoinette Jackson	45
Glenda Jackson MP	166
Margot James MP	157, 215
Baroness Margaret Jay	126
Baroness Anne Jenkin	107, 206
Prof Kate Jenkins	29
Debbie Jevans	34
Lynne Jones MP	87
Dame Tessa Jowell MP	93, 99
Malalai Joya MP	135
Noreine Kaleeba	130
Rhoda Kalema	137, 138
Zarghuna Kargar	123
Betsy Kawamura	132
Chris Keates	55

Name	Page No
Sally Keeble MP	61, 182
Barbara Keeley MP	185
Baroness Helena Kennedy	76
Oona King MP	184, 198
Julie Kirkbride MP	23
Vivan Kityo	134
Baroness Susan Kramer	50, 204
Aung San Suu Kyi	115
Dr Joyce Laboso MP	130
Eleanor Laing MP	23, 59, 159, 167, 196
Joan Lane	115
Andrew Lansley MP	158
Angela Larkin	122
Andrea Leadsom MP	189, 190, 212
Charlotte Leslie PPC	153
Ngawang Lhamo MP	131
Caroline Lloyd-Evans	40
Elfyn Llwyd MP	103
Tim Loughton MP	21
Prof Joni Lovenduski	36, 60
Caroline Lucas PPC, MEP, MP	146, 151, 213
Karen Lumley MP	179
Juliet Lyons	194, 197
Rachel Maclean PPC	141
Mary Macleod MP	17, 70
Fiona Mactaggart MP	30, 77, 86, 113, 172, 180, 184, 190, 211
Fungayi Jessie Majome MP	121
Seema Malhotra MP	26, 39, 115, 143, 174, 199
Judy Mallaber MP	68
Theresa May MP	38, 46, 53, 61, 111, 157, 183, 185, 210
Marg Mayne	130
Lindiwe Mazibuko MP	127
Kerry McCarthy MP	162
John McDonnell	32
Alison McGovern	112
Anne McGuire MP	200
Ann McKechin MP	171, 208
Esther McVey MP	91, 144, 179, 179, 196

Index by Name

Name	*Page No*
Alan Milburn MP	187
Ed Miliband MP	39
Maria Miller MP	22, 48
Bernadette Milliam PPC	146
Laura Moffatt MP	126
Madeleine Moon MP	76
Debbie Moore	91, 196
Margaret Moran MP	57, 89
Penny Mordaunt MP	115, 140, 144, 148, 163, 167, 205
Nicky Morgan MP	172
Mo Mowlam	118
Lisa Nandy MP	92
Brooks Newmark MP	26
Charlotte Newson	113
Baroness Lindsay Northover	94
Frances O'Grady	60
Philippa Oldham	31
Sandra Osborne MP	140, 191
Emmeline Pankhurst	27, 55, 111, 113
Priti Patel MP	38, 180
Claire Perry MP	18
Nancy Platts PPC	147
Stephen Pound MP	56
Lucy Powell MP	14
Baroness Margaret Prosser	64
Vicky Pryce	71
James Purnell MP	107
Carolyn Quinn	37
Sabrina Qureshi	199, 207
Dr Katharine Rake	23
Nick Raynsford MP	140
Rachel Reeves MP	63, 206, 211
Linda Riordan MP	200
Indhu Rubashingham	44
Amber Rudd MP	80, 83, 85, 175, 191

When There's a Woman in the Room

Name	*Page No*
Joan Ruddock MP	35, 100
Sheryl Sandberg	62
Anas Sarwar MP	125
Britta Schmidt	208
Rev Cannon Martin Seeley	32
Andrew Selous	109
Clare Short MP	53
Ryan Shorthouse	18
Margaret Sitta MP	121, 122
Chloe Smith MP	116
Iain Duncan Smith MP	91, 144, 179
Caroline Spelman MP	29, 52, 56, 61, 87, 88, 113
Andrew Stephenson MP	104
Iain Stewart MP	166, 169
Dick Stockford	187
Gisela Stuart MP	113, 157, 164, 205
Jo Swinson MP	49, 53, 57, 59, 94, 127, 135, 145, 163, 195, 198, 209, 215
Senator Fauzaya Talhaoui	122
Lady Margaret Thatcher	116, 167
Emily Thornberry MP	22, 154, 171, 203
Philippa Reiss Thorne	126
Sir Crispin Tickell	51
Sandi Toksvig	112
Ann Treneman	174, 181, 184, 205, 210, 213, 215
Baroness Pola Uddin	89
United Nations	120
Charlotte Vere PPC	146
Anastasia de Waal	15
Charles Walker MP	108
Diana Wallis MEP	56
Margot Wallstrom MP	137
Claire Ward MP	47
Helen Whately PPC	148
Emily Wilding Davison	112, 113, 117, 118, 175, 208
Andy Williams	59
Baroness Shirley Williams	41, 55, 137

Index by Name

Name	*Page No*
Stephen Williams MP	194
Jenny Willott MP	19
Dilys Winterkorn	205
Sue Woodsford	138
Tebereh Woldegabriel	136
Dr Sarah Wollaston MP	31, 142, 168, 189
Simon Woolley	55
Alison Worsley	82

SUBJECT INDEX

Index by subject only

Africa	3, 5, 32, 120, 122, 126, 127, 128, 132, 134, 136, 205, 213
All-Party parliamentary groups	13, 74, 75, 77, 79, 85, 89,103, 104, 134, 139, 180, 186, 190, 195, 197, 198, 199, 200
All-women shortlists	25, 26, 28, 43, 46, 49, 94, 97, 106
Alternative Voting System	215
Backbench business committee	210
Big Society	42, 212
Blair's Babes	43, 52, 111
Boardrooms	69, 70, 71, 95, 148
Borgen	203
Breast feeding (banned)	120, 121, 177
Brown, Gordon	49, 101, 103, 137, 154
Cabinet	6, 7, 8, 26, 29, 39, 48, 88, 90, 91, 92, 96, 99, 101, 120, 128, 167, 168, 186, 209, 217
Campaigning women	110
Campaigning	7, 26, 39, 59, 74, 78, 84, 85, 98, 110, 111, 112, 113, 118, 120, 125, 126, 134, 135, 138, 147, 150, 151, 153, 154, 185, 186, 198
Cameron David MP (Prime Minister)	7, 14, 17, 19, 26, 28, 29, 31, 48, 49, 62, 82, 88, 90, 91, 103, 120, 139, 140, 144, 157, 160, 161, 162, 165, 166, 168, 169,170, 171, 179, 185, 190
Central Lobby	16, 83, 110, 114, 115, 124, 125, 168, 172, 173, 175.
Chamber	6, 22, 40, 43, 57, 67, 91, 105, 119, 141, 146, 155, 156, 158, 168, 174, 177, 183, 184, 185
Child tax credit	19
Childcare	13, 14, 18, 19, 22, 23, 28, 98, 103, 148, 175
Chloe (If Chloe Can)	35, 39, 91, 115, 116, 144, 145, 175, 178, 179, 195, 196
Clegg Nick MP (Deputy PM)	13, 27, 94, 103,120, 144
Clock Tower (Elizabeth)	193
Congo	33, 121, 131, 199, 207, 208, 2011
Constituency	22, 36, 38, 40, 41, 63, 87, 116, 139, 140, 143, 150, 151, 153, 155, 159, 161, 167, 176, 177, 178, 187, 200

Subject Index

Creche	19, 47, 48, 98, 102
Dagenham Women (Ford)	62
Dangerous Dogs Act 1991	201
Discrimination	5, 25, 27, 28, 29, 54, 76, 91, 94, 95, 97, 100, 106, 116, 121
Domestic Violence	15, 53, 74, 77, 82
Education	14, 15, 20, 31, 39, 42, 50, 75, 94, 116, 121, 122, 123, 125, 130, 131, 133, 134, 135, 136, 141, 161, 170, 176, 177, 178, 198
Equal pay	60, 62, 63, 65, 66, 96, 100, 124, 179, 183
Equal Pay Act of 1970	62, 65, 96
Equalities Act	95
Europe	3, 5, 18, 30, 31, 51, 56, 69, 85, 86, 122, 132, 133, 134, 137, 147, 152, 167, 174, 190, 191, 198
Fawcett (Society)	24, 63, 147, 177
Female Genital Mutilation	74, 76, 79, 85, 102
Food Banks	139, 140, 160, 162
Forced Marriage	54, 74, 80, 81, 88, 89
Fringe event	77, 161, 197
Gay marriage	14, 168, 169
Gender	4, 15, 27, 36, 37, 60, 64, 65, 66, 68, 69, 75, 91, 95, 96, 97, 100, 121, 122, 132, 133, 134, 136, 148, 169, 177, 183
Government	14, 15, 16, 17, 18, 19, 20, 22, 23, 24, 26, 28, 29, 30, 38, 41, 42, 44, 47, 48, 55, 56, 60, 62, 63, 64, 65, 66, 67, 68, 69, 71, 74, 75, 76, 77, 78, 79, 80, 83, 85, 86, 87, 88, 90, 93, 94, 95, 96, 97, 99, 101, 102, 103, 104, 106, 107, 115, 119, 120, 122, 124, 125, 132, 133, 134, 135, 137, 140, 142, 143, 143, 149, 153, 154, 158, 159, 162, 163, 165, 170, 174, 176, 177, 181, 183, 186, 189, 189, 190, 194, 197, 198
Hansard	57, 58
Health	65, 75, 92, 93, 94, 109, 121, 123, 126, 131, 133, 134, 136, 141, 142, 143, 148, 156, 157, 160, 161, 170, 172, 173, 198
(Mental health)	134, 172, 189, 198

Home life	23, 177
Home Office	21, 74, 79, 86, 87, 183
Hours (MPs)	29, 40, 41, 43, 47, 64, 102, 146, 159, 160, 176, 183, 202, 203, 213
House of Commons	19, 20, 33, 53, 54, 57, 63, 72, 73, 76, 83, 105, 110, 114, 117, 132, 135, 150, 155, 157, 159, 160, 169, 171, 185
House Works of Art Committee	110
House of Lords	41, 50, 83, 115, 180, 196, 206
Human Rights (and Commission)	66, 69, 86, 106, 108, 122, 132
Immigration	158, 159, 198
International	9, 21, 23, 34, 49, 50, 52, 57, 67, 72, 75, 76, 79, 85, 90, 93, 106, 111, 117, 118, 119, 121, 122, 124, 125, 126, 127, 128, 130, 131, 131, 132, 133, 137, 141, 162, 183, 185, 186, 197, 198, 199, 206, 207, 208
International Parliaments	9, 132
Inter-Parliamentary Union	119, 121, 122
International Women's Day	51, 52, 57, 67, 85, 111, 117, 118, 119, 127, 128, 130, 133, 183, 185, 198, 199, 208, 211, 214
Iraq	163, 198, 199, 208
Ireland	90, 108, 109, 131, 197
Job share MPs	28, 31, 32, 36, 102, 68
Maiden speech	104, 116, 119, 145, 146, 155, 173, 174, 180
Male MPs	28, 36, 43, 200
Media	6, 7, 9, 17, 20, 21, 38, 42, 43, 44, 47, 57, 58, 70, 78, 93, 99, 108, 117, 139, 142, 148, 152, 163, 166, 170, 185, 195, 198, 201
Melon's gesture (Commons)	155
Miliband, Ed MP (Lab Leader)	39, 90, 92, 96, 120, 139, 157, 161, 162
Millennium Development Goals	120, 121, 134, 136
Million Women Rise	199, 202, 207
Modernisation Committee	102
Nagging	102, 103
National Minimum Wage	62, 106
Parents	17, 19, 22, 23, 24, 30, 98, 103, 104, 166, 169, 170, 183

Subject Index

Parliament	3, 5, 7, 8, 9, 13, 14, 19, 20, 25, 26, 27, 28, 29, 32, 35, 36, 37, 38, 39, 43, 46, 47, 48, 49, 50, 51, 52, 53, 55, 56, 57, 58, 59, 60, 61, 64, 72, 75, 77, 79, 81, 85, 86, 89, 90, 92, 97, 98, 100, 102, 103, 104, 110, 11, 112, 113, 114, 115, 118, 119, 120, 121, 122, 123, 126, 127, 128, 129, 130, 131, 132, 133, 134, 135, 136, 137, 139, 141, 145, 146, 148, 150, 151, 152, 153, 154, 155, 156, 157, 158, 159, 160, 164, 168, 172, 175, 178, 180, 181, 182, 184, 185, 186, 188, 190, 195, 196, 197, 198, 199, 200
Party Conference	149, 161, 197
Pay gap	64, 65, 68, 95, 98, 148, 183
Pregnancy	97, 108, 191
Press	9, 52, 96, 180
Press Gallery	37, 91
Prime Minister	13, 17, 23, 29, 41, 45, 53, 62, 82, 90, 93, 94, 103, 110, 116, 120, 137, 139, 140, 160, 161, 162, 167, 168, 170, 171, 173, 185, 190, 121
Prime Minister's Questions	17, 23, 139, 160, 168, 170, 173
Prospective Parliamentary Candidate	28, 47, 48, 58, 59, 141, 146, 148, 153
Prostitution	74, 85, 86, 132, 180, 183, 184
Public Policy	13, 18, 25, 29, 30, 53, 91, 102, 104, 139, 141, 188
Representation	7, 25, 26, 29, 30, 35, 43, 50, 53, 55, 57, 60, 69, 70, 93, 110,113, 123, 125, 128, 132, 133, 150, 178, 195
Scotland	41, 77, 92, 103, 169, 190, 197, 208
Select Committee	16, 26, 63, 68, 76, 80, 106, 118, 125, 129, 139, 158, 163, 164, 173, 186, 187, 188, 196
Sex	15, 21, 27, 31, 63, 65, 66, 75, 77, 79, 80, 81, 82, 86, 87, 97, 100, 102, 105, 106, 128, 155, 165, 166, 168, 169, 180, 184, 190
Sex Education (Ten Minute Rule) Bill	206
Shadow Cabinets	6, 26, 39, 48, 90, 91, 92, 96
Special Educational Needs Bill	206
Speaker's House	144, 208
Speaker's Chair	105, 159
Speaker's Conference	46, 47, 50, 98, 150, 202
Speakers' List	103, 213

251

Stalking	74, 75, 87, 88, 102, 103, 10
Statue	27, 107, 110, 111, 112, 113, 118, 185
St Mary Undercroft	110, 113
St Stephen's Hall	110, 113
Sure Start	13, 14, 20, 98, 103
United Nations	120, 121, 136
Upper Committee Corridor	111, 139
Violence	15, 53, 74, 75, 76, 77, 82, 83, 84, 87, 89, 100, 119, 120, 123, 124, 125, 128, 132, 133, 197, 199
Wales	68, 166, 180, 197
Welfare	15, 20, 84, 92, 96, 141, 142, 160, 162, 164, 165, 188, 203
Westminster	7, 8, 13, 22, 25, 28, 31, 32, 35, 37, 40, 41, 42, 43, 46, 48, 52, 56, 58, 59, 60, 80, 88, 90, 91, 97, 98, 102, 106, 107, 110, 111, 112, 113, 114, 115, 116, 118, 119, 120, 122, 124, 129, 137, 139, 143, 145, 146, 148, 150, 151, 152, 155, 162, 167, 168, 170, 172, 173, 174, 175, 177, 184, 186, 190, 194
Westminster Hall	80, 111, 115, 146, 150, 155, 175
Womenspeak	89
Women's Aid	89
Women2Win (Cons)	25, 26, 37, 38, 45, 46, 61, 107, 116, 148, 149, 180
Women in the World Today (Cons)	58, 74, 87
Wright Reforms	186